MOTORBOOKS
POWERTECH SERIES ™

How to Build & Modify

CHEVROLET
BIG-BLOCK V-8 ENGINES

TOM CURRAO

First published in 1997 by Motorbooks International Publishers & Wholesalers, 729 Prospect Avenue, PO Box 1, Osceola, WI 54020-0001 USA

Motorbooks International is a certified trademark, registered with the United States Patent Office

The information in this book is true and complete to the best of our knowledge. All recommendations are made without any guarantee on the part of the author or Publisher, who also disclaim any liability incurred in connection with the use of this data or specific details

We recognize that some words, model names and designations, for example, mentioned herein are the property of the trademark holder. We use them for identification purposes only. This is not an official publication

Motorbooks International books are also available at discounts in bulk quantity for industrial or sales-promotional use. For details write to Special Sales Manager at the Publisher's address

Library of Congress Cataloging-in-Publication Data

Currao, Tom.
    How to build & modify Chevrolet big-block V-8 engines / Tom Currao.
                        p. cm.
    Includes index.
    ISBN 0-7603-0203-0 (pbk. : alk. paper)
    1. Chevrolet automobile--Motors--Modification. 2. Chevrolet automobile--Performance. I. Title.
    TL215.C5C8724   1997
    629.25'04--dc21
97-22612

On the front cover: This impressive powerplant started life as a stock 454-cubic-inch engine. Along the way, the rat picked up Feuling heads, Feuling/A-R headers, KB flat-top pistons, a Fisher crankshaft damper, a Holley 850 carburetor, and, to top it all off, a K&N air cleaner. Nothing's as pretty as a modified Chevy big-block engine. *Tom Madigan*

Printed in the United States of America

CONTENTS

ACKNOWLEDGMENTS

To be a valuable resource in and of itself, a book like this requires input from many sources. Combined, the following people provided *hundreds* of years of experience researching, developing, building and modifying Chevrolet's ubiquitous big-block V-8. Many were there from the beginning back in '65 and know what works and what doesn't, so I know they have a solid foundation on which to build a book.

When it comes to world class engine builders, it's hard to find people more well-versed in Chevy big-blocks than Scott Shafiroff and John Lukovich, of Scott Shafiroff Racing Engines and Gianino/Lukovich Racing Engines, respectively. Both Scott and John took me under their wings, providing me with lots of great information that they use in their chosen professions daily. John's son Jeff also provided me with some insight into how Gianino/Lukovich prepares their racing engines. Thank you, gentlemen, for your thoughts, patience, and understanding. It was both an enlightening and enriching experience.

Dr. Rick Roberts, Edelbrock's director of engineering, was kind enough to supply me with his keen engineering expertise, for which I am very grateful. Dr. Rick, as he's known to insiders, has been a valuable resource for me and has a strong background with which to help lead Edelbrock on to even better products. Thanks, Rick. And once again, thanks go out to Edelbrock's Jim Losee for his help in this endeavor. Like Rick, Jim is one of those rare types who will go out of his way to help. Thanks for everything, Jim.

When it comes to pistons, you won't find a more knowledgeable man than John Levis of Wiseco Pistons. Thank you, John, for tirelessly answering all my questions over the past 18 months. I'd just like to know, how you're going to spend your time without me nagging you?

Mike Vendetto, of Moroso Performance Products, helped provide information on how that mix master we call the rotating assembly affects the lubrication system, as well as what strategies to use to optimize the system. Thanks for all your help, Mike.

Joey Lunati and Richard Woods, of Lunati Cams, were instrumental in providing their expertise relative to camshaft and valvetrain technology, as well as photos and photo props. Thanks for all your time and energy.

Thanks also go out to Tim Allen, of Cloyes Gear Company, for his assistance with camshaft drive system information and props.

Craig Davis of Brodix has also been a real help in supplying invaluable cylinder head information for this book. Thanks, Craig.

Heartfelt thanks also go out to Jim Davis of The Jim Davis Organization, Dick Maskin of Dart Machinery, Kevin Gallagher of K&N Engineering, Bill Taylor of Bill Taylor Engineering, Ted O'Bradovich of Extrude Hone, Todd Ryden of

FOREWORD

Autotronic Controls Corporation, Brad Cauzillo of Kinsler Fuel Injection, Mike Dunn of BHJ Dynamics, Bob Stratman of Crane Cams, Robert Roesé of Vortech Engineering, Scott Harrison of Mr. Gasket, Chris Wheeler of Crower Cams, John Brooks of Hooker Headers, Kathy Donovan of Donovan Engineering, Gary Dyer of Dyer's Connecting Rods and Machine Service, Len Allgaier, Russ Corley, Rick Vanlerberghe, Eric Lazarus, Holley Performance Products, and Flowmaster Corporation.

Although I have made a concerted effort to acknowledge all the people who have helped me with this particular book, I'm sure I have probably missed some. To them, I send both my apologies and my thanks.

On a personal note, I would like to thank John Petkovyat and George Dunn for their invaluable help and input on this book. They helped ask the right questions so I could provide the right answers. Thanks for all your assistance, fellas.

I'd also like to send a special "thank you" to Nicholas John Farrell, because without his help, this book wouldn't have been possible. Recovering all my computer files may have saved my life . . . it certainly saved my sanity. Thanks, Nick.

Most of all, I would like to thank Lea Anne and Alyssa, for whom this book is written and dedicated to. After all these years, I'm coming back home to you. And home is where I want to be.

This book provides guidance for building and modifying Chevrolet big-block V-8s produced from 1965 to the present, including Mark IV, Gen V, and Gen VI engines.

Even though this manual focuses on Chevrolet big-block V-8s, the big-block V-8s used in GMC trucks are in reality engineered and produced by Chevrolet. The same situation exists for some Chris Craft Marine, Crusader Marine, Flagship Marine, Hardin Marine, Indmar Marine, Marine Power Inc., Mercury Marine, OMC, Pleasurecraft Marine, Volvo-Penta Marine, and Yamaha marine engines. Consequently, the information contained in this book applies to them, as well.

Like any other science, engine hot-rodding is full of people with different points of view. One person believes a part should be this way, another believes it should be that way, and maybe a third holds a viewpoint somewhere between the first two.

All of the people I spoke with to develop this book have had considerable success in the manufacture, modification, and selection of parts for Chevrolet big-blocks, as well as engine building. Their differing philosophies and practices just prove there's more than one way to skin a cat. Therefore, this book presents information that although it may not totally align with all the beliefs of one particular part manufacturer or engine builder, it has all been proven on the street, track, or water.

INTRODUCTION

Technology has come a long way. In the late 1960s, Can-Am cars—the closest thing you could get to an unlimited road racing car—were pulling about 650 horsepower out of a 454. Today, a decent 468-cubic-inch bracket racing engine, one that you could put in your street car if you could put up with some relatively minor driveability problems, puts out 800-900 horsepower using a single four-barrel carburetor. The incredible difference between then and now is due to today's vast array of parts that work well right out of the box.

Besides all the extra knowledge that has been accumulated over the last 30 years, Computer-Aided Design and Manufacturing programs have reduced the learning curve dramatically. So parts are getting better, quicker. And Computer Numerical Control (CNC) machining helps put the finishing touches on parts in a methodical and consistent manner. It also allows for production of parts that were considered "custom" when Can-Am cars ruled the world.

But we can't escape from the past totally, because the vast majority of parts are a series of compromises based on the limitations of physics, engineering, manufacturing, and economies of scale. If tweaking a part a little here or there makes it a little less optimal for a specific application but increases its market appeal, it's usually done. This helps keep parts prices lower because of the broader range of audience.

And as in the past, the majority of power is produced by the parts in the "power path."

Power Path

The components that comprise the power path through the engine—induction system, camshaft, cylinder heads, and exhaust system—must all be selected to complement one another. Their operating range in terms of rpm must be similar to ensure the engine runs well. Dual-plane intake manifolds, oval port

This 632-cubic-inch rat in Scott Hocking's 1962 Impala will give you some idea of what a Chevy big-block is capable of. On gas, without the three-stage nitrous, this bad boy puts out 1,247 horsepower. Using the first two stages of nitrous bumps output to 1,725 horsepower. This equates to an incredible 7.68 at 181 miles per hour performance in the quarter-mile while moving 3,625 pounds.

heads, hydraulic cams, and small tube headers work well together for a strong running street engine with as much as 700 horsepower or so with excellent driveability. On the other hand, single-plane manifolds, rectangular port heads, mechanical cams, and large tube headers sing a harmonious song for a serious street/strip engine, or even a racing engine, depending on the exact components used. Almost everything else in the engine is devoted to turning that airflow into a rotating motion, waiting to be harnessed.

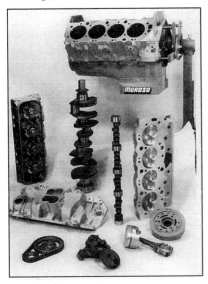

Selecting complementary engine components is essential to power output, driveability, and how happy you'll be with the finished product. Focus on how you're going to use the engine, then research and select components accordingly.

The difference between these two basic "packages" is the rpm range at which power is produced. The first provides lots of punch at low- and mid-rpm, then begins signing off around 6,500 rpm or so. The second shifts the usable power up the tach by about 1,500 rpm or thereabouts, providing little low-rpm power, but coming on strong in the midrange and topping out around 8,000 rpm.

Before building an engine, you need to remember that larger horsepower numbers usually come with increasing rpm. So, before purchasing parts, you need to be realistic about the maximum engine rpm you'd like to run the engine at, because as engine rpm increases, engine life drops. An engine that sees a maximum of about 5,500 rpm will last about twice as long as one that's frequently run to 7,000 rpm. Engines that hit 8,000 rpm on a regular basis are really only suitable for racing, because they wear parts out on a relatively frequent basis.

Assess Your Needs Honestly

With all the aforementioned information in mind, you need to be honest with yourself and provide answers to the following questions. Based on your answers, you'll have a better idea of what you want the engine to do and its operating environment. In turn, this will help set the parameters for the components that will provide the most satisfaction from your engine.

How Big Is Your Budget?

We'd all like to have an engine with the best of everything that produces enough power to circumnavigate the earth at warp speed. Unfortunately, this "dream" engine takes cubic bucks to build—bucks that most mortals haven't got.

As you try to establish how much money you have to spend, consider what jobs you can do yourself and what you'll need to farm out. Depending upon how well your garage is equipped, you can probably perform the majority of the prep work yourself, like grinding, port matching, cleaning, and assembly. When it comes to machining crankshafts, and porting heads, you're better off leaving such work to the pros.

Unless you're really strapped for cash, buy high-quality parts. Use of premium parts will add to your initial cost, but may actually cost less over the long haul because of their superior durability. Plus, you'll benefit from the increased reliability and performance they offer.

If you're on a limited budget, buy the parts that give the biggest bang for the buck first. Headers, free flow exhaust systems, free flow air cleaners, and distributor recurve kits all fall into this category. Next on your list should be a racier flat tappet cam, intake manifold, and fuel system.

But before you purchase those things, consider the possibility that you may want to upgrade a part or two at a time, and if you don't plan ahead, you could run into some compatibility problems.

If you want to leave your options open, take a look at performance "systems" offered by Edelbrock. The components in these systems are designed to work well with one another and let you add them as time and money become available. This approach can save you aggravation over the long haul, since you don't have to replace the parts you've already purchased with others that are more compatible with the new components you'd like to buy. All that's left to do is to create a short block that can handle the power the system provides with an added margin of strength in reserve.

As time goes on, more companies will probably follow Edelbrock's lead. They may even offer "emissions legal" packages that you'll be able to use on the street. So, if you're not sure of which parts to choose, or you simply want to purchase a system that has all the bugs worked out, look into one of these packages.

On the other hand, if you like a challenge and are up to the task, mix and match parts as your heart desires. Who knows, maybe you'll come up with a hot combination that everyone else will want to duplicate.

How Will the Engine Be Used?

Before you spend dollar one on components, you need to be realistic about how the engine will be used the majority of the time. Will it see duty in a vehicle that's used for daily transportation with a few stoplight grand prixs thrown in for good measure, or will it be a serious street machine that preys on the unsuspecting at 3 A.M.? Whatever the case, you'll be heartaches and dollars ahead by determining how the engine will be used, because it will help ensure all the parts you're going to use will complement one another. And that's the key to internal combustion happiness.

Also, the other vehicle systems must be compatible with the engine. If you have an engine that makes peak power at 5,000 rpm and has 25 inches of vacuum at idle, a stock automatic transmission, low three-series axle ratio and power brakes will complement it nicely. Or if you build an engine that provides its most serious grunt at 7,500 rpm and provides 10 inches of vacuum at idle (if it idles at all), you'll need a manual transmission, four-series axle ratio, and manual brakes, along with some headers to make the most of your rat.

What Type of Transmission and Rear Axle Will the Engine Be Mated To?

The type of transmission—manual or automatic—needs to be considered when selecting a camshaft. As a general rule, high-performance camshafts don't work well with an automatic transmission. However, you can make an automatic more compatible with an aggressive cam by installing a high-stall torque converter. To ensure they're compatible, ask both the prospective cam and torque converter manufacturers for their recommendations before you buy.

Manual transmissions are usually better to run behind a highly strung engine because you can keep the engine in the fat part of its power band. And no matter what type of transmission you choose, it has to have enough torque input capacity to take the punishment a hot rat can dish out.

How Much Does the Vehicle Weigh?

Vehicle weight affects engine component selection because some components work better with heavy vehicles than other parts. For example, single-plane manifolds, radical cams, and big-tube headers shift the power curve up the rpm band by a considerable margin. If you plan on moving a heavy vehicle (3,500 pounds or more), especially for street high-performance applications, you're much better off with a dual-plane intake manifold, a cam with no more than about 250 degrees duration, and 2-inch O.D. (outside diameter) headers.

What Octane Fuel Is Available?

Before you make some street screamer with an outrageous compression ratio, you need to know if it will live with the octane rating of the fuel that's available in your area. The octane rating has a direct bearing on how much compression you can safely design into your engine. The higher the compression ratio, the more power your engine can make.

If you plan on using premium unleaded gas, you should limit the compression ratio to about 9.5:1 unless you incorporate the "marine" combustion chamber modifications as outlined in chapter 10, *Cylinder Heads*, and run a moderate degree of ignition advance. Octane boosters allow you to raise compression ratio or advance ignition timing, but to what extent is dependent upon the type of booster you use and in what ratio.

How Much Time Do You Have?

The length of time it takes to properly select components, check and prepare them, and assemble them into a running engine must also be considered. This is especially true if you're transforming your daily driver into a Saturday night bomb. The "down time" that wasn't planned for can cause you to be without a ride, plus it puts lots of extra pressure on you to get the engine together quickly—and this isn't a formula for a strong running, long-running engine. So, allow lots of extra time to correct undiscovered problems.

What Are the Regulations in Your Area?

Before you run out and purchase any parts for a street-driven vehicle, you need to do two things—check your local regulations (emissions and otherwise) and make sure the parts you're buying fall within those guidelines.

Parts that are functionally equivalent to the stock parts they replace don't require any type of exemption and are legal to install in all vehicles anywhere in the country. Included in this list are some intake manifolds, ignition components, air filters, and other types of parts.

If you live in California, chances are most anything you do to increase engine performance may get you into trouble. Other states aren't so zealous in their fight against emissions. Whatever the case, as long as the parts you're installing have a California Air Resources Board (CARB) exemption in the form of an Executive Order (EO) number, you'll be within the legal guidelines of California. And since California regulations are the strictest in the country, you'll be within the regulations of the remaining 49 states. Parts that may require an EO exemption include carburetors, intake manifolds, camshafts, headers, catalytic converters, and some ignition system components.

Parts that provide the most performance are invariably those that can only be used on a racing vehicle, which may never be used on a street or highway. On the other hand, there are some areas of the country where big brother has been kept out of the high-performance garage (so to speak). In these areas, you may be able to slip some nonexempt parts into or onto your engine without generating much interest from the local police. Just keep in mind that it's up to you to install the parts that best meet your performance goals without running afoul of the law.

Likewise, if you're modifying an engine for marine use, make sure all the parts you use and any modifications you make meet or exceed U.S. Coast Guard safety standards. These standards ensure your safety.

For answers to questions about street legal parts and other aftermarket equipment, call the Specialty Equipment Marketing Association's Consumer Awareness Hotline at 1-800-514-SEMA. They'll be glad to answer your questions, or tell you who to contact to get answers.

CHAPTER ONE

COMPUTER SIMULATION

With the rising popularity of the personal computer, is it any wonder that some entrepreneurial gear-heads would design computer programs that would help you predict an engine's performance before you ever laid out dollar one? Don't be. Performance Trends has done just that. PT's Engine Analyzer has the ability to let you mix and match off-the-shelf Chevrolet parts, as well as some popular aftermarket components, so you can "assess" their performance without ever turning a wrench.

Performance Trend's Engine Analyzer is a surprisingly comprehensive program. For those who are simply curious about certain engine parts combinations, it provides a good range of parts from which to choose to build an engine. For those who want to take a deeper dive, numerous program parameters are modifiable to reflect the parts you plan on using.

After inputting parameters such as induction and exhaust systems, valve sizes, combustion chamber volume, port volumes, compression ratio, camshaft specifications, etc., this program will provide you with estimated information such as:

- horsepower
- torque
- brake specific fuel consumption
- volumetric efficiency
- vacuum at idle
- dynamic compression ratio
- cranking compression ratio

All of these factors are important in helping you decide what combination of parts best fits the intended use of your engine. And there are so many more modifiable features, you'll be truly amazed at what this program can do.

The best results are obtained when you know the values of all engine components that contribute to building horsepower. However, a number of default values are available in the program to help you get some amazingly accurate results even without inputting every last detail. Without customizing the program to any degree, I found that I could replicate the dyno figures from a number of advertised tests to within 1 to 3 percent. Pretty powerful stuff for a C-note or so.

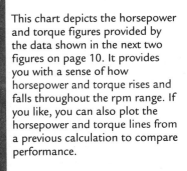

This chart depicts the horsepower and torque figures provided by the data shown in the next two figures on page 10. It provides you with a sense of how horsepower and torque rises and falls throughout the rpm range. If you like, you can also plot the horsepower and torque lines from a previous calculation to compare performance.

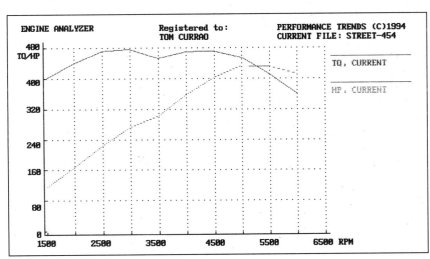

```
ENGINE ANALYZER v2.5        Registered to:       PERFORMANCE TRENDS (C)1994
HARDCOPY OUTPUT             TOM CURRAO            CURRENT FILE: STREET-454
DATE: 04-22-1997           TIME: 19:07:04

 ------  REPORT COMMENT: 468ci w/ stock rect port heads; 780cfm carb; 1 3/4x3

 ------  PROJECTED PERFORMANCE  -------------------------------------------------
RPM      1500   2000   2500   3000   3500   4000   4500   5000   5500   6000
BRK TQ    402    440    472    476    454    469    471    455    411    361
BRK HP    115    167    225    272    302    357    403    434    431    413
EX PRS     .3     .6    1.0    1.5    1.9    2.7    3.5    4.2    4.5    4.7
IN VAC     .2     .5     .6     .6     .6     .6     .7     .9    1.0    1.0
VE %     69.0   74.7   80.5   82.5   80.8   84.8   86.8   86.5   81.9   76.4
ACTCFM    150    217    293    360    411    493    568    628    655    667
FL FLW   54.8   79.1    107    131    150    180    207    229    239    243
BSFC     .478   .473   .474   .482   .495   .503   .513   .528   .554   .588
BSAC    6.012  5.946  5.969  6.067  6.230  6.324  6.456  6.644  6.967  7.405
FRN HP     12     18     27     38     50     66     84    105    128    153
MACH #   .124   .166   .207   .249   .290   .332   .373   .415   .456   .498
PSN SP   1000   1333   1667   2000   2333   2667   3000   3333   3667   4000
PSN GS    163    290    454    653    889   1162   1470   1815   2196   2613
OV %VE    3.1    4.7    5.5    3.6   -2.0   -1.8   -1.8   -1.9   -2.1   -2.2
IN VEL     77    103    129    155    181    206    232    258    284    310
IN TNP     .0     .1     .9    1.7    2.8    3.6    4.0    3.9    3.6    3.0
IN OVP    0.0    0.0     .0     .0     .0     .0    0.0    0.0    0.0    0.0
EX VEL    114    152    190    227    265    303    341    379    417    455
EX OVP    -.6   -1.6   -2.6   -2.7   -1.6   -2.4   -3.1   -3.4   -3.0   -2.4
SPKADV    21r    27r    32r     34     34     34     35     35     36     36

 ------  VALVE FLOW & CAM CALCULATIONS  -------------------- --INT-- --EXH--
OVERLAP AREA, SQ IN*DEG   21.8      TOTAL AVG FLOW COEF      .311    .263
TOTAL EXH/INT %           64.9      LOBE AREA, INCH*DEG     29.26   31.13
LOBE SEPARATION, DEG     108.5      VLV AREA, DEG*SQ-IN     355.1   230.3
                                    LOBE CENTRLINS, DEG     103.0   114.0

 ------  GENERAL ENGINE CALCULATIONS  -------------------------------------------
DISPLACEMENT, cc         7652.0     DISPLACEMENT, cu in     466.87
DYNAMIC COMP. RATIO        6.82     COMPRESSION RATIO         9.75
THEO. CRANK COMPRSSN,PSI    163     CLEARANCE VOLUME, ccs    109.3
CARB MINIMUM WOT RPM        220     EST IDLE VAC, ''Hg        10.4

 ------  'STARTING POINT' RECOMMENDATIONS @ 4000 RPM  ----  --AREA--  --DIA--
INTAKE DIMENSIONS ( FOR 1 RUNNER/CYLINDER ):
   REC INERTIA LEN, IN     18.7     REC AREA, SQ IN/IN       2.85     1.91
   SPEC INERTIA LEN, IN    10.0     REC AREA, SQ IN/IN       1.52     1.39
   REC LEN, 2ND PULSE      34.9     REC AREA, SQ IN/IN       5.31     2.60
   REC LEN, 3RD PULSE      25.1     REC AREA, SQ IN/IN       3.83     2.21
EXHAUST DIMENSIONS ( FOR 1 RUNNER/CYLINDER ):
   REC LEN, 1ST PULSE      68.0     REC AREA,300 FT/SEC      2.16     1.66
   REC LEN, 2ND PULSE      32.6     PRIMARY TUBE O.D.                 1.875
APPROX CAM FOR PEAKS ( based on current engine specs ):
   TQ PK, INT DUR @ .050    230     TQ PK, INT TAPPET LIFT   .326
   TQ PK, EXH DUR @ .050    249     TQ PK, EXH TAPPET LIFT   .368
   HP PK, INT DUR @ .050    198     HP PK, INT TAPPET LIFT   .261
   HP PK, EXH DUR @ .050    223     HP PK, EXH TAPPET LIFT   .311
```

These two pages of data on a 468-cubic-inch rat equipped with rectangular port heads, a 780-cfm carb, and 1-3/4-inch diameter x 34-inch long headers were calculated using Performance Trends' Engine Analyzer v2.5. Immediately under the heading "Projected Performance" are the horsepower and torque numbers and at what rpm they were established. Farther down, you'll also find numbers representing Brake Specific Fuel Consumption (BSFC). These numbers tell you how efficiently the engine is using fuel. You'll also find information on how much spark advance is used at what rpm. And under "General Engine Calculations" you'll find useful information such as dynamic compression ratio (6.82) and theoretical cranking compression (163 psi). Information like this is a great help in determining the effects of camshaft timing on engine compression. The documentation that comes with this program helps explain all the data so you gain a knowledge of what it means and how it impacts engine performance.

```
DATE: 04-22-1997           TIME: 19:07:04

 ------  REPORT COMMENT: 468ci w/ stock rect port heads; 780cfm carb; 1 3/4x3

 ------  ENGINE SPECIFICATIONS AND OPERATING CONDITIONS  --------------------

   BASE ENGINE SPECS:                  CAM/VALVE TRAIN SPECS,cont:
      BORE, INCHES          4.31       EXHAUST CAM SPECS:
      STROKE, INCHES           4          OPEN @.050, BBC (C)       60
      # OF CYLINDERS           8          CLOSE @.050, ATC (C)      12
      COMPRESSION RATIO (C) 9.75         MAX LOBE LIFT, IN         .36
      ACCESSORIES, 0-4 (C)     1          LASH @ VALVE, IN           0
                                          ROCKER ARM RATIO         1.7
   INTAKE SYSTEM SPECS:                ADDITIONAL CAM ADVANCE        0
      # VALVES/CYL             1
      VALVE DIAMETER, IN    2.19       SUPERCHARGER SPECS:
      PORT & RUNNER DIA, IN (C) 2         SUPERCHARGER PRESENT (Y/N) N
      PORT & RUNNER LENGTH, IN 11         S/C TYPE: CENT/RAC ROOTS/
      VALVE FLOW COEF (C)    .48            STR ROOTS/TURBO(C/R/S/T)  C
      RUNNER FLOW COEF (C)     2          BOOST LIMIT, ''HG         20
      INTAKE TYPE, 1-5 (C)     1          INTERCOOLER EFF, % (C)     0
      INTAKE HEAT (Y/N)        Y          CENT/ROOTS BELT RATIO (C)  2
      CARB-T/B FLOW RTNG, CFM (C)780      ROOTS VOL/REV, CU IN     227
      VAC SECONDARIES (Y/N)    Y          REL TURBO SIZE (S/M/L/X)   M

   EXHAUST SYSTEM SPECS:               ENVIRONMENTAL CONDS:
      # VALVES/CYL             1          BARO PRES, ''HG (C)     29.9
      VALVE DIAMETER, IN    1.88         INTAKE AIR TEMP, DEG F    60
      RUNNER DIAMETER, IN (C) 1.65       DEW POINT, DEG F (C)      32
      PORT & RUNNER LENGTH, IN 37        ELEVATION, FT (C)          0
      VALVE FLOW COEF (C)   .389         COOLANT TEMP, DEG F      165
      RUNNER FLOW COEF (C)   1.5       NITROUS OXIDE SPECS:
      EXH SYSTEM CFM RATING (C) 720       NITROUS OXIDE HP          0
                                          RPM TO START NITROUS    2000
   CAM/VALVE TRAIN SPECS:                 RPM FOR FULL NITROUS    4000
   INTAKE CAM SPECS:                   FUEL SPECS:
      OPEN @.050, BTC (C)     18          GAS/ALCOHOL (G/A)          G
      CLOSE @.050, ABC (C)    44          OCTANE (R+M)/2            94
      MAX LOBE LIFT, IN       .35
      LASH @ VALVE, IN          0
      ROCKER ARM RATIO        1.7
```

MR. GASKET'S Desktop Dyno Version 2.0G
Developed By Motion Software, Inc., Brea, California

FILE NAME: NO FILE NAME   TEST DATE: 04-22-1997

CALCULATED POWER FIGURES

RPM	HORSEPOWER	TORQUE
2000	172	451
2500	212	445
3000	248	435
3500	263	395
4000	255	335
4500	222	259
5000	171	180
5500	112	107
6000	41	36
6500	0	0
7000	0	0
7500	0	0
8000	0	0

ENGINE SPECIFICATIONS

SHORT BLOCK   Type: Manual Entry   Bore: 4.310   Stroke: 4.000
                                         Cylinders: 8   CID: 466.9

CYLINDER HEADS   Big Block/Stock Ports And Valves

VALVE SIZE   Intake: Auto Calc   Exhaust: Auto Calc

COMPRESSION   9.50:1   Cyl(cc): 956.3   Comb/Space(cc): 112.5

INDUCTION   Flow: 780 CFM   Description: 4/8-BBL Carb Or Fuel Inj

INTAKE MANIFOLD Dual-Plane Manifold

EXHAUST SYSTEM   Stock Manifolds And Mufflers

CAMSHAFT   Type: Stock Street/Economy   Lifters: Hydraulic

    Timing Measured At: Seat To Seat   Lobe Center Angle: 117
            IVO (BTDC):   12   IVC (ABDC):   62
            EVO (BBDC):   66   EVC (ATDC):   10
    Int Lift (@ Valve): 0.420   Exh Lift (@ Valve):   0.399
        Adv(+)/Ret(-):   0   Int Centerline Angle: 115

This data sheet was developed using Mr. Gasket's Desktop Dyno. It represents a stock 0.060-inch over-bored 454 and is provided as a baseline so you can see the effects of adding headers, then a high-performance street cam as illustrated in the accompanying data sheets. If you look carefully, you'll see that the 263 net horsepower peak is achieved at a low 3,500 rpm and horsepower is nonexistent at 6,500 rpm and above. On the other hand, torque is highest at 2,000 rpm and drops off substantially above 4,000 rpm. With this type of power band, high performance use isn't in the cards—towing is.

```
                MR. GASKET'S Desktop Dyno Version 2.0G
                Developed By Motion Software, Inc., Brea, California
------------------------------------------------------------------------
  FILE NAME: 468STK                              TEST DATE: 04-22-1997
------------------------------------------------------------------------

                        CALCULATED POWER FIGURES

         RPM                 HORSEPOWER              TORQUE
        ------              ------------            --------
        2000 .............. 193 .............. 508
        2500 .............. 232 .............. 487
        3000 .............. 274 .............. 480
        3500 .............. 302 .............. 453
        4000 .............. 303 .............. 398
        4500 .............. 279 .............. 326
        5000 .............. 242 .............. 254
        5500 .............. 192 .............. 184
        6000 .............. 126 .............. 111
        6500 .............. 56 .............. 45
        7000 .............. 0 .............. 0
        7500 .............. 0 .............. 0
        8000 .............. 0 .............. 0

------------------------------------------------------------------------

                        ENGINE SPECIFICATIONS

  SHORT BLOCK      Type: Manual Entry      Bore: 4.310   Stroke: 4.000
                                       Cylinders:  8    CID: 466.9

  CYLINDER HEADS   Big Block/Stock Ports And Valves

  VALVE SIZE       Intake: Auto Calc        Exhaust: Auto Calc

  COMPRESSION      9.50:1   Cyl(cc): 956.3   Comb/Space(cc): 112.5

  INDUCTION        Flow: 780 CFM   Description: 4/8-BBL Carb Or Fuel Inj

  INTAKE MANIFOLD  Dual-Plane Manifold

  EXHAUST SYSTEM   Small-Tube Headers With Mufflers

  CAMSHAFT         Type: Stock Street/Economy      Lifters: Hydraulic

  Timing Measured At: Seat To Seat      Lobe Center Angle:   117
        IVO (BTDC):    12                   IVC (ABDC):      62
        EVO (BBDC):    66                   EVC (ATDC):      10
   Int Lift (@ Valve): 0.420          Exh Lift (@ Valve): 0.399
        Adv(+)/Ret(-):  0             Int Centerline Angle: 115

------------------------------------------------------------------------
```

Mr. Gasket's DeskTop Dyno is a good program, as well. Although not nearly as sophisticated as PT's Engine Analyzer, it is much more intuitive for the first time user, allowing you to "build" an engine quickly and have a lot of fun doing it. The well-written guide that's included as part of the Desktop Dyno "package" helps tie the functions of the software to all the parameters that influence engine performance.

The real beauty of these programs is that they can help guide you to what you should spend your money on first, for the greatest performance increase, based on the components currently in use in or on your engine. Conversely, they also show you what type of "upgrades" will provide the least return for the money invested.

With some careful interpretation, you'll see how different components will move horsepower and torque up and down the rpm band. And that's important to selecting the right parts for the way your vehicle is geared.

After simply adding a set of small-tube headers with mufflers to the stock 454, horsepower improves markedly. At 2,000 rpm horsepower is up by 21 and peak horsepower is up by 40. Also notice that the horsepower curve has shifted up the rpm band by 500 rpm. Torque improves substantially as well with these headers—to the tune of 57 pound-feet at 2,000 rpm. Just as important, these headers provide as much as 77 feet-pound more torque as rpm increases. This really helps improve acceleration times.

For Further Parts Interchangeability Reading

For more detailed information on parts interchangeability, you may want to pick up a copy of the *Chevrolet Big-Block V-8 Interchange Manual*, available from Motorbooks International. In addition to lots of parts swapping information, it contains numerous charts that list thousands of factory and aftermarket components and their specifications. Think of it as one-stop shopping for your friendly rat. You could combine this information with a computerized engine building program, and "build" practically any type of engine you'd like before you ever ordered a single part. This "armchair engineering" could save you lots of money, so check it out.

For example, let's say you're building an engine for a car that will see a lot of daily driving, but want to substantially increase its performance over stock. Let's also assume the car is equipped with a transmission with an overdrive ratio, a low three-series rear axle ratio, and some 60-series tires. By swapping parts into and out of your hypothetical engine, you can find parts that will

With small-tube headers in place, a high-performance hydraulic street cam was added. Even though intake and exhaust lift are quite conservative (0.481/0.457), dropping down to an intake centerline (lobe separation) angle of 108 degrees really makes this rat come alive. Although horsepower is down by 13 at 2,000 rpm, by the time 3,000 rpm is reached, you're 4 horsepower to the good, and peak horsepower is up by 70. Not only that, there's a far greater abundance of horsepower across the rev range, and the rev range is extended by another 1,500 rpm. Torque is affected in a similar manner—although it is down slightly at 3,500 rpm and below, it's much stronger above that point and drops off at a much slower pace. Since this cam has shifted the power band up the rpm band significantly (like many other high-performance modifications), higher numerical gearing will help you take better advantage of the newfound breathing and power because they keep the engine operating at higher rpm.

increase power and torque below 4,500 rpm substantially—just what's required for this particular combination of parts to perform well.

Use of these programs will also allow you to directly see how the airflow path through the engine must be balanced in order to achieve optimum results. For example, slapping a single plane intake manifold and a big carb on a stock big-block won't net you nearly as much power as just adding a set of small-tube headers. That's because the exhaust side of the airflow path is considerably more restrictive than the intake side. So not only do the progams show which parts will best serve your needs, with some careful observations, you'll also know why. And that's fundamental to building great engines, no matter what the situation.

```
             MR. GASKET'S Desktop Dyno Version 2.0G
          Developed By Motion Software, Inc., Brea, California
-------------------------------------------------------------------------
FILE NAME: 468HDRS                              TEST DATE: 04-22-1997
-------------------------------------------------------------------------

                     CALCULATED POWER FIGURES

          RPM                HORSEPOWER            TORQUE
          ---                ----------            ------
          2000 ..............    180  ..............   472
          2500 ..............    226  ..............   474
          3000 ..............    270  ..............   473
          3500 ..............    316  ..............   474
          4000 ..............    354  ..............   465
          4500 ..............    373  ..............   435
          5000 ..............    368  ..............   386
          5500 ..............    337  ..............   322
          6000 ..............    291  ..............   255
          6500 ..............    236  ..............   190
          7000 ..............    173  ..............   130
          7500 ..............    107  ..............    75
          8000 ..............     30  ..............    20

-------------------------------------------------------------------------

                      ENGINE SPECIFICATIONS

SHORT BLOCK      Type: Manual Entry      Bore: 4.310    Stroke: 4.000
                                    Cylinders:   8       CID:  466.9

CYLINDER HEADS   Big Block/Stock Ports And Valves

VALVE SIZE       Intake: Auto Calc        Exhaust: Auto Calc

COMPRESSION      9.50:1    Cyl(cc): 956.3   Comb/Space(cc): 112.5

INDUCTION        Flow: 780 CFM    Description: 4/8-BBL Carb Or Fuel Inj

INTAKE MANIFOLD  Dual-Plane Manifold

EXHAUST SYSTEM   Small-Tube Headers With Mufflers

CAMSHAFT         Type: H.P. Street              Lifters: Hydraulic

  Timing Measured At: Seat To Seat   Lobe Center Angle:     108
            IVO (BTDC):      31             IVC (ABDC):      67
            EVO (BBDC):      67             EVC (ATDC):      31
       Int Lift (@ Valve):  0.481     Exh Lift (@ Valve):  0.457
          Adv(+)/Ret(-):     0        Int Centerline Angle:  108

-------------------------------------------------------------------------
```

With any of these programs, you can save each engine as it is "developed" for future comparisons or upgrading. You can also print out the data so you can compare all the various changes to one another to determine where in the rpm band the improvements lie—a very handy feature.

Since these programs are heavily math-based (which is nearly invisible to the user), a computer equipped a math coprocessor works much faster than one without. (How do you know if your computer has a math coprocessor? It's encoded in the processor model name. For example, if it reads *DX 486*, you're in luck. If it reads *SX 486*, you're not—but it can be upgraded if you so desire. If you have a Pentium-based machine, you're in luck, too, because all Pentium systems have math coprocessors.)

Overall, computer simulation programs put the power of the microprocessor to work for you, so you can make smarter choices in less time. Something we could all use more of.

Numerous aftermarket suppliers offer prepared blocks for street and racing applications. This particular block is a race ready Mark VI that's available from Lunati. Check what operations are completed and what needs to be done as you compare blocks. And be sure to ask what the return policy is if you're not happy with it. *Lunati*

CHAPTER TWO

CYLINDER BLOCKS

The modern big-block Chevy, as we know it, has been produced since 1965. The Mark IV was produced from 1965–1990. The Gen V that followed was a redesigned version of the Mark IV and was manufactured for model years 1991 through 1995. In 1996, Chevrolet made enough changes to the Gen V block that they felt a new name was in order. Since this new powerplant was based on the Gen V, it made sense to christen it the Gen VI. From a design standpoint, these blocks can be separated into two types, the Mark series and the Gen series.

Mark and Gen Series Production Blocks

Three significant differences exist between Mark and Gen series blocks: lubrication system, rear main seal design, and deck coolant passage shapes. These differences impact parts interchangeability, as well as certain modifications.

Mark IV blocks have oil routed to main bearings 1–4 via an oil gallery positioned on the left-hand side of the block, above the oil pan rail. The positioning of this oil gallery prevents using any main bearing caps with splayed outer bolts because they'll penetrate it, disrupting or stopping oil flow. Gen V and VI blocks aren't so limited, though, because the main oil gallery has been relocated to a position alongside the camshaft.

When Chevy redesigned the Mark IV, creating the Gen V, a larger diameter, one-piece seal replaced the two-piece seal used on Mark IV blocks. To accept the larger seal, the inside diameter of the rear main bearing cap was increased to 5.0625 inches. In turn, it also necessitated raising the rear main bearing cap 0.183 inch. This height increase

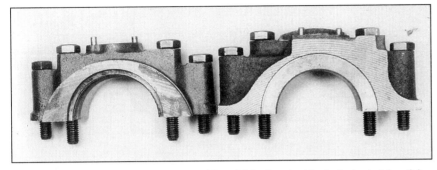

Another major difference between "Mark" and "Gen" series blocks is the height of the rear main bearing cap bolt bosses. Mark IV caps (left) are shorter than Gen series caps (right). The greater height of the Gen series cap is due to the larger diameter one-piece rear main seal used on these blocks and impacts oil pump selection.

On top is a Mark IV block and below is a Gen V block. As you can see, the coolant passage shapes are markedly different between these blocks. Each requires specific cylinder heads and cylinder head gaskets to prevent a coolant leak. Gen VI blocks have redesigned coolant passages that will accept all Mark IV and Gen series cylinder heads.

causes the body of a Mark IV oil pump to contact one of the main cap retaining bolts unless the boss for the offending bolt is reduced 0.183 inch. To avoid this less than optimal situation, use a Gen V/VI pump or an aftermarket pump.

This seal design impacted crankshaft interchangeability as well, because it meant only a Gen V crankshaft could be used. Sensing a marketing opportunity, aftermarket suppliers, such as Sallee Chevrolet, began offering a spacer that takes up the difference in diameters between the Mark IV and Gen V/Gen VI crankshafts. Its use allows a stock or stroker Mark IV crankshaft to be installed in a Gen V or VI block without any rear main seal problems.

The Gen V's deck coolant passages were also changed compared to the Mark VI. Where the Mark IV uses mostly round coolant passages, the Gen V provides irregular, tear drop-shaped passages. This difference in shape can result in coolant leaking into the lifter valley if production Mark IV heads are used on a Gen V block. When using factory-produced Mark IV heads on a Gen V block, you'll have to use an adapter kit, such as the ones produced by Sallee or Apple Chevrolet. The plugs in these kits are sealed to the block with silicone, then a premium Fel-Pro gasket for Mark IV engines is positioned over them.

This mismatch of coolant passage shapes isn't a problem with most late-model aftermarket heads because their coolant passages are usually designed to be compatible with both Mark IV and Gen V blocks. Just use the Fel-Pro 1047 head gasket (Gen V gasket) and bolt the head on—no adapters are needed.

When designing the Gen VI block, the coolant passages were resized so that all Chevy heads can be bolted on without fear of a coolant leak. No special head gasket kit is required.

A bonus with 502-cubic-inch Gen V and VI blocks is that they use siamesed cylinders. Instead of coolant passing between each cylinder, the cylinders are joined together. This strengthens the cylinders significantly and allows larger cylinder bores.

Mark IV cylinder blocks have been produced in a variety of styles. The standard performance blocks can be identified by their two-bolt main bearing caps. Four bolts secure the main bearing caps in high-performance blocks and are often designated as such by the PASS HIGH PERF or HIGH PERF PASS cast into the front of the block in the recess for the timing chain. In addition, they have two drilled and tapped bosses for oil cooler lines above the oil filter mounting boss. A 3/8-inch pipe thread is at the front and a 3/4-inch pipe thread is found further rearward. But don't use these as definitive evidence that the block has four-bolt mains. Instead, remove the oil pan and see for yourself.

Bow Tie Blocks

Designed for serious street or racing use, Bow Tie blocks are the strongest and most durable blocks Chevrolet manufactures. Compared to production blocks, all Bow Tie blocks have thicker decks and cylinders. The thicker decks provide a better clamping surface and the thicker cylinders allow for a larger bore—

Why do you think they call them Bow Tie blocks?

Bow Tie blocks use siamesed cylinder bores to increase block strength and to allow larger bores.

15

4.560 inches in Mark IVs and 4.600 inches in Gen V models. In addition, the cylinders in all Bow Tie blocks are siamesed, which allows larger cylinder bores while strengthening the cylinders significantly.

The decks on Bow Tie blocks are unique among GM-produced blocks. To begin, all the coolant passages are round and relatively small. This allows the use of any Mark IV or Gen series cylinder head provided the proper head gasket is used. However, if you want to use a Mark IV head on a Gen V Bow Tie block, you'll need to plug the vent holes at the front of each deck to prevent coolant from bypassing the

Looking through the water pump port, you can see the end of the cylinder head bolt boss doesn't open up to the water jacket. These "blind" head bolt holes, found on all Bow Tie blocks, helps strengthen the block while preventing coolant from working its way up the head bolt threads. All other blocks require the use of sealer on the head bolt threads to prevent leaks.

Bow Tie blocks (pictured) weigh 35–40 pounds more than standard production blocks due to their thicker bulkheads, decks, and cylinders. The average standard production block weighs about 230 pounds. Tall-deck blocks are about 10 pounds heavier.

CYLINDER BLOCK CASTING NUMBERS

Casting #	Engine Size	Block Design	Notes
364779	366	Mark IV	heavy-duty truck block, thick cylinder walls
3999293	366,454	Mark IV	
3855961	396, 427	Mark IV	2-bolt mains, cannister oil filter
3855962	396	Mark IV	4-bolt mains, thick cylinder walls
3902406	396	Mark IV	2- or 4-bolt mains
3902466	396	Mark IV	
3916323	396	Mark IV	2- or 4-bolt mains
39335440	396	Mark IV	2- or 4-bolt mains
3716323	396	Mark IV	2- or 4-bolt mains, spin-on oil filter
3955272	396	Mark IV	2- or 4-bolt mains
3968854	396, 402	Mark IV	2- or 4-bolt mains, medium cyl. wall thickness
3999290	396, 402	Mark IV	
6272177	402	Mark IV	
340220	427	Mark IV	
364776	427	Mark IV	4-bolt mains, heavy-duty truck block
473478	427	Mark IV	4-bolt mains, heavy-duty truck block
3782870	427	Mark IV	
3869942	427	Mark IV	2- or 4-bolt mains, thick cylinder walls
3904351	427	Mark IV	2- or 4-bolt mains, thick cylinder walls
3916321	427 (L88)	Mark IV	2- or 4-bolt mains
3935439	427	Mark IV	
3937726	427	Mark IV	4-bolt mains, heavy-duty truck block
3946052	427 (Al ZL1)	Mark IV	4-bolt mains, thin wall sleeves
3955270	427	Mark IV	2- or 4-bolt mains
3955276	427	Mark IV	4-bolt mains, heavy-duty truck block
3963516	427	Mark IV	
3969858	427	Mark IV	4-bolt mains, heavy-duty truck block
3999294	427	Mark IV	4-bolt mains ,heavy-duty truck block
361959	454	Mark IV	
3963512	427, 454	Mark IV	Relieved lower cylinders, thick walls
14044807	427	Mark IV	
3963513	454	Mark IV	
3999289	454	Mark IV	
14015445	454	Mark IV	4-bolt mains
10051107	454 (Bow Tie)	Mark IV	4-bolt mains, 1st Bow Tie w/ siamesed bores
10114182	454	Gen V	
10237297	454	Gen V	
14096859	502 marine	Gen V	4-bolt mains, thin main bulkheads
	7400	Gen VI	4-bolt mains

engine and returning directly to the radiator. Also, all the head bolt holes are "blind," meaning they have a "sealed" bottom. Therefore, no sealer is required on the head bolt threads.

For a no-holds-barred racing engine, Bow Tie short and tall-deck blocks are offered in a race-prepared state. These blocks are factory-blue-printed using CNC equipment and are ready to use "as is" after decking and honing. Above and beyond the "normal" Bow Tie features, these blocks have steel main bearing caps, main bearing cap studs and nuts, and enlarged main oil galleries. They also have head bolt bosses in the lifter valley. These allow the use of a sixth bolt around the combustion chamber—an important feature for keeping a good clamp on the cylinder heads when high compression ratios are used.

Casting Numbers

The block casting number denotes that a particular "raw" block

meets certain design specifications. In turn, Chevrolet has the option of machining that raw casting any way it sees fit to provide a specific part. When the part is machined, it's given a particular part number. Consequently, one casting can be used for a variety of different part numbers. And this is the reason you can't make a direct correlation between a *casting* number and a *part* number. For example, block casting 3968854 was used for both 396s and 402s, yet the 396 version has a different part number than a 402 because of the difference in cylinder bore diameters. So keep this situation in mind when selecting a used block.

Block Selection

As you're selecting a block, remember that maximum bore size is dictated by core shift. Core shift can be identified by comparing the relationship between the lifter bores and lifter bosses. If the bores are centered in the bosses, there is no core shift. The farther the bores are offset within the bosses, the greater the degree of core shift. The greater the core shift, the less the cylinders can be bored. To prevent cylinder bore cracking, the minimum cylinder wall thickness is 0.190 inch for street engines and 0.240 inch for racing engines. Also, remember that the quality of the ring seal is dependent upon the rigidity of the cylinder bores, which, in turn, is dependent upon cylinder wall thickness.

All factory production blocks (except early 396s) can be bored an additional 0.060 inch beyond the original bore size. Early 396s can usually be bored 0.125 inch without making the cylinder walls too thin.

Unlike regular production blocks that come fully machined, some new blocks require machining before they can be used. In some instances, the deck surfaces aren't square as shipped. These blocks will need to be decked for optimum performance. Mark IV Bow Tie blocks require a special fixture to locate the bore centers prior to honing, as well as the expertise to use it properly.

Also, a significant number of Mark IV and production Bow Tie blocks have lifter bores that aren't properly indexed to the cam. In order to use a roller cam in these blocks, the lifter bores will have to be trued. Although you can't tell simply by looking at them, set aside some money to have this checked and possibly corrected. Alternately, you can use the roller lifters offered by Crower or other companies that will compensate for minor amounts of misalignment. Late-model Gen V, and all Gen VI and Bow Tie CNC blocks don't have this problem because they're machined for roller cams at the factory.

New Versus Used

When a new block is cast, then machined, it develops internal stresses. The heating and cooling cycles that occur over thousands of miles of operation cause these stresses to be relieved gradually and the block becomes dimensionally stable. It's this dimensional stability that makes "seasoned" blocks the preferred foundation for a high-performance street or racing engine, because they're less likely to distort. New blocks haven't

When selecting a used block, check the position of the lifter bores within the lifter bosses. The closer the bores are to being centered within the bosses, the bettered centered the cylinder bores are within the block. This has a positive impact on how far the block can be bored.

been through these cycles, consequently, they distort somewhat after they're put into service. This distortion causes misalignment of components, increasing internal friction and reducing horsepower.

Factory Bow Tie and aftermarket blocks have numerous features that are desirable from a racing standpoint, but they're usually not available used. Aftermarket high-performance cast-iron blocks are available from Keith Black and World Products. Similar blocks made of aluminum can be purchased from Donovan or Rodeck. Some of these blocks can be outfitted with stroker cranks and oversize pistons to provide 750 cubic inches or more of blindingly fast rat. If you elect to go this route, plan on spending around $15,000 to get the engine together.

Two-Bolt Versus Four-Bolt

When selecting a block, you need to consider whether you'll need two- or four-bolt mains. A two-bolt main bolt block will hold up under about 550 horsepower, so it's a good basis for a moderate street motor. If the engine will be putting out more power than this, now, or in the future, get a four-bolt main block. Although a two-bolt main block can be con-

verted to four-bolt mains (since the blocks are otherwise identical), check into the price for this service. It may make more financial sense just to sell your two-bolt main block and buy a four-bolt main block instead.

For two-bolt main blocks subjected to 450 horsepower or more, or four-bolt main blocks subjected to 600 horsepower or more, use studs instead of bolts to secure the main bearing caps. Studs decrease the

Four-bolt main blocks should be used when power exceeds 550 horsepower.

load on the block compared to bolts.

When you move up to around 800 horsepower, such as with an all-out racing block, a crankshaft stroke of 4.500 inches or greater, or an engine that's heavily supercharged or nitroused, steel main bearing caps are required. Preferably, they should use angled (splayed) outer bolts for the number 2, 3, and 4 caps. Angling the bolts outward allows them to clamp into the sturdiest part of the block, minimizing cap movement and distortion of the bearing bores. These features are available in a Gen V Bow Tie blocks, as well as Donovan and World Products blocks.

Short-Deck Versus Tall-Deck

Except for the difference in deck height, passenger car and truck blocks are virtually the same. Passenger car blocks measure 9.8 inches between the crankshaft centerline and the top of the deck. Truck blocks (as in medium- and heavy-duty, *not* light-duty) are 0.400 inches taller than passenger car blocks at 10.200 inches.

Stroker Engines

The potential for increased engine displacement—that is, increasing bore and stroke—is one of the primary considerations when selecting a block. The block has to be able to accommodate the bore and stroke you need before you even consider it. With a maximum overbore of 0.060 inches for most production 396s, and all production 402s, 427s, 454s, and 502s, the maximum displacement increase you'll get from boring is a paltry 6–8 cubic inches. On the other hand, a 427 with a 0.060-inch overbore and a 4.250-inch stroker crank will get you up to 467 cubic inches—a substantial 40-cubic-inch increase. Pound for pound, an increase in displacement will get you more horsepower and torque more cheaply than just about any modification.

The best compromise for a short-deck stroker engine is a 4.250-inch stroker crank. Provided you use a factory rod, most blocks are already relieved near the oil pan rails to clear the rod bolts when using this crank. Also, there's usually sufficient clearance between the rods and the cam. This combination of 4.250-inch stroker crank with factory rods results in a torque monster between 3,000 and 3,500 rpm—just the ticket for that hot street ride or performance boat.

However, if you want to build an engine for high-rpm power, you'll want to use an aftermarket rod with a center-to-center distance described in Chapter 5, *Connecting Rods*. The caveat is that these rods may be somewhat bulkier (although stronger) than the factory rods. This usually isn't a problem with Mark IV blocks, but Gen V and VI blocks have less generous rod bolt reliefs alongside the oil pan rail, so you're going to need to do some grinding to clear the rods.

As far as stroker cranks go, a 4.375-inch stroke is the practical limit for a short-deck block. If you opt to go this far, you can still use a 0.400-inch longer rod to increase piston dwell time and reduce rod angularity. The best benefit of using a 4.375-inch stroke is that you can have an engine that looks like a 454 but is able to pack a punch of up to 510 cubic inches. Just the ticket for those Friday night drags down Main Street.

Although it's possible to use a 4.500-inch stroke crankshaft in a short-deck block, the piston skirt is almost entirely out of the bore when the piston is at BDC. In most situations, this will let the piston ring oil rails come partially out of the bore, which will spell disaster.

Use of a tall-deck block enables you to increase engine displacement more readily than a short-deck block. Depending upon the particular block and connecting rods being used, crankshaft strokes up to 4.250 inches will usually fit without any modifications. Use of stroker cranks longer than 4.250 inches, or some types of aftermarket rods, will require enlarging the existing notches at the bottom of the cylinder bores near the oil pan rail for connecting rod bolt clearance. On Mark IV blocks, just be careful that you don't cut into the main oil gallery on the left hand side of the block. And on all blocks, be sure to check the clearance of the rods to the camshaft. A 4.500-inch stroke crankshaft can be used in a tall-deck block, if rods with relatively narrow big ends are used and the oil pan rail area of the block is relieved to clear the rods and rod bolts.

Besides stroke, there are other considerations to using a tall-deck block. The extra 0.400 inch crank-to-deck difference requires the use of a longer distributor housing and shaft. It also necessitates using 0.400-inch longer pushrods for proper rocker arm geometry. And a wider intake manifold is needed too, since the taller decks position the cylinder heads farther away from one another.

Four-bolt main bearing caps with splayed (angled) outer bolts provide the best insurance that the crankshaft will stay put. This setup is required for ultra-high output and is used on some Gen V Bow Tie and World Products blocks, as well as this Donovan block.

Later production and service Mark IV blocks, along with all Gen series blocks, have cast-in reliefs to clear the connecting rod bolts. If your block doesn't have these reliefs, or the reliefs aren't sufficient to clear your particular rod bolts, you can grind them into the block.

Because there are very few performance intake manifolds that fit a tall-deck block, the most common way of dealing with this situation is to use a performance manifold that's designed for the short-deck block, along with a short-deck distributor (or height-adjustable aftermarket distributor) and pair of intake manifold spacers. Both Weiand and Moroso offer these spacers, available as part number 8204 and 65090, respectively.

Some tall-deck aftermarket blocks position the cam higher in the block to allow for a significant increase in crankshaft stroke without interference between the connecting rods and the cam. If you opt for one of these blocks, it will require a longer timing chain, or one of the trick belt-drive setups offered by the aftermarket. Mountain motor blocks, like those offered by Keith Black, Donovan, Rodeck, and World Products, offer sufficient acreage to build a 700-cubic-inch or larger monster. And the big ones require an extra-wide oil pan to fill the space between the oil pan rails.

Since Merlin blocks have stronger decks, they're preferred for supercharger applications, as well as truck-pull engines.

Aluminum Blocks

In spite of their higher purchase price, aluminum blocks offer a number of advantages over their cast-iron counterparts. Obviously, aluminum is lighter—about half the weight of cast-iron. Aluminum blocks can also last a lifetime, because they use replaceable iron cylinder liners. And if the block cracks, it can be repaired by a welder skilled in the use of MIG or TIG welding equipment.

Maybe the biggest drawback to using an aluminum block is that it costs some horsepower versus a cast-iron block since it dissipates heat faster. And heat is horsepower. Also, the cylinder walls don't stay nearly as round as those made from cast iron. So, you're trading away some power to save weight. However, sometimes weight is more critical than peak horsepower numbers. And that's when an aluminum block is preferred.

Since the design and construction of aluminum blocks can vary from manufacturer to manufacturer, clearance and torque specifications can vary considerably. Aluminum's thermal expansion rate also dictates that head gaskets with a coating such as graphite or teflon be used.

Recommendations

Mark IV, Gen V, and Gen VI blocks are a solid base for a street, marine, or semi-serious racing engine. When it comes to production blocks, each block works equally well for most applications. And factory production 502 cubic-inch Gen V and Gen VI blocks with siamesed bores will support 800 horsepower reliably.

If you'll be pumping out more power than this, or want to use a bore larger than 4.500 inches, go with a Bow Tie block or appropriate after-market block. These blocks should also be used when you can't get the displacement you want out of a regular production block, or the engine will be supercharged or turbocharged. Both Mark IV and Gen V Bow Tie blocks are preferred over production blocks for drag racing outputs greater than 650 horsepower, marine outputs greater than

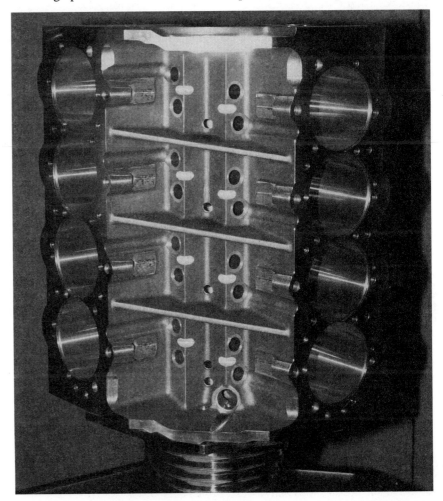

Aluminum blocks, like this one from Trick Flow Specialties, typically use reinforcing ribs between the cylinder banks to increase block rigidity. Aluminum blocks weigh around 120 to 130 pounds—about 50 percent less than their cast-iron counterparts.

600 horsepower, and all other forms of professional racing, because of their greater durability. Their extra durability comes from thicker decks, cylinder walls, and main bearing bulkheads.

Machining

Quality machine work is essential to the power output and life of any engine. And as power output rises, the quality of the machine work becomes critical. Slight imperfections that would never be noticed in a regular engine might spell disaster under the higher stresses inherent with a high-output engine. So, seek out a competent machine shop that has a strong reputation for quality, high-performance engine work. Whatever you do, don't buy machine work based solely on cost. Quality work takes time, and time costs money.

Before you send the block out to the machine shop, degrease it and then clean it with hot, soapy water so you can check it for any obvious flaws, like cracks in the cylinders, lifter valley, main bearing webs, or on the decks. Cylinder wall cracks typically run up and down in the cylinders, while lifter valley cracks usually run from front to rear. Sometimes cracks will appear between the bolt holes on the deck due to bolt overtorquing.

Also make sure all the motor mount bolt bosses are intact, as well as those on the bellhousing. If it passes these inspections, it's good enough to take to the machine shop. But before you do, remove all the freeze plugs and oil gallery plugs. Remove the freeze plugs by knocking them sideways, then levering them out with a seal remover or a pair of locking pliers. Doing this will ensure the cooling jacket is cleaned thoroughly.

Magnafluxing and Pressure Testing

The first thing to ask for when you roll your block through the shop door is to have it Magnafluxed. If it's cracked, you don't want to pay for machine work on a dead player. And unless you're sure the block is in good condition, have it pressure tested to check for any internal cracks. If it passes these tests, have it machined.

Hot-Tanking and Jet Cleaning

The next step is to have the block hot-tanked or jet-cleaned. This will further rid the block of grease and corrosion. If you opt for hot-tanking, the cam bearings will be destroyed, necessitating their replacement. And unless you have the proper tools and expertise to install new cam bearings, let the shop do it for you.

Align Honing

Align honing is a machining process used to correct main bore misalignment.

When a block is new, it has certain stresses in it as a result of the machining and casting processes. When crankshafts are fitted to these new blocks, minor discrepancies in the main bearing saddles and caps are corrected by selectively fitting thicker or thinner bearings to achieve the proper clearance. As the engine accumulates mileage, the stresses in the block are gradually relieved, causing the main bearing saddles and caps to move slightly. During this period, the bearings and crankshaft have time to adapt to these changes. All is well and good until you replace the bearings and crankshaft. These new or reconditioned parts haven't had the benefit of time to adapt to the changes in main bearing saddle and cap alignment. If this misalignment is severe enough, it can cause the bearings and/or crankshaft to die a premature death.

The time-honored way to check for this misalignment in your garage is to install the new or reconditioned crankshaft in the block onto new main bearings that have the proper clearance and have been oiled. After torquing the main bearing caps to specifications, the crankshaft should rotate freely without binding at any point. If it binds, the block needs to be align-honed.

While this test method is satisfactory for a normal rebuild, it's not suitable for high-performance work because it can't account for the wear caused by the constant pounding of the crankshaft on its power strokes. As a result of the untold power strokes that occur between rebuilds, the main bearing caps become slightly egg-shaped. And this prevents the main bearings from fully

transferring the heat to which they're subjected to the block. In turn, this can cause main bearing and crankshaft failure. Align-honing can remedy this situation.

Align honing is a process where a small amount of material (usually 0.005 inch) is taken off the mating surfaces of the main bearing caps and saddles. Then a self-centering abrasive stone on a long mandrel is passed through them to ensure they are perfectly round, and square to the block.

All blocks used for high-performance work (other than new CNC-machined blocks, which are just fine the way they come from the factory) should be align honed to ensure the crankshaft bearing bores are straight and true. Although you could get away with not having this done provided the block passed the test mentioned previously, if you have the machinist measure the alignment of the main bearing bores, it could cost more than half of what it would cost to have him align hone it. So, if there's a question about the straightness and trueness of the main bearing bores, just have the machinist align hone it and be done with it.

The catch about align honing is finding a machine shop with someone who's qualified to do it. Unlike cylinder boring, the quality of align honing is more dependent upon the machinist. Rarely will you find a shop that machines just regular, run-of-the-mill engines that has align-honing equipment and someone qualified to use it. And a bad job will do more harm than good. So, your best bet is to patronize a reputable machine shop that specializes in high-performance work.

If your block requires align honing, be sure that it's outfitted with the exact fasteners you plan on using so that the main bearing caps have exactly the same amount of clamping force applied to them. This will ensure the most accurate machine work.

Decking

Decking of the block entails machining of both cylinder deck surfaces. It accomplishes three things on Chevy big-blocks:

- Ensures the decks are flat and square to the centerline of the crankshaft
- Establishes the height between the flat part of the piston dome and the deck (deck height)
- "Indexes" the block, ensuring the decks are 90 degrees apart from one another, if a BHJ Blok-Tru is used.

Deck height is important to engine performance. If it's insufficient, the pistons may contact the heads, resulting in major engine damage. If it's too great, compression will be low and performance will suffer.

As with align honing, this type of work may not be necessary on a block that will see just street high-performance use. Checking the flatness of each deck with a machinist's straight edge and a feeler gage is usually sufficient. If warpage is less than 0.004 inch, the block will be fine. On the other hand, if warpage is greater than this, or you intend to use the engine for racing, the block requires decking. If decking is required, the block must be align honed first, because the decking operation is based on the position of the crankshaft in the block, and if the crankshaft bore isn't square within the block or is out-of-round, the decking will be off, as well. Engines that will see heavy doses of nitrous or supercharging can benefit by having the decks O-ringed at this point, too.

Also, keep in mind that if the block has been decked (or the heads have been milled), the mating surfaces of the intake manifold will need to be machined so it matches the heads and block, because either process moves the heads' intake manifold mating surfaces closer together.

Honing

Honing is required to ensure the cylinder bores are perfectly round, straight, and true to the crankshaft. Bores that are perfectly round are essential to gaining the most power possible from any engine because it ensures the best possible ring seal. Bore surface finish is just as important as roundness. Because modern rings are lapped at the factory, the smoothest bore finish possible will

Honing the block with torque plates bolted to the deck is the best way to ensure a good ring seal. The plates should be bolted down with your fasteners for best results.

result in the greatest horsepower gains. But cylinder finish is dependent upon the type of rings being used. And when it comes to boring and honing, there's no substitute for excellent equipment that's well-maintained and operated by a conscientious, experienced, machinist. For this process, the machinist will need your pistons so the bores can be matched to each piston specifically.

Use of torque plates when boring and honing is mandatory for a racing engine and is a good practice for a high-performance street engine. A good torque plate simulates the loads imposed by the cylinder head when it is bolted to the block. Honing the block to the final dimension with torque plates installed ensures that the cylinders will be round when the engine is actually run—not just sitting in a honing machine.

Whether you plan on using bolts or studs to retain the heads, make sure the torque plates are retained by the type of fastener you plan on using since bolts distort the block a little differently than do studs. Also, the same exact type of head gasket should be used underneath the torque plate as you'll be using underneath the cylinder heads, as each type of head gasket will load the block a little differently.

When considering an engine overbore size, keep in mind that standard overbore sizes (0.030- and 0.060-inch) have the greatest selection of ring types. If you choose to run a nonstandard overbore (such as 0.040-inch), you'll find no manufacturer offers file-fit rings for these applications. So if you're not happy with the ring end gaps as they come from the factory, you'll have two choices, stick with the available rings and settle for additional blow-by because the ring end gaps are too large, or scrap the nonstandard oversize pistons and have the block honed again for standard oversize rings and buy a new set of pistons and rings to fit—definitely bad options.

Plateau Honing

Plateau honing is performed after traditional honing. Using cork stones with embedded diamond dust mounted on the honing bar, the bar is passed through the cylinder five or six times. This helps remove the tiny, folded pieces of metal that occur with honing, resulting in an ultra-smooth cylinder bore finish that's great for all piston rings, except those with a chrome face.

After getting your block and pistons back from the machine shop, make sure you correctly identify which piston fits which cylinder. Both pistons and cylinder bores vary in size slightly, and if your machine shop was doing its job by matching the pistons to the bores, changing this relationship can make for less than optimum piston-to-bore clearance.

ENGINE DISPLACEMENT CHART

Engine	Overbore (in.)	Cylinder Bore Size (in.)	Displacement (w/stock stroke)	Displacement (w/ 1/4in stroker crank)	Displacement (w/ 1/2in stroker crank)
396	0.000	4.094	396	421	In most cases, a 1/2in
396	0.020	4.114	400	425	stroker crank will not fit.
396	0.030	4.124	402	427	
396	0.040	4.134	404	430	
396	0.060	4.154	408	434	
402	0.000	4.125	402	428	In most cases, a 1/2in
402	0.020	4.145	406	432	stroker crank will not fit.
402	0.030	4.155	408	434	
402	0.040	4.165	410	436	
402	0.060	4.185	414	440	
427	0.000	4.250	427	454	482
427	0.020	4.270	431	458	487
427	0.030	4.280	433	460	489
427	0.040	4.290	435	463	491
427	0.060	4.310	439	467	496
454	0.000	4.250	454	482	511
454	0.020	4.270	458	487	515
454	0.030	4.280	461	489	518
454	0.040	4.290	463	491	520
454	0.060	4.310	467	496	525
454	0.100 *	4.350	476	505	535
454	0.125*	4.375	481	511	541
454	0.250*	4.500	509	541	573
502	0.000	4.466	501	533	564
502	0.020	4.486	506	537	569
502	0.030	4.496	508	540	572
502	0.060	4.526	515	547	579

* Safe overbore only for Chevrolet bow tie and certain aftermarket blocks. For production blocks, recommended maximum overbore is 0.060in on blocks with minimal core shift. See the *Cylinder Blocks* chapter for more details.

Roller Cam Preparation

If the production block you're using wasn't machined for a roller cam from the factory, it will probably need some machine work if you want to use a roller cam. Numerous factory production blocks have lifter bores that aren't at an exact right angle to the camshaft. If you're using flat tappet lifters, this doesn't pose a problem, since the rounded feet on these lifters allow them to compensate for any minor misalignment. However, the roller wheel used on a roller lifter is perfectly flat, as is the cam lobe. So, if the lifter bore isn't at a 90-degree angle to the cam lobe, the edge of the wheel will cut into the cam lobe, possibly destroying them both.

To correct this problem, the lifter bores are enlarged and bronze sleeves are installed. The inside diameter of each sleeve is then reamed so the lifter is at an exact 90-degree angle to the cam. Later design Mark IV and Gen V Bow Tie blocks, as well as blocks that are machined using computer numerical-controlled (CNC) equipment, rarely have this problem.

To avoid this machining and its cost, Crower Cams has mechanical roller lifters that can accommodate lifter bore misalignment up to 0.002 inch. This makes them suitable for practically all blocks with lifter bore misalignment.

Block Preparation
Bore Blending

Bore blending is a process where the tops of the cylinder bores are relieved to unshroud the intake and exhaust valves. This "laying back" of the bore increases the flow into and out of the cylinder because it removes the step at the top of the bore. The factory performs a similar process on high-performance 396s and service 427 blocks. However, these can be improved upon by blending, as well.

How far the bore should be laid back depends upon the relationship between the bore size and the valve sizes, as well as combustion chamber design. A 454 with a 4.250-inch diameter bore with 2.19/1.88-inch intake and exhaust valves won't need to be laid back more than 0.150 inch at its widest point to appreciably increase intake valve flow. On the other hand, a 396 block with a 0.030-inch overbore using the same 2.19/1.88-inch valves would need to be laid back 0.200 inch at the top of the bore to achieve similar results. The area of the cylinder underneath the exhaust valve doesn't need to be laid back as far in either case, because the exhaust valve isn't as close to the side of the cylinder as is the intake valve.

If you're using open-chamber heads, it's also beneficial to lay back the top of the cylinder where it meets the edge of the combustion chamber. Closed-chamber heads won't benefit from this step because the edge of the combustion chamber, where the spark plug lies, is already inboard of the cylinder wall. All of this work improves engine breathing markedly, especially with 454 and smaller-bore engines.

Before you go to town with this procedure, you need to realize that any material that you remove will decrease compression because, in effect, you're making the top part of the cylinder part of the combustion chamber. But even with the decrease in compression, you end up with a net gain. You should also read the "Valve Unshrouding" section in Chapter 10, *Cylinder Heads*, to gain an appreciation of what you're getting into before you actually do it.

To perform this operation, clean both decks with some carb cleaner on a rag. Use a dark-colored permanent marker to color the tops of the cylinder bores on the deck so you can see the scribe lines you'll make later. Now lay the head gasket you're going to use over the dowel pins so all the gasket holes line up with the holes in the deck. Carefully scribe the outline of the head gasket on the deck where the valve reliefs are located, as well as the area where the combustion chamber would lie between them.

Now, measure how far down the top side of the top compression ring is from the deck of the piston. Subtract 0.050 inch from this figure and this is as far as the blending should extend down the cylinder. Never relieve the cylinder into the ring travel area or you'll lose your ring seal and the block will be scrap! Apply some duct tape to the cylinder to delineate this "no grind" zone and to protect the cylinder.

With the head gasket removed from the block, you can begin relieving the cylinder with a medium-grit grinding wheel chucked into a die grinder. Stay 0.030 inch inboard of the gasket outline to match the cylinders to the heads, as well as to prevent any problems with the head gasket hanging into the cylinder bores. Also, work to make the blend from the top of the bore into the

bore as gradual as possible. Finish the job by smoothing the grinding marks with fine grit sanding cones.

Stroker Crank Checks

Whatever block you use, you need to ensure that there's enough clearance between the crankshaft and the block. Mock-up the crank and piston assemblies in the block, then slowly rotate the crankshaft. With a stroker crank, interference between the rod bolts and the oil pan rail of the block is common. You can use a die grinder to obtain the required 0.050-inch minimum clearance, but you need to be extra careful if you're using a Mark IV-style block, because the main oil gallery in these blocks runs right along the left-hand oil rail. If you remove too much material from this area, you'll break into the oil gallery and be in deep trouble. Aluminum rods will require deeper reliefs in the block due to their larger size, so work carefully. For more checks when using a stroker crank, refer to Chapter 3, *Crankshafts*.

Deburring

To reduce the potential for stress risers, chamfer all the sharp edges on both the inside and outside of the block. A fine- or medium-grit grinding wheel mounted in a die grinder or drill motor can do the job here. Pay special attention to the areas around machined surfaces so you don't touch them with the grinding wheel. Masking tape can be used to protect these areas if you're not sure of your tool handling abilities.

The oil drain-back channels usually have casting flash inside them that reduces their size, and, in turn, can slow the rate at which the oil drains back into the crankcase. To improve this situation, remove all the casting flash with the grinding wheel and smooth the channels. Pay special attention to the oil supply holes where they make transitions from one plane to another. Any misalignment here can slow the flow of oil through the block.

Thread Chasing

Standard block preparation includes running a tap through all of the existing threaded holes to remove any residual sealer or grime.

This step can't be stressed strongly enough, because bolt torque is dependent on clean threads. If something increases the torque it takes to rotate a bolt, that exact amount of torque is taken away from the clamping force of the bolt. Since the bolt isn't as tight as it should be, the chances of a leak and/or gasket failure increase accordingly.

Lifter Valley Screens

Before cleaning the block, carefully measure and cut steel screens to fit over the drain back slots in the lifter valley. They serve to keep any major valve train debris out of the bottom of the engine should a problem develop. After the block is cleaned, epoxy the screens into position.

Cleaning

Cleanliness of the block is critical. Plan on cleaning the block at least twice: Once after disassembly and all the machining operations and grinding are complete so you can mock-up the engine when it's clean, and a second time just prior to final assembly. Inexpensive brushes made specifically for cleaning engine blocks can be purchased and make the task of cleaning all the long passages in the block possible.

A strong solution of liquid dish soap and hot water will go a long way toward ridding the block of all loose debris and oil residue. Pay particular attention to all the oil galleries and bolt holes to be sure they are absolutely clean. When all the surfaces are clean, you should be able to wipe a finger on any of them and not have any dirt or oily residue on your finger. Use a strong stream of water to flush all the residue out.

After washing, blow the block dry with compressed air to ensure no moisture remains. As soon as the block is dry, wipe the cylinder bores with a clean, lint-free rag that has been soaked in automatic transmission fluid (ATF). The ATF helps remove the fine dust left behind after the honing process. Spray the rest of the machined surfaces with a combination moisture displacer/rust preventative, such as WD-40. To prevent airborne dust and dirt from settling in the block, cover it with a large plastic garbage bag.

High-performance crankshafts like this one from Trick Flow Specialties have the leading edge of the counterweights tapered to reduce windage losses. Also notice the drilled rod journals to minimize reciprocating weight.

CHAPTER THREE

CRANKSHAFTS

A crankshaft in a high-performance engine is in for its fair share of work. The incredible loading it has to endure as a result of high rpm, high compression, and maybe even supercharging or nitrous oxide can put the wrong crankshaft—or one that's improperly prepared—in a world of hurt. The following information will help you decide what type of crankshaft is right for your engine and how to prepare it to last.

Internal and External Balancing

Big-block Chevy crankshafts are different than most other crankshafts because they can be either internally or externally balanced. Simply stated, this means either the crankshaft's counterweights are heavy enough to offset the weight of the crankpins plus the piston and rod assemblies, or weight must be added outside the crankshaft to do this. Chevy 396s, 402s, and 427s all use internally balanced crankshafts. That is, all the necessary counter-

weight is within, or *internal*, to the engine. The dampers, flywheels, and flexplates used with these engines need no additional weight to counterbalance the piston and rod assemblies and the crankpins.

When the 454 was born, the crankshaft pins were extended to provide another 0.240 inch of stroke. The problem was the crankshaft counterweights weren't heavy enough to offset the weight of the longer crankpins, and since there wasn't any room left in the crankcase to add extra weight to the crankshaft, the additional weight was added *externally*—to both the crankshaft damper and flywheel. Hence the name externally balanced. Whether the crankshaft is internally or externally balanced is an important point to remember, because if you use the wrong damper or flywheel, the crankshaft will self-destruct due to the imbalance.

In some situations, it's best to internally balance a normally externally balanced crankshaft. Why? Because at very high rpm (8,000+), the extra mass in the externally balanced flywheel and damper can cause the crankshaft to flex excessively. This flexing can cause the crankshaft to break or wipe out the main bearings, which will then cause the crank to fail. If you're building a high-performance street machine, you don't need to worry about this unless you're running the engine above 8,000 rpm for long periods of time.

Crankshaft stroke plays into this situation as well, because strokes greater than 4.250 inches tend to flex more at high rpm. And the greater the stroke, the greater the flexing. The uneven loads imposed by a counterweighted flywheel and damper only add to this problem. Consequently, strokes greater than 4.250 inches benefit most from internal balancing. But internally balancing a crank doesn't come cheap—on the order of hundreds of dollars.

So, you also need to consider what type of damper and flywheel (or flexplate) you already possess. If you have an externally balanced damper and flywheel, you'll probably want to keep the engine externally balanced as long as the crankshaft stroke is 4.250 inches or less. On the other hand, if you haven't yet purchased any parts and you want to use a crankshaft that has a stroke greater than 4.250 inches, the internally balanced route is the best way to go.

Internal balancing requires having the machine shop drill the counterweights and press slugs of tungsten into the drilled holes. These slugs are heavier than the metal they replace, allowing them to offset the weight of the crankpins and the piston and rod assemblies.

Cast and Forged Crankshafts

Most crankshafts are either cast or forged. A cast crankshaft can be identified by the thin "parting" line that runs down its center, on the non-machined surfaces. The parting line is simply the extra material that flowed out between the two halves of the mold when the crankshaft was poured.

Cast crankshafts offer numerous advantages over a forged crankshaft for a street performance engine. To begin with, cast cranks are more wear resistant than non-nitrided forged crankshafts by virtue of their physical chemistry. Also, cast crankshafts are less prone to cracking at intermediate and lower levels of stress because they can flex under load. And cast cranks cost significantly less. If you don't need the extra strength of a forged crankshaft now, or in the future, save your money for something else.

A cast crankshaft will fit the bill just fine for most high-performance street and marine applications where horsepower and rpm are kept to a reasonable level. Engines putting out more than about 350–400 horsepower with standard weight components, and high-performance boats that turn more than 5,000 rpm are best suited to using a forged crankshaft. Drag racers can get away with subjecting a cast crank to about 500 horsepower, since the loading is brief and the reciprocating weight in a drag racing engine is lighter than the norm.

A forged crankshaft has a wide parting line—about 1/2 inch— that runs the length of the crank on its unmachined surfaces. Forged cranks are made of steel and are punched out in a die using tons of pressure. The extreme pressure used in this process makes the crankshaft much stronger and more dense than a cast-iron crankshaft. But this extra density also makes it more prone to cracking at lower performance levels, unless it's Tufftrided or nitrided.

Tufftriding and Nitriding

Tufftriding is a chemical bath process that some factory high-performance crankshafts underwent to nearly double their fatigue resistance. Because it increased their surface hardness, it also made the rod and main bearing journals more wear resistant. Crankshafts that have been Tufftrided can be identified by the dull gray appearance of their unmachined surfaces.

Factory Tufftriding, which was applied after the machining process, varies from about 0.003 to 0.010 inch thick. Consequently, any grinding of the journal will remove the hardening. To eliminate the need for grinding, you can selectively fit undersize bearings to compensate for slight amounts of wear. This is accomplished by using bearings that are 0.001 inch thicker than standard bearings. In turn, by using just one of the oversize bearing shells, you can adjust bearing clearances by 0.0005 inch. However, if any of the surfaces are damaged severely enough to warrant grinding, the crankshaft can be treated again using the nitriding process. Nitriding provides the same attributes as Tufftriding, but without its negative impact on the environment, which is why Tufftriding has been legislated out of existence.

Cross Drilling

Normally, production crankshafts are manufactured with only one lubrication passage to connect each main bearing journal to each rod bearing journal. As the crankshaft rotates, the lubrication passage

Cross-drilling a crankshaft increases oil flow to the rod bearings. The welding rod that's in a near-horizontal position in the crank (left) illustrates the cross-drilling. The other crank has just the standard rod throw drilling.

in the main bearing journal can be up to 180 degrees away from the oil hole in the bearing that supplies pressurized oil.

This is okay in a low- or medium-performance engine that isn't heavily loaded for relatively long periods of time. However, if the engine is heavily loaded, the oil film that prevents the crankshaft journal from touching the main bearings can be compressed so greatly that it's squeezed out, allowing the crank journal and bearing to touch, which results in rapid bearing wear and could lead to crankshaft damage.

To prevent this, the crankshaft main bearing journals in high-performance big-block Chevy crankshafts are cross-drilled. As its name implies, this drilling crosses the normal lubrication passage to allow oil to flow from one side of the main bearing journal to the other, minimizing the possibility of a lubrication-related bearing or crankshaft problem.

Twist Versus Non-Twist

When most forged crankshafts come out of the dies that produce them, they move into a machine that twists them so the rod journals are "indexed" 90 degrees apart from one another while the crankshaft is still hot. This twisting instills unnecessary tension into the crankshaft, which can lead to crankshaft failure under extreme high-load conditions. In response to this problem, some companies manufacture crankshafts using dies that position the rod journals 90 degrees apart. Consequently, twisting of the crankshaft isn't necessary to position the rod journals. A non-twist crankshaft is the strongest type of crankshaft you can buy.

Weight

Crankshaft weight has a significant effect on engine acceleration. As we observed on the playground, it's easier to push a smaller kid than a larger one. The same is true for crankshafts. The lighter the crankshaft, the quicker we can rotate the flywheel, since less effort is expended getting the crankshaft moving. Going from an 80-pound crankshaft to a 65-pound crankshaft is like getting another 15–20 horsepower out of an engine.

This Lunati crank is a non-twist forging with tapered counterweights (not visible) and drilled rod throws to reduce weight. *Lunati*

When is a lighter crankshaft preferred? When a vehicle must be accelerated many times such as in sprint racing, or when it needs to be accelerated very quickly, as down the quarter mile. On the other hand, if engine speed stays nearly constant for long periods of time, such as in marine applications, engine acceleration speed really isn't important. In these cases, a heavier crankshaft will do just fine.

Balancing

As you're putting the big-block of your dreams together, you can mix and match crankshafts, pistons, and rods as you like. However, only after you've completed all the checks and work on the crankshaft, pistons, rings, rods, flywheel, and damper should you bring your parts in for balancing. Modifying any of these parts afterward will throw the balancing job out the window, unless the new modifications have a negligible effect on the weight of the parts, like chamfering the dome on a piston. Otherwise, you'll be forced to rebalance the assembly.

Also keep in mind that lighter pistons and rods can reduce or eliminate the need for external balancing as long as crankshaft stroke is 4.250 inch or less. That's because less weight is needed to counteract the weight of the piston and rod assemblies.

When balancing an engine, the parts that comprise the crankshaft assembly are separated into two categories: reciprocating weight and rotating weight. The pistons, rings, piston pins, and pin retainers move up and down so they're considered reciprocating weight. The crankshaft rotates, as do the connecting rod bearings, so they belong to the rotating weight group. Connecting rods are a little of each—the big end rotates, but the small end reciprocates. The whole idea is to have the mass of the rotating parts counteract the mass of the reciprocating parts.

After all is said and done, balancing is only a "best guess," because although it takes the weight of an arbitrary amount of engine oil into consideration, it can't really account for what happens to the oil in the crankcase. As testing by Moroso and others indicates, as the engine accelerates and decelerates, the oil moves around on the crank in different ways. This oil has mass, and this mass disrupts the "perfect" balancing that we all try to achieve. Still, precision balancing goes a long way toward engine longevity, especially in a high-performance engine.

Variety—The Spice of Life

Aftermarket crankshaft manufacturers offer a variety of crankshafts for different budgets and purposes. Most of these crankshafts are made from 4340 steel—one of the strongest materials available for a crankshaft.

Starting on the less expensive end are crankshafts that have generous 0.125-inch fillet radii, heat treating, nitriding, and minimal machining time. They're also usually the heaviest. Building on this foundation, the next step up would typically include cross-drilled main bearings and more extensive counterweight machining. Weight for these cranks is a little less than the first type due to the extra counterweight machining.

The next better crank may include radiused counterweight edges and extra lightening holes that extend through the crankpins. These steps further reduce crankshaft weight. And at the top of the crankshaft heap, you'll find even more lightening features including machined counterweight edges, center counterweight removal, and undercut counterweights. Obviously, these cranks are the lightest and most expensive.

Over this spectrum of crankshafts, weights can range from 80 pounds, at the cheap end of the scale, to about 55 pounds for the most expensive, depending on stroke. And strokes up to 5.200 inches are available for all you mountain motor fans out there.

In addition to features, crankshaft durability must be considered, especially when rev limiters are used. When a rev limiter engages, it begins to selectively cut the ignition to certain cylinders, and the crankshaft takes a terrific beating. Under these circumstances, a quality aftermarket crankshaft lives a considerably longer life than factory crankshaft. Callies, Cola, Crower, Lunati, Moldex Tool, and Trick Flow Specialties, among others, are well-known for producing quality crankshafts.

Interchangeability

Mark series crankshafts use a narrower and smaller rear main seal surface than Gen series cranks, consequently, they're not interchangeable with each other. However, Sallee Chevrolet manufactures a plate that adapts Mark IV crankshafts to Gen V and Gen VI blocks. Use of this type of adapter can lower your engine costs if you already have a usable Mark IV crankshaft in your possession versus having to buy a Gen V or VI crank.

Another thing to watch for as you're building a 396 or 402 is that they use a different counterweight design than 427s. Although they

Here's a side-by-side comparison of Mark series (left) and Gen series (right) crankshafts. The area on the Mark series crank where the rear main seal rides (just forward of the flywheel flange) is much smaller than the rear main seal on the Gen series crank.

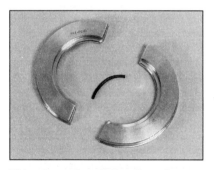

This adapter from Sallee Chevrolet allows you to use a Mark series crankshaft in a Gen series block.

share the same 3.76-inch stroke, the 396 and 402 crankshafts use a 7/16-inch wide #3 counterweight (third from the front). 427s have larger, heavier pistons, which require 7/8-inch wide counterweights at every position to counterbalance the extra weight. So, keep this in mind.

Stroker Cranks

One time-honored way of getting more power out of an engine is to increase its stroke. Use of a stroker crank can net you more displacement than simply boring the block. You also avoid ending up with cylinder walls that are too thin.

When considering a stroker crank, keep in mind that they work best with a longer connecting rod. There are three reasons for this: increased piston dwell at TDC, decreased rod angularity, and engine balancing.

To a point, increased piston dwell can provide more power

because the piston spends more time at TDC. And the longer it's there, the more time the ignited air/fuel mixture has to work on it.

Decreased rod angularity reduces friction, because the piston is pushed on a straighter path rather than out toward the cylinder wall.

Use of a longer rod also pays dividends when balancing the engine, because using a stock length rod with a stroker crank requires cutting the counterweights down to clear the piston when it's at the bottom of its stroke. So, just when you need to have more mass in the crankshaft counterweights to offset the longer crank throws, you're cutting the counterweights to clear the pistons. Although you can remedy this situation by adding a considerable sum of heavy metal to the counterweight, this is going to cost a few hundred dollars. The better route is to use a connecting rod with a longer center-to-center length, which avoids cutting the counterweights. For recommendations on rod lengths, refer to Chapter 5, *Connecting Rods*.

Although a 3.76-inch stroke crank works best in 427-cubic-inch and smaller rats, a 4.00-inch stroke crankshaft can be used in some 396s and most 402s and 427s, if you so desire. Just make sure the connecting rods will clear the lower end of the cylinders. A die grinder can be used to relieve this area to obtain the necessary 0.050-inch clearance. Alternately, these reliefs can be machined by a competent machine shop.

Later-model 427 and all 454 cubic-inch (Mark and Gen V and VI series) blocks have connecting rod reliefs and will accept a 1/4-inch stroker crank without any clearance problems, provided you use steel rods. However, if you use aluminum rods, they probably won't clear because they have a considerably larger "big end" circumference than steel rods. Due to the path it takes as it's rotating, the connecting rod or rod bolt will be closest to the block skirt and camshaft. The minimum clearance between these components is 0.050 inch. If clearance is marginally less than this, grind the block, rod or rod bolt at the offending area.

With stroker cranks, you'll also need to ensure that the crankshaft

counterweights won't contact the oil pump body as the crankshaft rotates. If a minimum clearance of 0.050 inch doesn't exist, carefully grind the pump body for clearance, or space it away using an aftermarket spacer kit, such as those offered by Moroso.

Another thing to remember with stoker cranks is that you'll need to use pistons with a different compression height. This is necessary to prevent the pistons from coming out of the tops of the bores.

Refer to Chapters 2, 5, and 6—*Cylinder Blocks*, *Connecting Rods*, and *Pistons & Rings*, respectively—for related information on using a stroker crank.

Reconditioning

Magnafluxing of the crankshaft should be performed before any machine work, so you'll know if any cracks exist. If they do, scrap the crank and buy another.

Aside from grinding the journals round and parallel, an important part of the machining process is grinding a wide radius at both ends of each journal. If this radius is too small or is ground away, significant strength is lost, increasing the potential for crankshaft breakage. Although the factory radius ranges from 0.020 to 0.045 inch, aftermarket crankshafts have a more generous 0.125-inch radius. Some crankshafts made specifically for supercharging have an extra-wide 0.140- or 0.150-inch radius to give them even greater strength.

Straightening

Big-block Chevy cranks should have a run-out of less than 0.003 inch, measured at the center main bearing journal. To check it, turn the block upside down, and with the main bearing upper shells in position and lightly oiled, put the crank in the block. Mount a dial indicator to the block, with the tip riding on the center crank journal, and slowly rotate the crank while watching the indicator. If runout is more than 0.003 inch, the crank requires straightening, which can be accomplished at a reputable crankshaft shop.

Although a straightened crank is all right to use in a high-performance street engine, it's not intended for use at the professional level.

Indexing

Indexing a crankshaft simply checks that the crankpins are exactly 90 degrees apart from one another, and machines them so if they're not.

When production crankshafts are manufactured, sometimes the crankpins aren't machined exactly 90 degrees apart from each other. Although this isn't anything to worry about for a non-competition street or marine engine, it does present a problem for a serious racing engine.

If the crankpins aren't exactly 90 degrees apart from one another, the pistons won't be at the proper point in the cylinders relative to the induction and ignition cycles. Since this presents a "piston timing" problem, some cylinders will be making more power than others. In a racing engine, all cylinders must contribute equally for the engine to produce maximum power. Consequently, if it's a racing engine you're building, you'll probably want to look to the aftermarket for a crankshaft.

Why is that? Well, years ago new GM crankshafts used to be cheap relative to aftermarket crankshafts. Consequently, you could have a lot of prep work performed (like indexing) on a GM crankshaft and still be money ahead versus using an aftermarket crankshaft. But times have changed. New·GM crankshafts have grown appreciably in price, while the cost of aftermarket crankshafts have dropped. So the pricing gap has narrowed significantly. As a result, when you include the cost of all the prep work that's necessary for a racing engine, like indexing and internal balancing, aftermarket crankshafts are usually the most cost-effective. And this doesn't even address the superior metallurgy that aftermarket crankshafts offer.

Polishing

Main and rod journal finish has a significant effect on bearing durability. The smoother the finish, the longer the bearings will last. It also helps reduce friction. To polish a crankshaft, cut a strip of 600-grit wet-or-dry sandpaper the width of a crankshaft journal. Wrap the paper around the journal, then wrap an old shoe lace around the paper twice. By pulling on alternate ends of the shoe lace, the sandpaper will polish the journal.

Polishing the journals after machining helps remove burrs that increase friction and bearing wear. Here, some 600-grit wet-or-dry sandpaper polishes the journal courtesy of a shoelace and some elbow grease.

Chamfering

After all the manufacturing and machining operations, a crankshaft has lots of sharp edges, which are great places for cracks to begin. To prevent cracking, chamfer all the sharp edges with a die grinder equipped with a medium-or fine-grit grinding stone.

When it comes to the lubrication passages, just remove the sharp edges. Taking off more material than this can weaken the crankshaft. And be careful not to nick the journals.

Pay special attention to the edges of the crankshaft counterweights. As the crankshaft rotates, the leading edge of the counterweights push lots of air. You can feel the same effect when you pass a tractor-trailer on the the freeway in your car. As you begin to pass the tractor, the air that it pushes with its blunt front end forces your car to the side of the lane. This is exactly what happens in the crankcase as the crankshaft counterweights rotate. Instead of cutting through the oil, the "windage" it produces pushes the oil to its sides. It

Crankshaft oil lube holes shouldn't be flared outward where they meet the journals because it reduces crankshaft strength. Just chamfer the sharp edges as you see here.

also causes the oil to hang onto the crank and rods. And this absorbs horsepower. By putting a 1/8-inch radius on the edges of the counterweights, you streamline them, causing a reduction in windage.

Cleaning

After all the grinding and other prep work has been completed, clean the crankshaft. Using an appropriately sized brush from one of the aftermarket engine brush kits, clean all the crankshaft oil passages with solvent. Scrub them until the solvent comes out clean. Finish up by cleaning the entire crankshaft, including the oil passages, with hot, soapy water. When you've finished, blow all the passages out with compressed air, then spray the entire crankshaft with some WD-40 or LPS-2.

Assembly Checks
End Play

Crankshaft end play must be checked as it allows hot oil to escape from the thrust bearing. If the clearance is too tight, oil flow through the engine will be disrupted. If the clearance is too loose, the crankshaft will move back and forth in the block and cause bearing problems.

To check crankshaft end play, clean all the main bearing saddles, then install the bearings. Put a very light coating of clean engine oil on the bearings, then lay the crankshaft in the block. Next, install the thrust bearing into the rear main bearing cap and position the cap onto the block. Tap the cap into position on the block with a lead or rawhide hammer. Then use the hammer against the front and rear of the crank to align the thrust faces of the upper and lower bearing halves with one another. A couple of firm taps in each direction should do.

Now, with the rear main bearing cap bolts installed and torqued to specifications, pry the crankshaft forward by using a pry bar between a counterweight and the block. Then measure the end play by slipping the largest feeler gauge you can fit between the bearing and the crankshaft thrust surface.

If end play is insufficient, lay the thrust bearing on a piece of 600

Crankshaft end play has an impact on engine oil flow and bearing life. After forcing the crankshaft forward, you can check this clearance with a feeler gauge. End play should be 0.006–0.010 inch.

grit wet-or-dry sandpaper that's backed up by a flat surface. With some clean engine oil for a cutting fluid, move the thrust surface of the bearing over the sandpaper in a "figure 8" motion to provide more clearance. Work both upper and lower halves equally and check your work frequently to prevent removing too much material. After you've finished, clean the bearings thoroughly with carburetor cleaner.

If there's too much clearance, the machine shop can usually weld up the crankshaft thrust flange and then machine it for proper clearance.

Main Bearing Clearance

As with any other engine, proper main bearing clearance in a big-block Chevy is critical for long engine life. If bearing clearance is insufficient, the crankshaft and bearings may touch each other when the engine is heavily loaded. At the least, it's a situation you want to avoid. At the most, it could take the crankshaft out, as well as the rest of the engine. On the other hand, if main bearing clearance is too large, oil pressure will drop accordingly. Also, too much oil could end up on the cylinder walls, causing an oil consumption or detonation problem. So, you want to be careful when setting clearances.

To check the main bearing clearances, clean the bearing bores with carburetor cleaner. The bores must be absolutely free of any residue for the most accurate readings. Then do

the same for the bearings, and blow them dry. Now slip the bearings into position. Remember, the upper main bearings are grooved, the lowers are not. Next, install the caps and torque their retaining bolts to specifications. Torque them first to 20 pound-feet, then 40 pound-feet, then to the final specs to ensure the most accurate measurement. (Note: final torque specifications vary depending on whether you're using bolts or studs, and from fastener manufacturer to manufacturer).

Using a dial bore or telescoping gauge, check the inside diameter of each bearing bore. If you're using telescoping gauges, be sure to take two readings, each 90 degrees apart from one another and about 45 degrees away from the point where the upper and lower bearing shells meet each other. This "parting line" area is marginally thinner than the rest of the bearing and will give you inaccurate measurements. Write your readings down on the Engine Build Sheet (Appendix A) found at the rear of this book. Work carefully and make sure your measurements are repeatable.

After you've measured the main bearing bores, measure the main bearing journals on the crankshaft. Using a micrometer, measure each journal in at least two places, 90 degrees apart from one another. Again, repeatability of readings will tell you that your measurements are accurate. When you have all the figures, subtract the crankshaft journals' outside diameters from the inside diameter of the respective main bearing bores. The result is the main bearing clearance.

In rats with a crankshaft stroke of less than 4.500 inches, strive for a main bearing clearance of 0.0026–0.0028 inch, although you can get away with a maximum of 0.003 inch. When the crankshaft stroke is 4.500 inches or greater, main bearing clearances should be 0.0029–0.0032 inch. This extra clearance will allow for the crankshaft and main bearing cap flexing that's inherent with long strokes.

If you don't have access to the types of measuring tools mentioned earlier, there's another, less accurate way to check main bearing clear-

Main bearing clearance should be within specifications for best engine life and to control oil flow into the crankcase. With the bearing caps torqued to specs, measure the inside diameter of the bearings in two places, 45 degrees away from the bearing parting lines. Measuring the bearing diameter at the parting line is misleading because the ends of each bearing shell are tapered.

ances, and that's with Plasti-gage. Plasti-gage is a soft plastic material that compresses at a controlled rate. It's available in three color-coded thicknesses to check a variety of clearances. To check both main and rod bearing clearances, you'll need the green Plasti-gage.

To use it, insert the crankshaft into the dry main bearings. Lay a 1-inch length of the Plasti-gage on the top of the journal and parallel to its length. Then install the bearing cap and torque the bolts to specifications. Now, carefully remove the cap and measure the width of the Plasti-gage at its widest point by comparing it to the markings on the Plasti-gage envelope. The width of the Plasti-gage should fall between the 0.0025- and 0.003-inch markings.

You also need to ensure that the bearing doesn't ride on the journal radius. Do this by placing the bearings in the block, then laying the crankshaft over them. If the edges of the bearing are inboard of the crank journal radii, then you're all set. If not, you'll have to scrape the edge of the offending bearing area away with a knife. If this doesn't sound like a lot of fun, Callies Performance Products offers bearings with sufficient clearance for large journal radii—no modifications are needed.

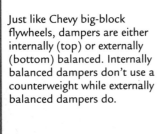

Just like Chevy big-block flywheels, dampers are either internally (top) or externally (bottom) balanced. Internally balanced dampers don't use a counterweight while externally balanced dampers do.

CHAPTER FOUR

FLYWHEELS, FLEXPLATES, AND DAMPERS

Just like the crankshafts used in big-block Chevys, the flywheel, flexplate, and damper must be matched to the engine balancing strategy—either internally or externally balanced. If they're not, the engine will vibrate itself to death in short order.

Big-block Chevys that are internally balanced use no balancing weights on the flywheel, flexplate, or damper. Because they have no balancing weights, these parts are called "neutral balanced." Rats with a displacement of 454 cubic inches and larger require counterweights on both the damper and flywheel (or flexplate) to help counterbalance the greater mass of the crankshaft and piston and rod assemblies used in these engines. These counterweighted parts are considered externally balanced.

Flywheels

All Mark IV flywheels will interchange with one another, provided they use the same type of balancing—either neutral or externally balanced. However, Gen V and VI factory-produced flywheels (and dampers) are different. Since they're particularly sensitive to the natural resonant frequencies produced by different crankshaft materials, they must be matched to either a cast or forged crankshaft. If they're switched, crankshaft breakage will occur. This limitation doesn't usually apply to aftermarket flywheels and dampers due to the different materials and designs used.

Flywheel material is another consideration. Normal-duty factory flywheels are made of cast iron, which is fine for moderate street use. Higher grade materials such as nodular iron, billet steel, and aluminum are more resistant to exploding at high rpm, which makes them the preferred choice for high-performance and racing applications.

Nodular iron has a denser grain structure than cast iron, which makes it better able to withstand the rigors of

This factory-issued Mark IV flywheel (part number 3963537) is scalloped to reduce inertia and provide quicker acceleration. Although this flywheel is for externally balanced engines (as evidenced by the counterweight at the top) a similar flywheel is offered for internally balanced engines. If acceleration isn't a top priority, such as a marine application, you may want to use a heavier flywheel for greater engine durability.

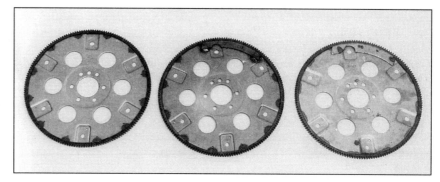

These three flexplates cover just about all Mark and Gen series engines. The neutral-balanced flexplate on the left is for internally balanced engines like 396s and 427s. The flexplate in the center has an external counterweight for 454 Mark series engines. The flexplate on the right is also counterweighted, but it's for a Gen series engine. The Gen series flexplates are specific to either cast or forged crankshafts. Make sure you buy the right flexplate for your particular application.

high rpm. Chevrolet nodular iron flywheels, in new condition, have been tested to 10,000 rpm; consequently, they're preferred over cast-iron flywheels for high-performance use.

Aftermarket flywheels are usually manufactured of billet steel or aluminum. Billet steel flywheels are very explosion-resistant and are offered in weights up to about 50 pounds, which makes them great for launching a heavy car down the quarter mile, or propelling a boat across the water. Aluminum flywheels are not as durable as billet flywheels, but are considerably lighter. A lighter flywheel helps a vehicle accelerate faster from corner to corner, but requires the clutch to be slipped more when starting out to prevent engine stalling.

If you're installing a used flywheel, you need to make sure that it hasn't been severely overheated. If it has, stress cracks will be visible at the bolt holes and may even radiate to the friction surface. These cracks can cause the flywheel to explode at high rpm, making it very dangerous for use. *Any flywheel with this type of damage must be scrapped!* If they explode, they can maim or kill you, so don't take a chance. As additional insurance, be sure to equip your transmission with a blow-proof bellhousing or transmission blanket to ensure your safety if a flywheel or flexplate does explode.

Flexplates

Flexplates are available in two basic versions—standard and heavy-duty. Standard versions use a center plate that's about 0.070–0.080-inch thick. Heavy-duty versions are considerably thicker—on the order of 0.125 inch. Use of a thicker center plate is necessary to combat the effects of high-stall torque converters and high rpm, which could cause a standard flex plate with its thinner center plate to crack.

Two different flywheel and flexplate diameters are available—14 and 12-3/4 inches. The 14-inch version has 168 teeth around its circumference, while the smaller version has 153 teeth. Because of the difference in diameters, each design necessitates a starter with a particular nosepiece. The 14-inch versions use a starter nose with mounting bolt holes that are offset from one another. The 12 3/4-inch model requires a starter nose whose mounting bolt holes are straight across from one another. Although the starter mounting pad on most blocks have three bolt holes to accommodate either of these designs, take a look to be sure. If not, they can be drilled and tapped to accept either starter.

Dampers

Crankshafts are big chunks of metal, so you wouldn't expect them to bend, but they do. That's the reason machine shops store cranks vertically. And that's why a damper is required. The pulsing of the pistons as they move down the cylinders during each power stroke causes the crankshaft to deflect a certain amount, based on crankshaft material and load. As the piston continues downward, the crank arm springs back in the other direction. All this loading and unloading causes the crankshaft to accelerate and decelerate constantly. If uncontrolled, this twisting, which is felt as a vibration, will cause the crankshaft to break. And as engine output or rpm rises, damper selection becomes more critical.

Stock dampers use a cast-iron hub surrounded by a malleable iron inertia ring. This inertia ring is connected to the hub by a rubber ring with a specific amount of elasticity. As the crankshaft twists on the power stroke, the rubber gives slightly then stops. In a kind of mechanical crack the whip, the

A compact starter like this can provide more room for headers while providing more grunt to crank high-compression engines.

crankshaft tries to pull the inertia ring along with it. However, the weight of the ring works against this acceleration, retarding it to an acceptable level. As the crankshaft springs back in the other direction, the same thing happens with the damper. This "damping" of the forward and backward motion helps keep crankshaft torsional vibration to an acceptable level.

To combat torsional vibration, both the weight of the inertia ring and the elasticity of the rubber that secures it to the crankshaft hub are tuned to provide the greatest resistance against the point at which the crankshaft vibrates the most on its own. Any changes to the weight of the flywheel, and to a lesser extent, the pistons and connecting rods, will change the natural frequency at which the crankshaft vibrates. In turn, this necessitates a change in damper tuning.

Stock dampers are limited in their "tune-ability." By design, they're tuned to a counteract a specific vibrational frequency based on crankshaft weight and material, as well as all the rotating and reciprocating weight connected to the crankshaft including the piston assemblies, connecting rods and flywheel or flexplate. When the weight of any of these components changes, a stock damper must be rebalanced.

Stock dampers are suitable for most street and marine applications where high-rpm operation occurs on an intermittent basis. However, a number of racing classes exclude the use of stock dampers because of the possibility of the inertia ring separating from the hub or exploding at high rpm.

Aside from potentially exploding, another problem with this type of damper is that the rubber that's used eventually dries out and splits. If this problem is severe enough, the inertia ring will slip relative to the hub. Sometimes it will stay aligned with the hub and simply rotate on it.

If this is the case, the timing marks will be way off when you check the ignition timing, but the engine will be running fine. Other times, the inertia ring will move backward or forward (e.g., front to rear) on the hub—a sure sign that something bad is about to happen. If any of these problems occur, you'll need to replace the damper.

Ten factory dampers have been fitted to production big-blocks over the years. With Mark IV engines, their usage depends on whether the engine is internally or externally balanced. Since all Gen V and VI engines are externally balanced, usage depends on whether the crankshaft is made of nodular iron or forged steel. If these dampers are switched, the crankshaft may break due to the difference in natural frequencies between nodular iron and forged steel.

For high-performance street, marine, or racing use, an "all-steel," viscous, or internally counterweighted damper will provide the best insurance against crankshaft breakage. They can also increase horsepower and extend crankshaft bearing life.

Another thing many people fail to consider is that the front of the crankshaft is connected directly to the camshaft via the timing chain or gears. If crankshaft vibration isn't adequately controlled by the damper, its oscillations are transferred to the camshaft. In turn, these oscillations cause the cam to move erratically and since the valvetrain can't keep up with all the monkey motion, horsepower drops. It also adds extra fatigue to these parts, shortening their life.

An "all-steel" damper is a high-performance variation of the stock damper. Using a billet steel hub, forged steel inertia ring and a special rubber bonding process to hold these two pieces together, it can withstand sustained high rpm that would destroy a stock damper. Depending upon which model is ordered, it can be used in street, marine, and racing applications.

The viscous damper uses a housing filled with silicone fluid. As the crankshaft twists back and forth it shears the silicone fluid. This fluid acts much like the brake in a revolving door—it only allows the door (crankshaft) to move so fast, then it

Current factory high-performance dampers are 8 inches in diameter and have degreeing marks. This damper is for an externally balanced engine, as evidenced by the counterweight on the backside.

This "all-steel" damper from Pro Street is SFI certified for racing use.

won't let it move any faster. Viscous dampers are not tuned to a specific vibration frequency and are therefore not affected by changes in engine reciprocating weight. They also extend crankshaft and main bearing life, as well as reduce valve timing variations that result from crankshaft torsional vibration.

Dampers that use rubber to mount the inertia ring have the same weight when rotating as when they are standing still. Those that use silicone to surround the inertia ring, such as the Fluidampr®, have about only two-thirds the static weight when rotating as when they are standing still, due to the cushioning

effect of the silicone. In effect, this lightens the load the crankshaft has to turn, allowing quicker engine acceleration.

When handling a viscous damper, make sure that you don't damage the exterior shell. If a dent is deeper than about 3/32 inch, it can actually cause the exterior shell to contact the inertia ring which will interfere with its damping ability.

The Rattler is an internally counterweighted damper that absorbs crankshaft vibration. This design claims to absorb more crankshaft vibration over a broader rpm range than any other damper available. I can't vouch for that, but the people I've talked to about it say that it does an excellent job.

ATI, BHJ Dynamics, Fluidampr, Pro Street, and TCI all offer high-performance dampers for Chevrolet big-block engines.

The Bottom Line

The flywheel, flexplate, and damper you should use depends on how you use your vehicle. As with all the other reciprocating and rotating components connected to the crankshaft, the lighter and smaller the flywheel or damper, the quicker the engine will accelerate and decelerate. This provides a strong advantage for light drag cars and sprint cars where engine rpm must climb as rapidly as possible. It's also an advantage on the street, as well, but not to the same extent

This Fluidampr uses silicone fluid to dampen engine vibration. It also helps reduce variations in valve timing caused by reciprocating assembly vibration.

because street-driven vehicles are also used on the highway. If engine rpm is more or less constant for long periods of time, such as in marine use, a larger and heavier flywheel and damper will help keep engine rpm more constant and improve durability.

Talk about a disaster! This rod became fatigued, let loose, and took the engine out with it. Proper preparation and inspection—plus keeping engine rpm to a safe limit—can help prevent this situation.

CHAPTER FIVE

CONNECTING RODS

If you've ever seen a movie about medieval England where someone's put on a rack to "correct" their way of doing things, you'll begin to appreciate the life a connecting rod leads. As the piston assembly approaches the top of the cylinder, it wants to continue on through the head and through the hood. The only pieces preventing this from happening are the piston pin, rod, and rod bolts. These loads rise exponentially as engine rpm climbs, which is a good argument for using the lightest piston assembly available. It's also a good reason to select a strong, light rod with high-quality rod bolts.

When selecting a rod, pick one that most closely matches the use of your engine and its horsepower rating, while keeping future modifications in mind. Buying a rod that's good for 1,000 horsepower when your engine will never put out more than 600 horsepower is a waste of money. Some aftermarket manufacturers, such as Crower, list the maximum horsepower and torque a particular rod is capable of handling. Information like this can help you select the rod that's right for your specific engine.

Design Features
Processing
All high-performance connecting rods undergo certain processes to increase their strength and durability. For example, the two factory high-performance big-block rods Chevrolet offers are magnafluxed and shot-peened. Aftermarket high-performance rods usually undergo a number of additional processing steps to further ensure rod durability and quality, including stress-relieving,

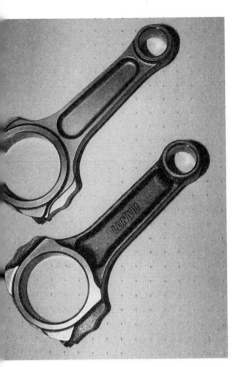

These high-performance rods from Lunati provide extra camshaft clearance when using a stroker crankshaft. Because these rods use cap bolts, there are no bolt heads on the top side of the rod to interfere with the camshaft.

CNC machining, X-raying, and sonic testing. Generally speaking, the greater the number of processing steps, the greater the cost and quality.

Magnafluxing highlights cracks in ferrous metals. An electro-magnetic field is induced in the rod and finely powered metal is sprinkled over the part. The powder will cling to any detected surface cracks. *Wet magnafluxing* is a variation of this process; after the part is magnetized, a liquid containing phosphorus is poured over the part. The phosphorus will highlight any surface cracks when viewed under a black light.

Shotpeening reduces the potential for cracks. Steel shot the size of miniature BBs are sprayed against the part under air pressure. This compresses any minor surface imperfections in the metal, making the rod more crack resistant.

Stress-relieving relaxes metal. Rods are heated to a high temperature for a period of hours to relax any torsional stress that may exist after the manufacturing process. Final

machining is performed afterward to increase part accuracy.

CNC machining helps remove surface imperfections which can lead to cracking. It also provides consistently repeatable machining, which helps minimize weight differences between rods.

X-raying helps detect internal flaws in the metal. It works the same way on rods as it does on your body parts, highlighting flaws that could be potentially dangerous to your engine's health.

Sonic-testing detects internal flaws in metal by using sound waves. Think of it as an ultrasound for your engine.

Material Considerations

Connecting rods use various materials (4340 steel, aluminum, and titanium) depending upon their application. Each has its advantages and disadvantages, but some are more suitable for certain uses than others.

For street high-performance and marine use, as well as endurance racing applications, a forged steel rod is best, because it has a much higher strength-to-density ratio than aluminum and is much more cost-effective than titanium. Steel rods also have a much longer service life than aluminum rods, and eliminate the budget and time-consuming task of frequent rod inspection and replacement required with aluminum rods.

Aluminum rods are a different matter, because there are three conditions that warrant their use: compression ratio over 13.5:1, use of nitrous oxide (or supercharging), or a manual transmission. If your engine and vehicle have at least two of these conditions, the engine should use aluminum rods. These conditions place a significant amount of stress in the connecting rods. Due to the forgiving nature of aluminum, aluminum rods are able to absorb some of this stress without failure. In turn, this helps prevent the rod bearing from being hammered to death. So in these situations, aluminum rods are preferred over steel rods.

You'll also need aluminum rods if engine stroke is greater than 4.500 inches and any one of the above conditions are present. That's because

the longer the stroke, the greater the friction. And the greater the friction, the more heat that's produced. If this extra heat was passed along to the bearing, it would lose its crush, causing it to spin. Since aluminum dissipates heat at a faster rate than steel, aluminum rods allow the rod bearing to run cooler.

The disadvantage of aluminum rods is that they require regular replacement because of their relatively low fatigue resistance (compared to steel rods). And their big and small ends go out-of-round faster, too. Consequently, their replacement schedule depends upon the particular type of rod and how it's used. Good-quality aluminum rods are good for 250 to 300 passes down the quarter mile before they require replacement.

Aluminum rods are also engineered a little differently than steel rods. Due to their considerable thermal expansion rate and growth at high rpm, aluminum rods are usually 0.010 inch shorter than the factory dimension for steel rods. And because of their thermal expansion

Lunati Race Prep connecting rods like the one shown here are based on blueprinted GM forgings and are available in a variety of conditions that best fit your needs and budget. *Lunati*

Aluminum rods are designed for high rpm drag racing and similar applications. They need to be replaced on a frequent basis, so they're really not for street applications unless the engine and vehicle meet the criteria explained in this chapter. These rods are available from Manley.

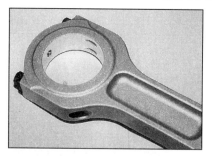

Because aluminum expands significantly when heated, aluminum rods have pins to prevent the bearing inserts from spinning. You can see it here at the center of the rod cap.

rate, all aluminum rods have pins to prevent the main bearings from rotating in the bearing bore. Accordingly, this requires bearings with holes to accommodate the pins.

Titanium rods are available for those with a rat that produces over 1,000 horsepower and revs beyond 8,500 rpm. These extremely lightweight rods are more durable than aluminum rods, and are stronger as well. Unfortunately, these rods are considerably more expensive than either steel or aluminum rods and should only be considered for serious racing efforts backed by big budgets.

Weight Considerations

Generally speaking, most aftermarket I-beam rods made from billet stock are significantly lighter than factory-issue rods. Aftermarket H-beam rods are about as heavy as factory rods, but are considerably stronger. Heavier rods can be a detriment on tracks where the engine has to be accelerated and decelerated constantly, because it will take more time to reach a certain rpm. Where rpm is virtually constant, like long tracks or marine racing, this extra weight isn't really a problem. In these cases, as well as street high-performance applications, it's far better to sacrifice some engine acceleration to gain durability.

Piston Pins

Connecting rods can use either a pressed or floating piston pin. With pressed pins, the pin is locked in the small end of the rod, and the piston rotates on the ends of the piston pin. Pressed pins work well in most street and marine engines because they

eliminate the potential for a piston pin lock to come loose and wedge itself between the piston and the cylinder wall. However, with pressed pins, piston removal sometimes results in a ruined piston, since a press or heat must be used to separate the two.

Connecting rods designed for a floating pin have a small end that's about 0.0005–0.0007-inch larger in diameter than the piston pin. This allows the pin to rotate freely or "float" within the rod. To keep the pin from sliding out of the piston, wire retainers are used on each end of

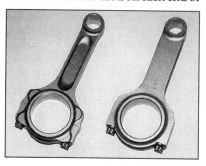

This photo shows the significant differences between an I-beam rod (left) and an H-beam rod (right). I-beam rods are for more "normal" applications, while H-beam rods are best for endurance applications.

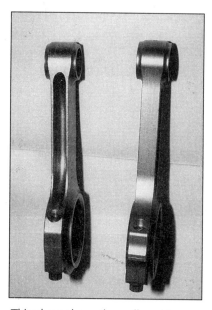

This photo shows the scalloped beam of an H-beam rod along with the smooth beam of the I-beam rod. Both of these Manley rods offer more camshaft clearance than stock rods.

To ensure adequate piston pin oiling, each of these aluminum rods have an oil feed hole above the piston pin. A similar 1/8-inch diameter hole with a 1/4-inch counterbore can be used in steel rods to enhance pin oiling.

the piston pin boss. This design allows for easy removal of the piston without the use of a press, saving time and money.

If you have pressed-pin rods but you'd prefer floating pins, a competent machine shop can convert them for you.

Lubrication

Rods with floating pins can benefit by the addition of a 1/8-inch-diameter lube hole in the small end of the rod above the piston pin. When counter-bored with a 1/4-inch-diameter drill bit to a depth of 1/8 inch, this hole acts as a funnel to direct oil to the piston pin.

Rod Bolts

When a big-block is spinning at high rpm, the load on each rod runs in the thousands of pounds. The only things keeping the rod cap on the rod are the rod bolts. In light of this, a set of quality rod bolts is probably the best insurance policy you can buy for your engine. Their superior materials, and in some cases, design, are just what the doctor ordered for this most-highly stressed of all engine bolts.

Rod bolts are manufactured to different levels of performance and cost, both at the factory and in the aftermarket. Standard performance rod bolts have knurled shanks, which help keep them in the rod during the assembly process and compensates for minor manufacturing tolerances in the bolt holes. Although it usually isn't a problem in moderate street and marine applications, the knurling can cut into the rod, causing stress risers. This can lead to rod

Dimples in the ends of the rod bolts allow the use of a rod bolt stretch gauge during engine assembly—an important feature. Most aftermarket high-performance rod bolts have them. Whenever dealing with rod bolts, handle them carefully. A small nick that may seem inconsequential can cause a stress riser that leads to a catastrophic failure. And when a rod bolt fails, it goes away big time, taking your crankshaft, block, and wallet with it.

failure when the engine is run at high rpm or is highly loaded for extended periods of time.

In performance applications where the rod will be stressed near or to its limits, you'll want to use a set of ARP WaveLoc rod bolts. Instead of knurling the shanks, the shanks have metal "waves" that help compensate for differences in hole sizing without creating stress risers. In extreme situations, this can mean the difference between finishing a race and buying a new engine.

As you're selecting rod bolts, you may find yourself correlating bolt tensile strength with durability. However, the two are not the same. Tensile strength is expressed in pounds per square inch (psi) and is the maximum amount of tension a bolt is capable of withstanding before it's literally pulled apart. Durability describes a bolt's resistance to bending. As a bolt is moved from side-to-side at its fatigue limit, it starts to crack. If the loading continues, the crack keeps moving until the bolt breaks in two. Bolt material is the major determinant of fatigue resistance. Aftermarket bolts are almost always manufactured from high-

quality alloy steel, which has superior fatigue resistance when compared to all the factory rod bolts except the 7/16-inch diameter boron bolts. Manufacturers of quality rod bolts include ARP, Milodon, and SPS.

Rod-to-Stroke Ratios

All factory rods have a center-to-center length of 6.135 inches. That's the distance from the center of the crankshaft bearing hole (big end) to the center of the piston pin hole (small end). The rod-to-stroke ratio compares the center-to-center length of the connecting rod to length of the crankshaft stroke. For example, if the center-to-center length of the rod is 6 inches and the stroke is 3 inches, the rod-to-stroke ratio would be 2:1. Production big-block Chevys use a rod-to-stroke ratio of 1.53–1.63:1, depending upon the particular engine.

Using a rod that's longer than stock helps increase power output, because the piston spends more time at top dead center (TDC). This longer dwell time provides more opportunity for combustion pressure to build before pushing the piston down the cylinder. And this creates more power. It also requires that piston pin compression height (the distance between the centerline of the piston pin and piston deck) be reduced to compensate for the increase in rod length.

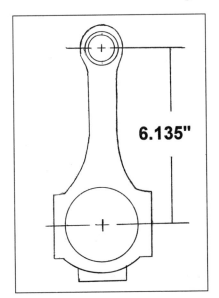

Stock big-block rods have a center-to-center length of 6.135 inches. Rods with a longer center-to-center length are beneficial when crankshaft stroke is 4.00 inches or greater.

Another benefit of using a longer rod is reduced piston-to-bore friction because rod angularity is less severe. And piston-to-bore friction is one of the largest contributors to internal engine friction.

Optimally, you want to use the longest rod that will fit in the engine, but with big-block Chevys, you can reach a point of diminishing returns. If the piston stays too long at TDC, the flow through the induction system is interrupted, because the air/fuel mixture keeps starting and stopping instead of constantly flowing during the intake stroke. And this reduces power.

Surprisingly, engines with a 3.76-inch stroke crankshaft (396s, 402s, and 427s) like the stock length rod best. On engines that use a 4.00-inch stroke crankshaft (454s), a connecting rod with a center-to-center length of 6.385 inches (0.250 inch longer than stock) is best. If you choose to use a connecting rod that's 0.400 inch longer than stock with this crankshaft, you gain nothing.

A 4.250-inch stroke crankshaft can use a rod that's 0.250 inch longer than stock but works best with a rod length of 6.535 inches (0.400 inch longer than stock). Although you can use a rod that's 0.600 inch longer than stock with this crank, it's actually a detriment because the piston dwell time at TDC is too long, upsetting the signal in the induction system, as mentioned previously.

For all you prospective mountain motor owners, crankshafts with a stroke of 4.500 inches respond to a 6.535-inch rod, but work best with a 6.635–6.735-inch long rod. Crankshafts with a 4.625-inch stroke thrive when 6.800-inch long rods are used. As stroke goes beyond 4.625 inches you run out of block, so you have to compromise on rod length.

The great thing about these increased rod-to-stroke ratios is that they add power through the rpm range of the engine, not just at the low or high end. Just keep in mind that when you're buying longer rods, you're buying pistons as well, because you have to move the piston pin up to compensate for the increase in rod length.

In some cases, the use of longer rods requires that the piston pin be raised beyond practical limits. To go further, you'll need to use a tall deck block. Longer-than-stock rods can also cause interference problems with the camshaft, and may require using a smaller base circle cam. Rods specially designed to reduce or eliminate this problem are available from the aftermarket. Typically, these rods use bolts that thread into the big end (rather than using a separate nut). This allows the offending part of the rod to be sculpted to provide more camshaft clearance.

Factory and Aftermarket Rods

Six different factory connecting rod designs have been produced over the years. Although they all share the same major dimensions, some are more desirable than others, so you need to select one based on your particular needs.

Unless you plan on adding some significant stress via turbocharging, supercharging, or nitrous oxide injection, there's a factory rod for your street machine or boat. The only problem with using factory rods for serious competition work is that they may need to be reworked significantly enough that their price equals or exceeds quality aftermarket rods designed for racing. Or you may need a rod for a special purpose. For instance, drag racers may want to use an aluminum rod to help reduce the

weight of the reciprocating assembly. Or, as noted in the "Rod-to-Stroke Ratios" section, those of you with a 4.00-inch or longer crankshaft stroke may want to take advantage of a rod with a longer center-to-center length. For situations like these, you need to look to the aftermarket.

The first and second design factory rods use a plain beam and 3/8-inch diameter rod bolts. They're suitable for use up to 525 horsepower provided you chamfer all the sharp edges and replace the factory bolts with a set of 3/8-inch performance rod bolts, such as those made by ARP, Milodon, or SPS. These bolts are considerably stronger than stock rod bolts and can take a lot of abuse.

Trucks rods are the strongest factory rods that use 3/8-inch diameter rod bolts. To endure the rigors of commercial trucking, their beam section is considerably wider above the big end than the other rods fitted with 3/8-inch diameter rod bolts. Truck rods are suitable for performance street and marine use, as well as mild racing applications, when fitted with aftermarket rod bolts.

The best factory rod is the L88 rod. Compared to the other factory rods that use 7/16-inch diameter rod bolts, this third design rod features thicker main beams for greater strength. In addition, it has been heat-treated, magnafluxed,

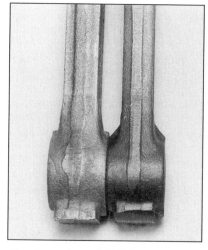

The Gen series rod (right) is considerably narrower than the Mark series rod (left).

and shotpeened to reduce its potential for cracking. Up top, this rod accommodates a floating piston pin. On the big end, it uses shotpeened 7/16in diameter boron rods bolts with profile-ground shanks and a tensile strength of 220,000 psi. These bolts also feature dimples on both ends to allow accurate measurement of rod bolt stretch. These bolts can be quickly identified by the single bump on each side of their beam, in combination with their dimpled bolts and are available as part number 3969804.

The fourth and fifth designs are the early- and late-model LS6/LS7 rods, respectively. The early LS6/LS7 rods are a good choice for high-performance street and limited racing use, provided you upgrade the rod bolts to a quality aftermarket type. The late-model LS6/LS7 is an improvement on the early LS6/LS7 rod and is currently used in Gen V and VI high-output engines. Available as part number 10198922, this rod features a strengthening rib directly under the piston pin boss and has one bump on each side of the beam. These rods are also factory machined for pressed piston pins, magnafluxed, shotpeened, and use heavy-duty 7/16-inch diameter rod bolts with knurled shanks. Late model LS6/LS7 rods are sturdy enough to be used in high-performance street and marine engines, as long as nitrous isn't used.

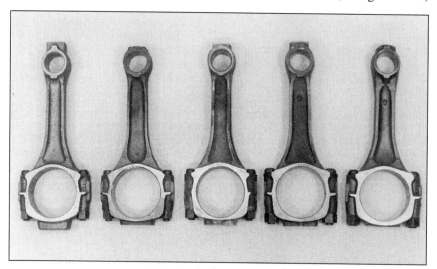

Here are five of the six connecting rods Chevrolet has produced. From left to right: first design, truck rod, second design, third design (L88), and fifth design (LS6/LS7/Gen series). All of these rods (except the L88 rods) will benefit from the use of aftermarket high-performance rod bolts like those available from ARP, Milodon, and SPS. The L88 rods are already fitted with high-performance 7/16-inch-diameter boron bolts as they come from the factory.

Reconditioning

Before you take your rods to the machine shop, take a close look at them. If any of them have a polished look in the main bearing bore, throw them out and buy new ones. It's not possible to recondition rods with this type of wear without angle-cutting the cap, which can lead to rod failure.

Used rods that are going to spend most of their time in mild to moderate performance street engines should be reconditioned by a competent machine shop. Before any work begins, the rods should be Magnafluxed. If any surface cracks exist, the rod can be scrapped without incurring any other machine shop expenses.

If money's tight, steel rods that have been in use without any evidence of causing an uneven wear pattern on the crankshaft bearings or piston skirt can usually be placed back into service after replacing the rod bolts and nuts.

Squareness

Squareness compares the alignment of small end of the rod to the big end. They must be perfectly aligned with each other to prevent overloading the piston skirt against the cylinder. A competent machine shop can check your rods for squareness.

Bend and Twist

Straight connecting rods are essential to any engine. Bent or twisted rods sap power by increasing piston-to-cylinder wall friction. They also disrupt the sealing between the piston rings and the cylinder wall, creating more blow-by of the air/fuel mixture. How do you know when a connecting rod is bent? By checking the wear pattern on the piston skirt. Wear on one skirt that's a mirror image of the opposite side indicates the rod is bent. If the piston isn't attached to the rod, your local machinist can check rod alignment. This step is mandatory for any high-performance engine rebuild.

Align Honing

Align honing trues and sizes the rod big end and is a worthwhile step for used rods that will see over 6,000 rpm on a regular basis.

With all the up-and-down motion a rod sees over a number of years, the big end can become oval-shaped. And with the relatively low octane of today's gasoline, the potential for detonation is high. Detonation places abnormally high loads on the rods (as well as the pistons, rings, bearings, and crankshaft) and can cause them to distort. As distortion increases, so does bearing wear, along with the potential for a spun bearing.

To avoid this situation, the machine shop will grind a few thousands of an inch off the rod cap, bolt the cap onto the rod, torque the bolts to specifications, then pass a hone through the big end. It's preferable to take a minimum amount of material off the cap to prevent weakening it. On the other hand, you want the inside diameter of the bearing bore to be at the low side of specifications so the bearing shells are clamped as tightly as possible. So once again, a compromise is involved.

After align honing, the distance between the main bearing and piston pin bores is less, slightly decreasing static compression ratio.

Preparation

Connecting rod preparation is key to engine survival at high rpm. As engine speed rises, the inertial loading on the rod increases significantly. This loading causes the big end of the rod to grow into a slightly oval shape parallel to the rod beam. If engine rpm climbs high enough, the metal where the rod and cap meet moves inward, causing the bearings to "pinch" the crankshaft pin. If the pinching is severe enough, the bearings will catch on the crank, and the crank will spin them in the rod bore causing a "spun" bearing. To reduce the potential for this, put a 45-degree bevel on the inside edges of the mating surface of the rod and cap. Using a file here will provide greater control than a grinder.

You can increase rod durability and lighten it at the same time by carefully grinding the parting line off the rod beams with a die grinder. Working in the direction of the rod beam will prevent a crosswise cut in the beam that could cause failure down the road. When the parting line is just about flush with the surrounding area, use a fine grinding cone to polish the beam smooth.

After grinding and polishing the beams, you'll need to have them shot-peened. Shotpeening compresses the surface of the metal, making it harder for cracks to form and gives the rods a flat, textured appearance.

The areas where the rod bolt and nut seat deserve a little extra preparation as well. To ensure the load is spread evenly across the bolt head and nut, their respective seats must be flat and square to the big end bore. This isn't a concern with new rods because they're manufactured this way. However, used rods can have surface irregularities due to the tightening and loosening that occurs

High-performance rod prep requires removal of the forging line followed by shot peening. Work in the direction of the beam to prevent causing any stress risers.

When prepping rods, take care to chamfer the areas around the rod bolt and nut seats (right). Put a gentle radius on all the sharp edges to prevent stress risers.

To check rod side clearance, measure the length of each crankshaft journal. Then stack the big ends of each mating pair of rods together (#1 and #2, #3 and #4, etc.) and measure them. Subtract the paired rod measurement from the respective journal measurement and the difference is the rod side clearance.

Side clearance with steel rods should be in the range of 0.015–0.018 inch. Side clearance for aluminum rods needs to be marginally larger—0.020–0.025 inch—to allow for thermal expansion of the rod.

If clearance is inadequate, increase it by sanding the sides of the rod big ends. Use 600-grit wet-or-dry sandpaper laid over the bed of a drill press or a thick piece of glass to do this. Sand a little at a time, then measure the rods again to be sure you don't take too much material off. If clearance is excessive and you have rods where the side clearance it too tight, try swapping them to gain the proper clearance. For best performance, stay near the minimum clearance.

during every engine tear down, mock-up, and build-up. Take extra care ensuring that any sharp areas where the bolt head and nut seat are carefully chamfered, to prevent cracks from forming in these highly critical areas.

If you're using new rod bolts, take a look at the area where the shank meets the head. Some rod bolts use a radius in this area to gain strength. However, if the top of the rod bolt bore won't accommodate this radius, the bolt won't be properly seated which can cause it to loosen and fail. If your rod bolts are radiused like this, relieve the top of the bolt bores with a die grinder to accept them.

Assembly Checks
Rod Side Clearance
Connecting rod side clearance is another area that deserves attention. Too little clearance and the oil supply from the crankshaft will be insufficient to lubricate the sides of the rods, cylinder walls, piston skirts, and cam lobes. Too much clearance and oil pressure will drop significantly. It can also lead to detonation if too much oil

gets thrown up on the cylinder walls and overwhelms the rings. Once this oil gets into the combustion chambers, it's a short trip to detonation city.

Piston-to-Rod Clearance
The clearance between the top of the rod and underside of the piston should also be checked if you're using non-stock rods or pistons. Some

Rod journal width plays an important part in rod side clearance. Measure it carefully, then subtract the width of the paired rods to determine this clearance.

rods, especially aluminum rods, are quite thick on their small end. This extra material can contact the underside of the piston as the rod rotates, especially if the piston pin compression height is lower than stock. It can also rub against the piston pin boss, potentially cocking the rod and causing a rod bearing failure.

To ensure there's sufficient clearance between the top of the rod and the underside of the piston, rotate the piston back and forth on the rod until the piston skirt almost touches the rod. If the piston doesn't rotate freely, note where the interference is and carefully grind a radius on the rod that will allow full piston movement. Since the rods aren't centered under pistons in a big-block Chevy, push the rod against both piston pin bosses and then rotate it to ensure that piston movement isn't inhibited.

To check for rod contact against any of the piston pin bosses, install the crank and piston/rod assemblies into the block. As you slowly rotate the crank, you should be able to push the rods side-to-side without them touching the piston pin bosses. If they touch, the side of the rod small end or piston pin boss can be milled (or sanded as described in "Rod Side Clearance" if the interference is minor) to obtain adequate clearance.

Rod-to-Block Clearance

If you plan on using a crankshaft with a longer-than-stock stroke, you'll need to check that sufficient clearance exists between the rod bolts and the block when the crankshaft is near the bottom of its stroke. If you can fit a 0.050-inch thick feeler gauge between the rod and the block when the rod is closest to the block, then clearance is sufficient. If there's not enough clearance, use a die grinder on the block (preferred) or rod bolt/nut. Remove the minimum amount of material that will provide sufficient clearance.

Rod-to-Cam Clearance

The area between the top of the rod bolt and the camshaft is another place where clearance can be insufficient. Check this clearance by mocking up the short block with the crank, rods, and pistons. Also install the cam and timing chain set you plan on using. Be sure the cam is timed the way you want to use it, as this is critical to obtaining an accurate clearance measurement. Now lay a 1/8-inch thick strip of modeling clay over the top of the innermost rod bolts on all the rods.

With the clay in place, rotate the crankshaft four complete revolutions to ensure all cylinders have gone through one complete combustion cycle. If you can't rotate the crankshaft at any time, stop to see why. It's possible the rods are touching the cam. Once the crankshaft has completed at least four revolutions, take the rods out of the engine and measure the clay at its thinnest point.

If the clay is at least 0.050 inch thick, everything's cool. If it's 0.050–0.010 inch thick, carefully grind the rod bolt head to gain the required clearance. Just remember, only take the minimum amount of material off the bolt head to prevent weakening an already highly stressed component. And be sure to polish the ground area to prevent stress risers. If rod-to-cam clearance is less than 0.010 inch, you'll need to use a cam with a smaller base circle diameter, or a stroker rod. Stroker rods are recontoured in this area of interference, or they use a bolt that slips in through the cap and screws into the rod, which eliminates the bolt head on the top side of the rod.

Rod bolt stretch is the most reliable indicator that the bolt is stretched into its elastic range. However, the rod bolts must be dimpled to accept a stretch gauge.

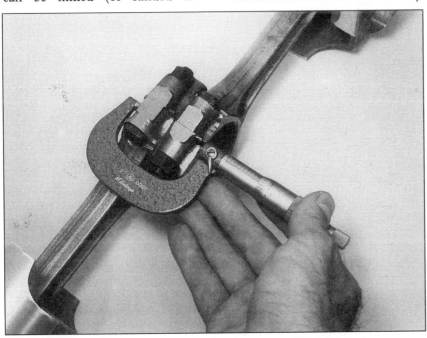

Proper rod side clearance helps prevent overlubricating the cylinder walls. If too much oil gets on the cylinder walls it can overwhelm the rings, get into the combustion chambers, and cause detonation. Be sure to measure each pair of rods that fit on one common journal.

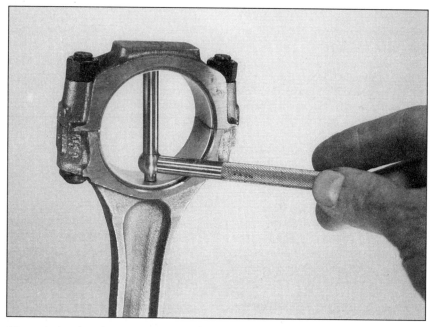

Like main bearing clearance, proper rod bearing clearance is essential to engine life and oil control. Take two or three measurements to ensure your readings are accurate and the rod's bore is round.

Bolt Torque

For a bolt to stay tightened, it must be loaded into its elastic range. The elastic range is the range in which the bolt is stretched so that it remains in tension, but not so far that it's permanently stretched. And this relates directly to bolt torque. Rod bolts present one of those rare instances where you can directly measure bolt stretch. And bolt stretch is the best indicator of load (torque).

Some rod bolts have a dimple in both ends. These dimples accommodate the tips of a rod bolt micrometer so bolt stretch can be measured directly. If the rod bolts you're using don't have dimples, or you don't have access to a rod bolt micrometer, apply clean, 30 weight oil to the bolt threads and nut seat on the cap before installing and torquing the rod nuts. This will reduce friction sufficiently between these surfaces to ensure an accurate torque reading. Factory 7/16-inch diameter boron rod bolts should be torqued so they stretch 0.009 inch, or to 73 pound-feet.

Rod Bearing Clearance

Use the same technique you used to check the main bearing clearances to check the rod bearing clearances. To torque the rod bolts to specifications, you'll have to hold each rod in a soft-jawed vise.

Rod journal diameter should be checked in two places, 90 degrees apart from each other to check for egg-shaped journals. Likewise, check both sides of the journal to ensure the journal isn't barrel-shaped. Egg-shaped journals can occur as the engine wears, but barrel-shaped journals are due to improper machining.

Racing engines like this
Gianino/Lukovich-prepared rat
provide astounding performance.

CHAPTER SIX

PISTONS AND RINGS

Through the miracles of modern engineering, metallurgy, and machining, pistons harness the power of expanding 2,000-degree gasses and tons of pressure to propel your shorts down the drag strip or across the country.

Before purchasing pistons for your rat, you need to keep the intended use of the engine in mind. Street high-performance engines will have different requirements than marine or racing engines. And nitroused or blown engines may have even greater needs. The idea is to purchase pistons (and other components) that fit these needs without buying more or less than required.

As you go through the selection process, keep any future engine performance upgrades in mind. Nitrous oxide, superchargers, and turbochargers make power by increasing cylinder pressure significantly. And this increases piston loading. Frequent or full-time racing also takes its toll on pistons by causing

more fatigue and stress, which can lead to piston failure. So, buy the pistons that will accommodate future performance modifications, and be money ahead.

Piston Types

Two types of pistons are available: cast and forged. These names describe the manufacturing processes that give pistons certain physical properties. Hypereutectic pistons, which are a variation of cast pistons, have some of the benefits of forged pistons with a lower cost. Over the years, cast, forged, and hypereutectic pistons have all been used in production Chevy big-blocks.

Cast Pistons

Cast pistons are manufactured by pouring aluminum alloy into a mold that is slightly larger than the final size and shape of the piston. To control piston expansion as engine operating temperature rises, a steel strut is positioned in the mold

before the piston is poured. Because the steel strut controls piston expansion so well, typical piston-to-bore clearance can be set at about 0.002 inch. This helps prevent piston slap when the engine is cold, reducing engine noise. It also helps keep the rings flatter against the cylinder wall, increasing ring performance and life, while helping to control exhaust emissions. After the pistons are cast, they're machined to specifications.

How sturdy are cast pistons? Well, some 400-horsepower big-blocks were outfitted with them, but this was probably a concession to budget limitations. Cast pistons were never intended or designed for true high-performance work. Consequently, you need to choose between hypereutectic and forged pistons, based on how your engine will be used.

Hypereutectic Pistons

The beauty of hypereutectic pistons is that they have strength that's comparable to a forged piston. In addition, they also have excellent wear and scuff resistance and are cheaper than forged pistons.

What makes hypereutectic pistons possible is silicon (sand, to you and me) and a special casting process. Like most forged pistons, hypereutectic pistons rely on hard silicon to provide more resistance to scuffing and ring land deformation. But the addition of silicon comes with a price—the more silicon that's used, the more brittle the piston becomes. When a hypereutectic piston fails, it breaks rather than simply bending or melting, which is what happens with forged pistons. Typically, the silicon content of a hypereutectic piston ranges from approximately 10–17 percent, with higher percentages providing more resistance to scuffing and ring land deformation.

Hypereutetic pistons also have lower thermal conductivity and a lower rate of thermal expansion than cast or forged pistons. This allows tighter piston-to-bore clearance. Besides reducing piston noise, this tighter clearance can have a positive effect on power output, because it helps keep the rings more square to the cylinder. In turn, they seal better and provide more power.

Hypereutectic pistons are available in standard and performance versions. Standard versions use slots behind the oil control ring to keep heat away from the piston skirt. In turn, this enables a tighter skirt-to-bore clearance when the engine is cold. The down side is that it makes the skirt weaker. Performance hypereutetic pistons use holes instead of slots behind the control ring. This gives the skirt more strength, but it also requires greater skirt-to-bore clearance to prevent scuffing when the engine is at normal operating temperature.

Although high-performance hypereutectic pistons offer greater strength than forged pistons, they aren't strong enough to survive piston operating temperatures of 600 degrees Fahrenheit or more. Therefore, hypereutectic pistons should only be used where high loads are intermittent and infrequent.

Forged Pistons

Forged pistons are used when superior strength and durability are required, such as in racing and marine applications, where piston operating temperatures can and do exceed 600 degrees Fahrenheit. Forged pistons fail at a considerably slower rate than other pistons, due to their greater ductility. However, forged pistons cost more than other types of pistons and may cause increased piston noise when the engine is cold because of the required "loose" clearances.

Forged pistons are manufactured from a solid slug of aluminum alloy that's pressed into shape using 3,000 tons of pressure. This makes for a very dense and therefore, strong piston—about 40-60 percent stronger than cast pistons. Today's forged pistons are stronger than in the past, thanks to tighter quality control that weeds out more of the metal impurities. And like most things in life these days, a computer has had its hand in the design and manufacture of these pistons.

Use of Computer Numerical Control (CNC) equipment allows more precise machining of the raw forging, which equates to lighter pistons that can be run at higher speeds. A tolerance for higher operating temperatures and tighter piston-to-

For racing engines, it used to be common practice to keep the skirt clearance loose to gain power. This worked when piston skirts were ground, but computer-aided modeling and manufacturing have enabled piston manufacturers to optimize skirt shape, thereby reducing skirt-to-wall clearance without increasing friction. So now you can run skirt-to-wall clearances that used to be just for street engines in a racing engine and gain even more power through better ring sealing. *Lunati*

bore clearances are other added benefits of the marriage between better alloys and CNC machining. In fact, some forged pistons have piston-to-bore clearances that are in the ballpark of cast pistons. In part, this is due to the diamond tooling that produces almost identical pistons, one after the other.

Another way of controlling piston-to-bore clearance when the engine is cold is through the use of slots in the root of the oil ring groove. These slots help isolate the piston skirt from the heat absorbed by the rest of the piston, allowing the skirt to be more flexible. In turn, this allows a tighter bore clearance when the engine is cold. On the other hand, when the piston oil holes are drilled instead of slotted, the piston has greater strength. However, this causes the piston skirt to be less flexible, necessitating greater bore clearance when the engine is cold. As a result, cold engine exhaust emissions are higher with this type of forged piston.

From a practical standpoint, any engine that's being built for high-performance use will have to have the cylinders honed (with torque plates for best results) to ensure they're as straight as they can be. Straight cylinders are essential to a good ring seal, and a good ring seal is essential to power production. Since the cylinders will be larger after honing, new pistons will be required. Although cast pistons could be used for mild street performance applications, take this opportunity to purchase either a set of hypereutectic or forged pistons. This will allow you to upgrade engine performance in the future without potentially having to replace pistons. Refer to the "Piston Selection Guidelines" chart on page 53 for recommendations.

Skirt Clearance

The clearance between the piston skirt and cylinder wall will influence how well the rings seal. The tighter the clearance between the skirt and cylinder, the more square the rings are to the cylinder wall. This aids in achieving a good ring seal, and better ring sealing leads directly to more power. The reverse is also true. When clearances are loose, the piston tilts slightly in the bore, so the face of the rings can't seal as well against the cylinder wall. In turn, this can allow some of the burning air/fuel to blow past the rings, decreasing power.

The optimal skirt-to-cylinder wall clearance will keep the piston square in the bore without being so tight that when the piston is heavily loaded, the skirt will push tightly against the cylinder wall. Excessively tight clearances will lead to piston scuffing. Scuffing occurs when one metal is temporarily welded to another through friction and then is torn away. The metal from one surface is actually transferred to the other—a condition you definitely want to avoid. On the other hand, excessively loose piston clearance, in addition to wasting power, can also cause abnormal cylinder wear and even cylinder bore cracking in severe cases.

Piston skirt-to-cylinder wall clearance is dictated by piston type, material, and design, as well as intended engine use. Engines that see street duty operate at various temperatures because they're loaded in different ways for differing lengths of time—full throttle operation, cruising, idling, and everything in between. If pistons with a high

This is one way to check piston skirt clearance, but a better way is to measure the piston skirt 90 degrees from the piston pin bore, then measure the cylinder bore with a dial bore gauge. The difference between the two is the skirt clearance.

expansion rate are used in this application, power will be down at all times except when the engine is loaded sufficiently enough to heat the piston as it was designed to be heated. Consequently, hypereutectic pistons are prime candidates for street engines. However, the trump card in all of this is how the engine will be used. If hypereutectic pistons don't possess the stamina required, as indicated by the "Piston Selection Guidelines" chart on page 53, you shouldn't use them.

An alternative is to use forged pistons that require as little skirt clearance as possible. This will help keep the ring square under more engine operating conditions than loose fitting pistons while providing you with the strength and ductility your engine requires. Typical forged pistons require a skirt clearance of 0.006–0.0075 inch. The tighter versions use a skirt clearance of about 0.004–0.0055 inch.

Other Considerations

Other than deciding on which piston type is best for your engine application, you also have to consider whether you will be using closed or open chamber cylinder heads, what the desired compression ratio will be, the dome design, and piston weight.

Closed and Open Chamber Designs

Due to changes in emission regulations in the early seventies, Chevrolet big-block heads evolved from "closed chamber" to "semi-open chamber" to "open chamber" designs. Basically, this meant the combustion chamber became larger and larger to expose itself to a greater area of the piston. This made more of the air/fuel mixture accessible for combustion, reducing exhaust emissions while providing more power due to more complete combustion.

However, the larger combustion chambers caused compression ratios to drop markedly. To regain compression ratio, the piston domes were enlarged to fill the chambers more fully. Because of this, pistons designed for open chamber heads will not fit the smaller combustion chambers used in closed chamber heads. If you try this combination, the pistons will come in direct contact with the head. However, since the piston domes on closed chamber pistons are smaller than those used on open chamber pistons, they can always be used with open chamber heads, but you'll lose some compression in the process and put a damper on the flame front. The neutral parties in all this are flat-top and dished pistons—they can be used with either open or closed chamber heads.

The piston on the left is for closed chamber heads because its dome doesn't extend all the way to the piston edge. The piston on the right is for open chamber heads because its dome extends to the edge of the piston. Although closed chamber pistons can be used with both closed and open chamber heads, open chamber pistons can't be used with closed chamber heads because they'll hit the unrelieved area of the combustion chamber. *TRW*

Short dome pistons are preferred for rats because they help move the air/fuel mixture for better combustion and more power. Sometimes high dome pistons are required to reach a specific compression ratio, depending upon combustion chamber volume. This Lunati forged piston is made from high silicon aluminum but is also available in 2618 aluminum. *Lunati*

Piston Dome Shape

Piston dome shape has a considerable impact on how gasses flow in the cylinder. Before you can select a piston dome shape for best flame front travel, you have to consider what occurs during the combustion process.

As the piston moves up the cylinder on the compression stroke, the air/fuel mixture is squeezed into a smaller and smaller space. This groups the air and fuel molecules closer together. It's this close proximity of air and fuel molecules that allows the mixture to burn.

When the spark plug ignites the air/fuel mixture, it begins burning at the plug then travels across the piston dome. If the dome interrupts the burning process (because of its height or shape), small pockets of the air/fuel mixture won't burn. And you have to burn all of the available air/fuel mixture for best power output and lowest emissions. Consequently, the shape of the piston dome needs to be selected carefully to prevent shrouding of the air/fuel mixture.

When it comes to big-block Chevys, a small dome (0.150–0.250 inch) works best, with a dished piston coming in second place. Both the dome and the dish help initiate swirl of the air/fuel mixture, which leads to more complete combustion. However, in some racing applications, you'll need to use pistons with a dome height around 0.500–0.700 inch to achieve the necessary compression ratio. On high-compression, open-chamber pistons, a flame trough is

cut into the spark plug side of the piston dome to direct the ignited air/fuel mixture over to the other side of the dome. To avoid this situation, the trend is toward using shorter combustion chambers combined with the smaller domes mentioned earlier.

The strategy for piston dome height is different for relatively small inch motors (454 cubic-inches and smaller) than it is for larger motors. For small-inch engines, you'll need to use a higher dome to get the compression you need. With larger engines, the dome doesn't have to be as high, because the cylinder bore is larger. Therefore, with equally sized combustion chambers, the larger engine already has a higher compression ratio due to the greater bore size.

For best flame front travel, you want the piston dome to fit closely to the sides of the combustion chamber. This helps eliminate dead spots where portions of the air/fuel charge can lay dormant. It also helps reduce exhaust emissions.

If you're opting for dished pistons to achieve a certain compression ratio, the shape of the dish should mirror that of the combustion chamber to increase turbulence of the incoming air/fuel mixture.

Flat-top pistons come in a distant third in the quest for power. Since flat-top pistons don't impart any turbulence to the air/fuel mixture, pockets of the mixture aren't ignited. This leads to premature detonation, which robs power. It also leads to higher exhaust emissions.

Compression Ratio

Compression ratio compares the volume of the area above the piston when the piston is at the bottom of its stroke versus the volume above the piston when the piston is at the top of its stroke.

Compression ratio is one of the leading factors in achieving a desired level of engine performance. The more compression an engine can run, the greater its power output will be. Compression ratio can be increased by using domed pistons or heads with smaller combustion chambers (of which a wide variety exist for the big-block), milling the heads, or using a thinner head gasket. Detonation (the uncontrolled burning of the air/fuel mixture) is what limits compression ratio and can destroy a piston or an engine in a matter of seconds. High compression, overly advanced ignition timing, low-octane fuel, and combustion chamber deposits can all contribute to detonation.

Supercharged and turbocharged engines don't use a high static compression ratio because the supercharger or turbocharger supplies extra compression in the form of increased cylinder pressure. Although static compression ratio will vary depending upon the level of boost, it typically falls in the 7.5:1–8.0:1 range for most street applications. To achieve a compression ratio in this range may require the use of dished pistons, depending upon combustion chamber volume and bore size.

Realistically, street-driven vehicles using 92 octane fuel shouldn't run a compression ratio of more than 9.0-9.5:1. Long duration camshafts lower cylinder pressure, so you can increase compression to about 10.0-10.5:1 on street-driven vehicles, if you use this type of camshaft along with 93-94 octane fuel and apply the combustion chamber modifications outlined in Chapter 10, *Cylinder Heads*. Other types of high-performance vehicles, such as Pro street cars and bracket racers, should limit their compression ratio to about 13:1, depending upon the camshaft used and the fuel octane that's available.

Before purchasing a particular set of pistons, you must also consider the lift, duration and lobe separation angle of the camshaft you plan on using, because they each directly affect the dynamic compression ratio of your engine—the actual compression ratio of your engine when it's running. Consequently, dynamic compression ratio is more important than static compression ratio. If it's too low, your engine will run like a slug. If it's too high, you'll

When tall piston domes are required to obtain a certain compression ratio, they'll have a "flame trough" cut into them, like this Wiseco piston. This trough allows the burning air/fuel mixture to get over to the other side of the piston for more complete combustion.

need to run high octane fuel, or you may burn holes in the pistons.

Let's say you plan on building an engine for a tow vehicle so it has lots of low end grunt. Increasing the compression ratio can help provide some of this, as will a camshaft designed for tow vehicles because they both increase cylinder pressure. However, if you increase static compression substantially and use the towing camshaft, cylinder pressure

could rise dramatically—far enough, in fact, that you might need to run octane booster, if the pistons don't melt down first. Keep in mind that the higher the compression ratio, the greater the potential for piston failure due to detonation.

Moving to the other end of the spectrum, let's imagine your engine's compression ratio is 9:1 and you've installed a real hot cam with lots of duration because you wanted more power and speed. The result? A real dog of an engine. Long duration cams reduce cylinder pressure significantly by virtue of both intake and exhaust valves being open together for long periods of time. This valve overlap reduces dynamic compression. If this effect isn't offset by a higher static compression ratio, engine performance will be disappointing. For more related information, see the "Piston Compression Height" section and Chapter 8, *Camshafts and Lifters*.

Calculating Compression Ratio

To determine compression ratio, you'll need to know the volumes of four different things: cylinder bore; head gasket; combustion chamber; and piston dome (or dish). Determining the volume of the cylinder bore and head gasket will be straightforward because they can be calculated using the formula for displacement. However, determining the volume of the combustion chamber and the piston dome (or dish) will be somewhat more difficult because of their shapes. This CC'ing operation will require a 1-inch-thick piece of clear plexiglass about 6 inches square; a graduated burette (or syringe); some windshield washer fluid; and some clean grease.

For purposes of explanation, we'll use an engine with a 4.250-inch bore and 4.00-inch stroke outfitted with domed pistons. And let's say the combustion chamber has a volume of 123.2 cc. To determine combustion chamber volume of your heads, refer to Chapter 10, *Cylinder Heads*.

Piston Dome Volume

Unless you're using flat top pistons (or the manufacturer provides information on piston dome volume),

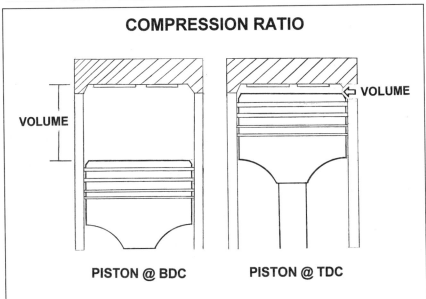

COMPRESSION RATIO

VOLUME

VOLUME

PISTON @ BDC   **PISTON @ TDC**

Compression ratio compares the volume above the piston at bottom dead center (BDC) with the volume above the piston when its at top dead center (TDC). This static compression ratio is different from the dynamic compression ratio, which takes the effects of camshaft timing into consideration. The higher the compression ratio you can run, the greater the power output.

the next step is to measure piston dome volume.

To do this, rotate the crankshaft to bring the piston (with the top compression ring in place) about halfway down the cylinder. Then wipe a light film of grease over the cylinder wall and bring the piston up the bore until its quench area is exactly 1 inch away from the deck. Using the formula to calculate cylinder volume, determine how much volume this 1 inch long cylinder provides. Then wipe off all the grease that remains on the piston and cylinder walls without allowing the piston to move in the cylinder.

Now apply a thin film of grease to the deck around the entire perimeter of the cylinder bore. With the block angled so one edge of the cylin-

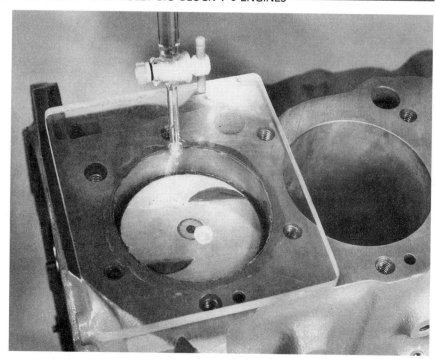

After applying a light coating of grease around the perimeter of the cylinder, position the measuring plate so its fill hole is at the top side of the cylinder and press it firmly into place. Then fill the cylinder with the colored alcohol or washer fluid and note the volume.

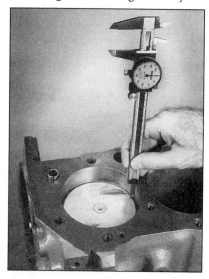

When determining piston dome volume, the top ring must be installed on the piston, and the cylinder must be lightly greased to prevent the measuring fluid from leaking out of the cylinder. Also, the piston must be set a measured distance down the cylinder. Exactly 1 inch from the deck is a good location.

der is slightly higher than the other, hold the plexiglass plate so its fill hole will be at the high side of the cylinder and press it firmly into place. After filling the burette with windshield washer fluid, fill the cylinder with the fluid and note the reading.

If you put less fluid in the cylinder than a 1-inch cylinder should hold (as determined earlier) the difference between the two readings is

the volume of the piston *dome*. If you put more fluid in the cylinder than a 1-inch cylinder should hold (as determined earlier), the difference between the two readings is the volume of the piston *dish*.

For example, using the formula for cylinder volume:

Cylinder volume = 0.7853981 x (bore x bore) x stroke

We can calculate the volume of a 4.250-inch diameter bore 1-inch long is 14.186 cubic inches. To convert this to CCs, multiply it by 16.387 (14.186 x 16.387 = 232.47 cc). However, since our piston had a healthy dome, it took only 191.1 cc of alcohol to fill the cylinder; therefore, our piston dome has a volume of 41.37 cc (232.47 - 191.1 = 41.37).

Cylinder Volume

Now, calculate total cylinder volume:

Cylinder volume = 0.7853981 x (bore x bore) x stroke

Using our 4.250-inch bore and 4.00-inch stroke, the formula would then be: 0.7853981 x

18.0625 x 4.00 x = 56.745cu in. To be able to use this result to calculate compression ratio, we have to convert it to CCs by multiplying it by 16.387 (56.745 x 16.387 = 929.88 cc). So our total cylinder volume is 929.88 cc.

Head Gasket Volume

To calculate the volume of the cylinder head gasket, simply use the cylinder volume formula substituting compressed gasket thickness for stroke, then multiply the result by 16.387 (cylinder volume = 0.7853981 x [bore x bore] x compressed gasket thickness x 16.387). For example, if the bore is 4.250 inches and the compressed gasket thickness is 0.039 inch, the formula would be: (cylinder volume = 0.7853981 x 18.0625 x 0.039 = 0.5532638 cubic inch). To convert this to CCs, you would multiply it by 16.387 (0.5532638 x 16.387 = 9.066 cc).

Deck Volume

Unless the quench area of the piston is even with the top of the deck, there's one last thing that needs to be computed and that's deck volume. With the piston at TDC, use a dial caliper to measure how far down the bore the piston is. Typically, big-block Chevys with steel rods are set up so the piston is 0.005 inch below the deck. Using this 0.005-inch deck clearance as an example, the formula would be the same as the one you just used for head gasket volume (cylinder volume = 0.7853981 x [bore x bore] x deck height x 16.387). Working the equation, it would look like this: 0.7853981 x 18.0625 x 0.005 x 16.387 = 1.162 cc.

Determining Static Compression Ratio

Now you can use all of your figures to determine static compression ratio. Remember that static compression ratio compares the volume of the area above the piston when the piston is at the bottom of its stroke (BDC) versus the volume above the piston when the piston is at the top of its stroke (TDC).

To begin, add all the volumes above the piston when it's at BDC (Refer to chart below).

Finally, divide the total volume at BDC by the total volume at TDC to calculate the compression ratio: 1020.776cc÷92.058cc=11.09

So our hypothetical engine has a static compression ratio just shy of 11.1:1.

Piston Pins

Two types of piston pins have been used in big-block Chevys: pressed and floating. Pressed piston pins are locked into the end of the connecting rod by an interference fit of about 0.0015 inch. As the piston moves up and down in the cylinder, the piston pivots on the pin. This type of design is used in the vast majority of big-block engines.

Unlike a pressed pin, a floating piston "floats" in a bushing in the small end of the connecting rod. A clearance of about 0.0005-0.0007 inch allows this to happen. A similar clearance exists between the ends of the piston pin and the piston. To prevent the pin from moving out from the piston and contacting the cylinder wall, two wire retainers are fitted into each end of the piston. These retainers are usually either of the Tru-Arc or Spirolox variety.

Tru-Arc retainers are basically internal snap rings. If these are used, one must be positioned so its open end is at the 12 o'clock position and

the open end on the other should point toward 6 o'clock. If these rings are positioned so their open ends are anywhere near horizontal, the forces acting on the piston as it accelerates and decelerates can actually compress the rings and cause them to move out of the piston pin bore. Once this happens, your Visa card will hit its redline immediately.

A Spirolox retainer is a flat spring that's nearly two revolutions long. To install these in the piston, they need to be wound in. And because they're so long, they have no "opening" which makes them considerably more resistant to moving out of piston pin bore. This resistance is a mixed blessing, however, because it makes them quite difficult to remove.

The biggest advantage of floating pins is that they make it easy to remove the pistons whenever you choose, without damaging them, unlike pressed pins.

Pin Material

Piston pins are available in a number of different materials for big-block Chevys, but three types are predominant: standard chrome moly, tool steel, and 4340 chrome moly. As with pistons, you must select piston pin material based on the intended use of the engine.

Standard chrome moly pins are used in most street applications because they offer good durability and are relatively inexpensive. Marine applications are different, though. Unlike street engines, marine engines are always loaded, so the environment they live in is more severe. Consequently, engines used in pleasure boats (and oval track racing) require thick-wall chrome moly pins, while racing boats require tool steel pins.

Tool steel is used to manufacture thin-wall piston pins for the race car set. Their thin wall design allows them to be significantly lighter than standard chrome moly pins. In turn, this allows the engine to accelerate quicker. However, thin-wall tool steel piston pins lack long-term durability, so they shouldn't be used in engines destined for street or marine applications.

Piston pins made from 4340 chrome moly are at the top of the

Combustion chamber volume	123.20 cc
Head gasket volume	9.066 cc
Cylinder volume	+929.88 cc
Subtotal volume @ BDC =	1062.146 cc

Then subtract the piston dome volume from this total.

Subtotal volume @ BDC	1062.146 cc
Piston Dome Volume	- 41.37 cc
Total volume @ BDC =	1020.776 cc

Now add all the volumes above the piston when it's at TDC, including:

Combustion chamber volume	123.20 cc
Head gasket volume	9.066 cc
Deck volume	+1.162 cc
Subtotal volume @ TDC	133.428 cc

Then subtract the piston dome volume from this total:

Subtotal volume @ TDC	133.428 cc
Piston dome volume	-41.37 cc
Total volume @ TDC =	92.058 cc

Besides using different materials, piston pins can be of straight (left) or tapered-wall design. Generally speaking, straight wall pins are used for all street, marine, and other applications where endurance is the number one priority. Taper-wall pins are used in racing applications where reciprocating weight is most important and parts are inspected and changed relatively frequently.

When longer rods or a stroker crank are used, the piston pin needs to be moved up in the piston to keep the piston below the block deck. The piston on the left has the pin bore in the typical location. The piston on the right has a raised pin bore. Since it extends into the oil ring rail, buttons are required on the ends of the pin to seal it.

heap because they offer superior strength and durability compared to the other types of pins. They're the way to go for engines with superchargers or turbochargers, as well as endurance racing applications. Just be prepared to pay a premium for them.

If you're not sure what type of pin material to use for your particular application, be sure to contact the piston manufacturer for their recommendations. They know what works best.

Piston Compression Height

Piston compression height is the distance between the center of the piston pin bore and the piston quench area (the flat part of the piston at its top).

In order to use the same length connecting rod when changing crankshaft stroke from 3.76 inches to 4.00 inches, Chevrolet merely moved the piston pin higher in the piston. You need to do the same when your search for more cubic inches leads you to a crankshaft with a longer than stock stroke. If you fail to do this, the pistons may extend past the deck of the cylinder block and may even contact the cylinder head—a sure recipe for disaster.

To determine the difference required in piston compression height to achieve normal deck clearance, subtract the old crankshaft stroke from the new crankshaft stroke, and divide

this result by two ((new stroke - old stroke) ÷ 2 = difference in upward and downward strokes).

For example, let's say you have a 427 and you want to increase the stroke by approximately 1/4 inch by using the crankshaft from a 454. The stroke of the 454 is 4.00 inches and the original stroke of the 427 is 3.76 inches. The difference between these two figures is 0.24 inch, which is the total difference in stroke. To determine how much farther up and down the cylinder the piston will go, divide the total stroke by two. In this case, the result is 0.12 inch. So you need to use pistons whose compression height is 0.12 inch less than your original pistons because the upward and downward strokes are 0.12 inch longer. Now, you need to find a set of pistons with this amount of pin offset. Information on piston pin compression height can be found in the *Chevrolet Big-Block V-8 Interchange Manual* or at your local speed shop.

In some instances, the piston pin will need to end up somewhere under the oil ring groove to achieve an optimal rod/stroke ratio. This may look a little scary, but it won't cause any problems because it's isolated from the effects of cylinder compression. To provide more support for the underside of the bottom oil rail, the oil ring groove is

machined 0.030 inch wider and a spacer ring is positioned below the bottom of the oil rail.

Deck Height

The distance between the quench area of the piston and the deck of the block is what is called deck height. If the quench area of the piston is even with the deck, the deck height is called "zero." If it's above the deck, the piston is called "out of the hole." Conversely, if it's below the deck, the piston is said to be "in the hole." Generally speaking, a piston that's 0.005 inch "in the hole" is preferred for steel connecting rod engines, while a piston that's 0.020 inch "in the hole" is used for engines equipped with aluminum rods. Aluminum rod applications require the piston to be farther in the hole to compensate for the greater stretch inherent with aluminum rods.

Deck height determines the distance between the quench areas of the piston and combustion chamber. As the piston approaches TDC on the compression stroke, the air/fuel mixture that's squeezed in this area is pushed out into the combustion chamber, adding to the charge turbulence. The smaller this clearance can be (without allowing the piston to hit the combustion chamber) the higher the charge turbulence will be.

Weight

Although the intended use of your engine must be the primary factor in selecting cast, hypereutetic or forged pistons, you should also consider piston weight.

As the piston assembly reaches the top of its stroke, it wants to continue up and out of the cylinder. And the heavier the piston, the greater the urge. The tremendous inertial loading imposed by the piston assembly continues until the piston is well on its way back down the cylinder and rises exponentially as engine rpm climbs.

The heavier the piston, the greater the force on the rod and main bearings, reducing their life. More weight squeezes out more of the oil film out from between the bearings and crankshaft. If this film of oil is squeezed hard enough, the bearings will contact the crankshaft, shortening both their lives.

Lightweight pistons put less strain on the crankshaft and bearings and increase both the acceleration and deceleration speeds of the crankshaft. This translates into free horsepower.

Factory pistons range from about 655 to 875 grams, depending upon bore size, dome configuration, and whether the piston is cast, hypereutectic, or forged. Aftermarket forged pistons average about 650 grams for a 4.250-inch bore size, without a piston pin. Drag racing pistons can weigh about 100 grams less, because of their thinner decks.

Keep in mind that a thicker deck is required in street applications so it can transfer enough heat to the oil (via the rings) to keep it from failing. If it's too thin, combustion heat will destroy the heat treating. Once this happens, stress cracks will appear in the top of the piston and the piston fails. On average, piston deck thickness for street engines is around 0.225 inch. In drag racing applications, the decks don't need to be as thick because the pistons are loaded for such a short period of time. Typically, deck thickness for naturally aspirated drag racing engines is about 0.180 inch. Drag racing engines fed nitrous require piston decks that are about 0.200 inch thick to stand up to the "juice."

Since the lightest racing pistons usually have the shortest life span, it may prove more economical to use pistons that are a little heavier than what would be considered optimal.

Piston Speed

No matter how much air your engine can flow, piston speed is what determines maximum engine rpm before it lets go like a huge hand grenade. How far is too far? That depends on the designs and materials used for the crankshaft, connecting rods, and pistons.

Generally speaking, 4,000 feet-per-minute is the limit for a big-block equipped with a cast-iron crank, stock rods, and cast or hypereutectic pistons. Typical high-performance street engines outfitted with a forged crank, high-performance rods and rod bolts, and forged pistons have a maximum piston speed of about 4,500 feet per minute. Although these speeds can be exceeded once in a while for bursts of a few second or so, they should be considered the maximum limit. Piston speeds are calculated in feet per minute using the following formula:

$$\text{Piston speed (fpm)} = \frac{\text{Stroke (in inches)} \times \text{rpm}}{6}$$

For this example, let's say your engine uses a 4.00-inch stroke crankshaft and you want to determine piston speed at 7,000 rpm. Our formula looks like this:

$$\text{Piston speed (fpm)} = \frac{4.00 \times 7000}{6}$$

These Ross pistons illustrate some different ways to support the piston pin bosses. The piston on the left lacks the reinforcing section used on the inboard areas of the other piston pin bosses. The right-most piston has even beefier bosses than the one in the center. The additional weight of the bosses, though welcome strength-wise, limit maximum piston speed.

Multiply the stroke by the engine rpm at which you want to check piston speed and divide this result by 6 (4.00 x 7,000 divided by 6 = 4,667 fpm). Using the information provided above, you can see that piston speeds this high will require a forged crank, high-performance rods, and forged pistons. You could push an engine with a cast-iron crank and pistons this high, but you'd be taking a chance that it might let go. Drag racing engines can push this limit to 5,500-6,000 feet per minute, but that's with the best components that are inspected frequently and replaced on a regular basis.

When to Buy

If you plan your work so you have at least two months to build the engine, don't order your pistons until you've prepared the combustion chambers as outlined in chapter 10, *Cylinder Heads*, and have CC'd them. This will help you select the pistons that will provide you with the desired static compression ratio. If you buy the pistons before you do any combustion chamber work, the static compression ratio may be lower than you require due to the increased combustion chamber volume.

Shop Work
Dome Machining

In some instances, it will be necessary to cut the piston valve reliefs to ensure sufficient clearance between the valves and the pistons. Before you have this operation performed, call the piston manufacturer to see how much material can be removed from the valve pockets before piston dome strength becomes questionable. Some pistons can have more material removed than others, so you need to check. Generally, piston dome thickness must never be less than 0.200 inch for street applications and 0.180 inch for racing applications. And to minimize the potential for stress cracks, make sure the machine shop you're sending the pistons off to uses radiused cutters to cut the reliefs. Information on how to check valve-to-piston clearance can be found in Chapter 9, *Valvetrain*.

Piston Preparation

The top of a piston is exposed to combustion temperatures over 2,000 degrees Fahrenheit. Any sharp edges on the dome will heat more readily than the surrounding areas. As these edges become hotter, they can actually ignite the air/fuel mixture on their own. The flame front from this auto-ignition air/fuel mixture will actually battle the flame front started by the spark plug. This pre-ignition leads to engine-destroying detonation. To avoid this situation, carefully chamfer all the sharp edges on the dome.

Sharp edges on the remainder of the piston act as stress risers and can cause cracks to form. To prevent this from happening, radius all the sharp edges. A die grinder outfitted with a fine grit sandpaper cone will do the job here, as will a Dremel Moto-Tool.

Assembly Checks

Because of the myriad number of possible piston compression heights, dome configurations, bore sizes, and stroke combinations, it is impossible to predict what will work in all situations. In light of this, you need to mock up your engine with the crankshaft, bearings, camshaft, and timing gears you plan to use, as well as one cylinder head with the proper gasket, and the valvetrain for one cylinder to see if all the clearances are within specifications. If they're not, now is the time to do something about it.

Piston-to-Combustion Chamber Clearance

For optimum performance, you want to ensure the piston dome isn't closing off any part of the combustion chamber. To check for this, mock up the piston and rod for one cylinder and assemble it onto the crankshaft. Then roll out strips of modeling clay about 1/8 inch thick and place them around the dome. With the cylinder head on top of the head gasket you plan on using, torqued to specifications, slowly bring the piston up to top dead center. Finally, remove the head and check the thickness of the clay. There should be no areas of the clay that are less than 0.080 inch thick. If there are, the piston dome will interfere

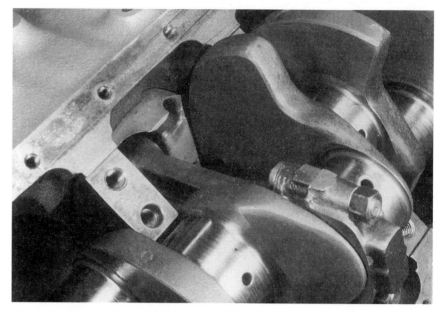

Check the clearance between the bottom of the piston and the crankshaft counterweights. A minimum of 0.050 inch for steel rods and 0.100 inch for aluminum rods is required.

with flame travel. Carefully remove the offending material with a grinder or file until sufficient clearance is obtained. When you're finished, smooth the reworked areas to eliminate any sharp edges that could cause preignition.

Some piston domes can be lightly massaged with a grinder or file to fit, then dressed with 400-grit sandpaper. Others may require machining. Just remember, once you modify the pistons, you won't be able to return them. And not all pistons can be modified in a major way without compromising their strength and durability. So, check with your local supplier to be sure the pistons you have can be modified, and if so, what modifications are allowable and to what extent.

Skirt-to-Counterweight Clearance

In addition to checking clearance on the top side of the piston, you also need to check the piston skirts to ensure they don't contact the crankshaft counterweights when the pistons are at the bottom of their stroke. Unless this interference is less than 0.050 inch (0.100 inch for aluminum rods), which can be handled with a file and some 400-grit sandpaper, the crankshaft counterweights will have to be

machined for clearance. A little pre-planning on your part can avoid this expensive situation.

Custom piston manufacturers such as Arias, JE, Ross, or Wiseco can make practically any piston you may need. Call them for further information if necessary. (See Appendix B for address information.)

And remember, some pistons increase exhaust emissions, which makes them illegal for vehicles used on public highways. Generally speaking, if the piston compression ratio, dome height, and style are the same as the original, you shouldn't have any problems. If they've changed, you'll need to check with the piston manufacturer or supplier before spending any money.

Piston Rings

Piston rings seal the space between the piston and cylinder wall, as well as the space between the piston ring grooves and themselves. Both of these jobs are critical to power production. If the combustion gasses leak through either area, horsepower and torque will drop.

Piston rings are available in a number of different widths, materials and designs. What is most appropriate for your engine depends on its intended use.

PISTON SELECTION GUIDELINES

Piston Type	Application							
	Standard service	Light truck & towing	Moderate street perf.	Oval track claimers	High perf. street/strip	Pro Street & brackets	Blowers & nitrous	Fast ovals & drags
Cast								
Hypereutetic								
Forged - with slotted oil groove								
Forged - with drilled oil groove								

Key:

- Not normally used for this application
- May be marginal due to cost or strength
- Will work, but exercise caution with ignition timing & air/fuel mixture
- The best choice for this application

General Guidelines: Modifications which dramatically increase cylinder pressure, such as very high compression, blowers or nitrous usually require drilled type forgings. Engines that see only occasional wide open throttle use, as in towing or moderate street performance applications, are best off with hypereutectic pistons. Applications which fall between these extremes can used either piston type, with the decision based on cost, desired strength and future plans for the engine/vehicle.

Chart courtesy Federal Mogul Corporation

Width

Ring width and the outward pressure that a ring exerts has a direct correlation to internal engine friction. The wider the rings and the greater the outward pressure, the higher the friction. However, rings must have a minimum width and outward pressure to provide acceptable ring life and sealing qualities.

For all street driving and a number of competition classes, standard width rings work best. When talking big-block Chevy, that equates to 5/64-inch wide compression rings and a 3/16-inch wide oil control ring. Those wanting to gain an extra edge on the competition may want to use 1/16-inch thick compression rings. These rings offer reduced friction at the expense of increased wear. Also consider that as ring width decreases, it's more likely to not seal as well if

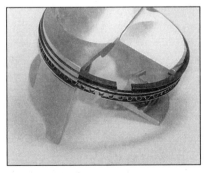

These "gapless" rings from Total Seal use a thin rail beneath the second compression ring to improve cylinder sealing. A leak-down rate of 1 to 2 percent is common with these rings.

piston-to-skirt clearance is on the high side. That's because there's more opportunity for the edges of the ring to roll away from the cylinder wall.

Material

Piston ring material impacts ring life and the ring's sealing qualities. Molybdenum (moly) has been the ring coating of choice for years, because it decreases friction between the ring and the cylinder wall. It does this by trapping oil between the voids on its surface and the cylinder wall, allowing the ring to glide on a thin film of oil. The film also prevents scuffing, which is more common in higher performance applications.

Rat rings are typically available in conventional (single moly), double moly, and plasma moly configurations. In conventional moly ring sets, only the upper compression

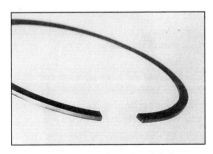

Moly rings use an inlay of molybdenum to improve cylinder sealing and reduce friction. The moly has small voids in it that capture and retain engine oil. When gapping these rings, always file from the outside of the ring inward to prevent chipping the moly.

ring has a pure moly inlay. In double moly ring sets, both the upper and lower compression rings have a pure moly inlay. Moly rings use a gray iron base material, which works well in standard performance applications.

Plasma moly rings are the latest innovation in piston ring design. These rings are manufactured by plasma spraying molten molybdenum onto a ductile iron top compression ring. Unlike standard moly rings, the molybdenum used in plasma moly rings is combined with nickel to increase its service life. The ductile iron top compression ring has a relatively high level of elasticity, which allows it to bend rather than break under severe operating conditions. It's also three

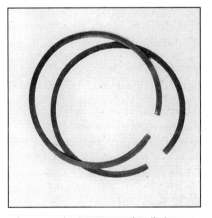

Plasma moly rings use a ductile iron base that's three times stronger than the gray iron used for other types of moly rings. This helps them resist damage from detonation.

times stronger than a gray iron ring. So these rings are best in severe duty applications like marine use, supercharging, turbocharging, racing, and with nitrous oxide.

Second compression rings typically use grey iron as a base material because they don't have to deal so directly with the heat of combustion. Higher quality ring sets have plasma moly second compression rings while lesser quality plasma moly sets use a non-coated cast-iron ring. High-performance engines equipped with nitrous, blowers or turbos, or used for racing or high-performance marine applications should use plasma moly second rings. All other applications should be fine with the non-coated cast iron second compression ring.

Just remember moly rings should never be used in an aluminum bore due to the possibility of ring scuffing.

Perfectly round cylinder bores are essential to achieving maximum power. Therefore, the use of a Sunnen CK10 automatic honing machine, along with torque plates bolted to the block, is essential for maximum ring sealing. Plateau honing should also be used, as long as chrome rings won't be part of the engine package.

Sizing

Piston ring end gaps must fall within a particular range. If they're too close together at room temperature, they'll butt against one another when the engine reaches normal operating temperature and scuff the cylinder wall. If they're too far away from each other, combustion gasses and pressure will leak between the ends into the crankcase, lowering power output and increasing exhaust emissions.

Conventional rings are designed so that when they're placed in the cylinder, they provide an end gap that usually falls within the recommended end gap specification. However, you should always check them to be sure.

Leading manufacturers of piston rings, like Speed Pro, offer two different styles of plasma moly rings. One is a conventional style in that the ring end gaps are established for a particular size bore. Other than checking the end gaps to ensure they fall within the end gap specifications, you basically install them as they are, right out of the box.

File-fit rings are for those of us seeking a little extra power. As their name implies, they have to be filed to provide the proper end gap for a given bore size. This is because they are marginally longer than conventional rings.

Why are file-fit rings preferred over conventional gap rings? Because blow-by of the air/fuel mixture through the ring end gaps can extract a small penalty in regard to power loss and engine emissions. File fit rings can help minimize these problems because the engine builder is responsible for measuring and adjusting ends gaps as they see fit.

Rings that are adjusted toward the minimum end gap specification reduce blow-by of the air/fuel mixture, increasing power, while simultaneously reducing emissions.

Gapless rings are another type of design. Instead of having an open gap between the ends of the ring, a step or rail is used underneath the second compression ring. This makes it more difficult for combustion gasses to get past the rings, resulting in less blow-by and lower emissions. Total Seal and Childs & Albert both offer high-quality gapless rings.

Checking Fit

In order for piston rings to do their job effectively, they have to seal against the bore *and* the piston. Many people spend lots of time making sure the cylinder bores are round and true, but they forget to check how the ring seals against the piston. And this can cost some horsepower. Let me provide some background.

When the piston is on the compression stroke, the top ring is forced down against the ring land. Combustion pressure gets behind the back side of the ring and pushes it outward against the cylinder. This augments the pressure provided by the ring in the first place. If the clearance between the ring lands and the ring is too great, some of the combustion pressure will blow right past the ring, lessening the seal against the cylinder wall and reducing power. It also invites oil into the combustion chamber, just the ticket for engine-damaging detonation.

To prevent this from happening, ring side clearance should be about 0.002 inch. However, too much side clearance doesn't necessarily mean the piston needs to be scrapped. If the engine is used mostly for stoplight races, you could have the ring land machined oversize and use a flat steel spacer to take up the gap. But this isn't the optimum fix.

You also need to make sure the rings rotate in their lands smoothly. If they don't, they can't seal against the lands effectively. Carbon or burrs on the ring lands or bent ring lands are usually the cause of this type of problem. Carbon deposits can usually be removed with solvent. Burrs can be

addressed using a fine file, but only remove the burr and nothing else. Bent ring lands may be able to be repaired with a ring file, but you never really know what internal damage is lurking within the land. For this reason, it's always best to replace a piston with a bent ring land.

Gapping

Proper ring end gap is critical to engine power and life. If the gap is too great, combustion pressure will blow past the rings into the crankcase. If the gap is too tight, the ends of the rings will butt and damage the cylinder walls. This is especially critical with the top compression ring because it's closest to the heat of combustion. It also has to deal with the higher heat load that's transferred from the top of the piston. All this heat causes the top ring to expand at a greater rate compared to the other rings. If ring end gap is insufficient, the ends of the ring will contact one another and push outward against the cylinder, damaging it.

To set ring end gap, the general rule of thumb is to allow 0.0045 inch for every inch of cylinder bore diameter. That means if cylinder diameter is 4.310 inch, ring end gap should be 0.0194. However, this rule only holds true for naturally aspirated gasoline-powered engines. If the engine is loaded with nitrous, or is supercharged or turbocharged, end gap must be increased about 0.003 to 0.004 inch to compensate for the additional heat loading. If you're ever in doubt about ring end gaps being too tight, it pays to err to the loose side so the engine doesn't go south on you. And always follow the ring manufacturer's specifications.

Ring gap isn't as critical for the second compression ring as the first since it's further away from the heat of combustion. Nevertheless, you shouldn't become careless when you're gapping it.

The time honored way of setting end gaps is with a fine toothed, flat bastard file. The file is mounted in a vise and the ends of the ring are compressed against the file while pushing the ring across it. This is still a good method, but it's time consuming.

PISTON RING SELECTION GUIDELINES

Piston Ring Type	Application									
	Standard service	Light truck & towing	Moderate street perf.	Oval track claimers	High perf. street/strip	Pro Street & brackets	Nitrous, Blowers & turbos	Fast ovals & drags	Pleasure boats	High perf. marine
Conventional Moly	■	■	■	■	□				■	□
Plasma Moly	□	□	□	□	■	■	■	■	□	■

Key:

■ The best choice for this application

□ Not normally used for this application

General Guidelines: Modifications which dramatically increase cylinder pressure, such as very high compression, blowers, turbos or nitrous require plasma moly rings, as do engines with siamesed cylinder bores. Engines that see only occasional wide open throttle use, as in towing or moderate street performance applications, are best off with conventional moly rings. Applications which fall between these extremes should consider double moly rings, with the decision based on current and future plans for the engine/vehicle.

Piston ring selection guidelines, by application and ring type.

Ring grinders, both manually and electrically powered, are available.

If the gap is smaller than it needs to be, you'll need to carefully file it until it has the proper spacing. There are two things you need to watch for as you're doing this: One, the ends of the ring must remain parallel to each other to ensure the proper end gap; two, file the ring from the front to the back to avoid chipping the face of the ring. File a little at a time and keep rechecking the end gap to avoid removing too much material. When the end gap is correct, lightly chamfer the edges of the ring ends with a stone to prevent scratching the cylinder bore.

After all the end gaps are set and the engine is ready for assembly, keep in mind that the end gaps need to be positioned properly to minimize blow-by. Generally, this means positioning the end gaps 120 degrees away from each other when installing the pistons.

Leakdown Testing

After all your hard work ensuring the ring seal will be as good as possible, you should quantify the results with a leakdown test after the engine is broken in. A leakdown test will tell you how much pressure is actually getting past the rings—and the less, the better. Leakdown testing also provides a baseline with which you can compare if something seems to go awry down the road.

A racing engine with excellent sealing qualities will have a leakdown rate of 2 percent. Those with a leakdown rate of 3 to 5 percent are considered to be good. Any cylinders with a reading of more than about 8 percent need to be checked further to find the cause of the problem. For high-performance street and marine engines, add about 2 percent to these values to determine sealing efficiency.

Check piston ring end gap by squaring the ring about an inch down from the top of the cylinder using the skirt of a piston. It must be square in the bore to accurately determine end gap. Take your time ensuring the gap is within specifications to ensure best power and performance.

Dry sump systems use an external pump and reservoir to supply engine oil. Although they take more power to operate than a wet sump system, they ensure the engine gets a steady supply of oil under nearly all conditions. *Moroso*

CHAPTER SEVEN

LUBRICATION SYSTEM

A properly engineered and functioning lubrication system is critical to engine life. Thankfully, Chevrolet did its homework before producing the Mark and Gen Series big-block V-8s, so no real rework of the system is necessary. Instead, there are some things that can be modified to enhance the system for the particular circumstances a high-performance engine encounters.

Wet Sump and Dry Sump

There are two flavors of engine lubrication systems: "Wet sump" and "dry sump." Wet sump systems store oil underneath the crankcase in the "sump," or oil pan, as it's commonly called. The oil pump sits in the oil in the sump, so it can ingest and deliver the oil throughout the engine. Almost all Chevy big-blocks, either stock or racing versions, use a wet sump system.

Dry sump systems are so-named because hardly any oil is actually carried in the "sump." The oil pan used with dry sump systems merely collects the oil returning to the crankcase. Engine oil is carried in a remote reservoir and is sucked out of and pumped into the engine via a belt-driven pump mounted at the front of the engine. A dry sump system has many advantages over a wet sump system.

For example, when a vehicle accelerates, brakes, or turns aggressively, the oil in the pan moves away from the oil pump pickup. When these loads reach a certain point, the oil will move away from the pickup totally. Instantly, the pickup will suck in only air (and your wallet), making short work of your engine thanks to oil starvation. Baffles and trapdoors in a wet sump pan are a good defense against this, but they can do only so much.

Dry sump systems rise above this problem because the pressure stage of the pump draws oil out of

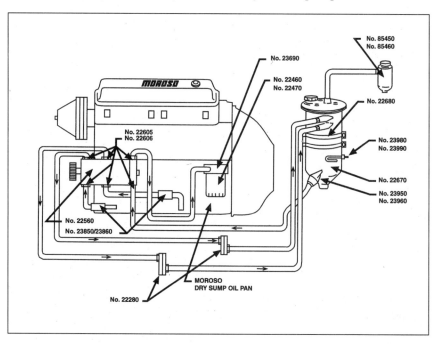

the remote reservoir, pressurizes it, and pushes it into the block's oil passages. So there's no worry about running out of oil during high-G maneuvers. As this is happening, the scavenge sections (called stages) draw the oil out of the pan and route it back to the reservoir.

Another advantage of a dry sump system is that the volume of oil that's available for engine operation isn't dictated by the area available below and around the crankshaft. Since a remote reservoir is used, more oil can be stored where vehicle packaging can accommodate it. This greater volume of oil (typically twice as much as a wet sump system) takes more time to pass through the engine. In turn, this provides more time for any air that may be in the oil to dissipate. It also gives the oil more time to cool, which is one of the oil's most important functions.

On the downside, it takes more horsepower to run a dry sump system. So you have to trade away some power to get more reliability during extreme vehicle maneuvers. And like a number of things in life, dry sump systems cost a considerable sum of money—well over $1,000. So realistically, they're cost-prohibitive for street-driven vehicles.

Pressure Reservoirs

One way to guard against temporary oil starvation in a wet-sump engine is to use a pressure reservoir system, such as Moroso's Oil Accumulator. This accumulator provides an additional three quarts of pressurized oil to the engine when oil pressure drops below a certain point. When oil pressure rises again, it forces the additional oil back into the accumulator for later use.

An oil accumulator, such as this Moroso unit, can feed oil to the engine when oil pressure drops below a predetermined point. *Moroso*

Oil Pans

Admittedly, an oil pan seems like a pretty simple device; all it has to do is hold engine oil. But because of all that happens within the engine as it's operating and all the external forces acting on the chassis, there's much more to it than that. The right oil pan can increase horsepower and extend engine life.

Because of the different ways the oil moves on the reciprocating assembly as engine rpm rises and falls, more than one strategy is required to control the oil. Baffles, windage trays, and crankshaft scrapers help provide this defense.

Baffles

The baffles in an oil pan help keep oil near the oil pump pickup during severe vehicle maneuvers, such as during flat-out acceleration or braking. Two types of baffles are used: stationary and trapdoor. And both types can be used in one pan.

A stationary baffle is a metal plate that's positioned horizontally in the sump and has a cut-out section to clear the oil pump and pickup. This baffle helps trap oil so it can't move away from the pickup.

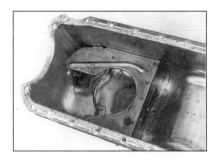

This LS7 oil pan uses both a trapdoor and stationary baffle to control oil. It has a 5-quart capacity and is intended for use with the flat windage tray shown on page 58.

A trapdoor baffle is hinged so it only opens toward the oil pump pickup. Most street performance pans position this baffle just forward of the pickup, to allow oil to open the door and gather around the pickup as the vehicle accelerates. When the vehicle slows, the door swings shut, trapping the oil around the pickup, ensuring a plentiful supply. Wet sump road race pans typically use these baffles on the sides of

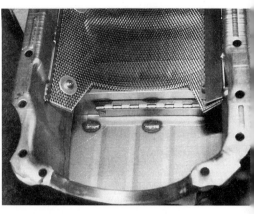

This Moroso oil pan uses a trapdoor in the bottom of the sump to keep oil near the oil pump pickup. The louvered windage tray is one of the most effective ways of keeping oil away from the crankshaft. The more oil you can keep away from the crank, the more power that's available to the flywheel.

the pickup as well as the front to trap oil during high lateral loads.

Windage Trays

As the crankshaft and connecting rods rotate, the oil that's on and around them eventually enters a state of turmoil. Below 2,500 rpm things are pretty calm. However, as engine rpm increases, the air (windage) moved by the spinning crankshaft counterweights pushes the oil so violently that the oil can take the shape of ropes, dragging on the crankshaft and connecting rods. This parasitic drag can cut horsepower 3 to 7 percent—a significant amount when you consider this could be worth 18–42 horsepower on a 600-horsepower engine.

A windage tray reduces this problem by separating the oil from the spinning crankshaft. In turn, this increases the horsepower available to the most important end of the crank—the flywheel end.

The most common type of windage tray is made of flat or curved sheet metal and is held in place by extra-long main bearing cap bolts. Recently, the aftermarket has begun offering screened and louvered trays. Although these trays keep the oil and the crankshaft separate like a solid tray, they're designed to allow oil to pass through them during drain-back but prevent the oil from moving back toward the crankshaft.

A flat steel windage tray helps reduce the oil that gets on the crank below 7,000 rpm. Above this speed, a screened or louvered tray with a block-high scraper is the best strategy for reducing windage losses.

The most efficient type of windage tray for a particular use depends on how the engine will be used. Street/strip engines operated below 7,000 rpm work all right with flat or curved solid windage trays. As engine speed rises above 7,000 rpm, or crankcase volume or crankshaft stroke increases, a screened or louvered windage tray with a block-high scraper is best. And when you reach the Competition Eliminator or Pro Stock ranks, a dry sump system with a full-length windage tray is the way to go.

Crankshaft Scrapers

Crankshaft scrapers (aka wipers) are another way of combating errant crankshaft oil. A scraper is simply a strip of sheet metal that wipes the oil off the crankshaft counterweights. Two types of scrapers can be used: oil pan-mounted and block-high. Although both of these scrapers run the length of the crankshaft, the oil pan-mounted one is flat and is found in some high-performance oil pans. The block-high scraper has reliefs cut into it that just clear the crankshaft counterweights. Mounted on the right-hand side of the block between the oil pan and the block, it literally scrapes oil off the counterweights as the crankshaft turns. For maximum effectiveness, the gap between a scraper and the counterweights should be within about 0.100 inch.

This experimental Moroso oil pan was used to study oil flow throughout the rpm range of a Pro Stock engine. It was found that oil moves differently within the crankcase at different rpm ranges. Three pan-mounted scrapers combine with a louvered windage tray and a block-high scraper to control windage.

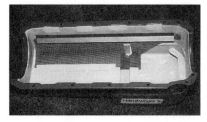

The oil scraper on the right-hand side of this pan helps peel the oil off the crankshaft as it rotates—another way of reducing parasitic power losses.

Block-high scrapers have the greatest value when engine speed rises above 7,000 rpm, especially if the crankshaft counterweights haven't been massaged to reduce windage. In terms of power, a crank scraper equates to 3–5 horsepower improve-

ment—insignificant when running on the street, but a good part of a power raising strategy for a race engine.

Kicked-Out Pans

For a street high-performance or marine application, the first thing you want to do is increase oil capacity. Marine applications allow the greatest latitude for oil pan size and shape, because there's usually lots of room underneath the engine. This provides another benefit, because the farther you can move the oil away from the spinning crankshaft in a wet sump application, the better. Conversely, the closer the oil is to the crankshaft, the greater the potential for the windage generated by the crankshaft to blow the oil

back onto the crankshaft and rods.

Boat owners are lucky because they can use a deep "box-type" oil pan, maybe the ultimate shape for an oil pan. With a land-based vehicle, the front crossmember usually limits how you can increase pan volume. To increase ground clearance or oil capacity in these applications, some aftermarket pans use a "kick-out." This boxed extension on the lower sides of the sump takes advantage of what area is available on most cars and trucks to add oil capacity.

Starter and Flywheel Considerations

Aside from having all the requisite features your particular application requires, you need to make sure that your oil pan is compatible with the starter and flywheel (or flexplate) you intend to use. Some pans may not provide enough clearance for a stock starter or 168-tooth flywheel, so you may need to use a compact starter or a 153-tooth flywheel to provide sufficient clearance.

Stroker Engine Considerations

Stroker engines have special requirements when it comes to oil pans. As crankshaft stroke grows beyond 4.00 inches, the potential for the crankshaft, connecting rods, and rod bolts contacting the sides of the oil pan increases proportionately. Aftermarket oil pans designed for stroker cranks, such as those made by Hamburger, Milodon, and Moroso, are manufactured with notches in these areas to clear the crankshaft counterweights.

The sides of the pan aren't the only area of concern when using a stroker crank. The crankshaft counterweights can contact the bottom front area of the pan as well. To be sure there's enough room, buy a pan that's designed for a stroker crank, and follow the checking procedure at the end of this chapter.

Factory Oil Pans

Factory pans use one of two basic designs. Standard performance Mark and Gen series pans use a stationary baffle to help keep oil around the oil pump pickup. The Mark IV pan holds 4 quarts of oil, but has lim-

ited use for high-performance applications, because there's not enough room at the front of the pan to accommodate a windage tray and mounting studs. It's also too small for use with a high-volume oil pump. The Gen V pan was used in light-duty trucks and holds 6 quarts.

The high-performance, 5-quart LS7 oil pan uses both stationary and trapdoor baffles. To maximize oil control, a flat windage tray (part number 3967854) is included with it, but you'll need to buy the mounting studs for it.

The oil pans for Mark series engines are different than those used on Gen series engines, consequently, they can't be interchanged. Mark series oil pans are longer than Gen series pans and use a three-piece oil pan gasket versus the one-piece gasket used on Gen series engines.

When you consider both factory and aftermarket oil pans, there's a rather large variety of pans available for Mark series engines, and the choices for Gen series engines are expanding quickly.

Aftermarket Oil Pans

A wide variety of Chevy big-block oil pans are available from the aftermarket— street/strip, drag racing, road racing, circle track, marine, you name it, and the aftermarket almost surely has it. They also offer a variety of configurations and features including notched pan rails for stroker cranks, crankshaft scrapers, kicked out sumps, trapdoor baffles, and numerous types of windage trays. Suppliers of these pans include Canton, Hamburger, Milodon, and Moroso.

Oil Pressure

For a high-performance Chevy big-block, the general rule of thumb is that 10 psi of oil pressure is required for every 1,000 rpm when the engine and oil are at normal operating temperature. So, if an engine is run at 7,500 rpm, oil pressure should be about 75 psi. And remember, oil viscosity has a direct bearing on oil pressure—thicker oils raise oil pressure and thinner oils reduce it.

The bypass spring in the oil pump cover is what controls oil pressure. If oil pressure is insufficient, shim the spring using small washers. Just don't

use so many that the bypass piston can't uncover the bypass port in the pump cover or you may blow out the oil filter seal or casing when the engine is cold. High oil pump pressures also cause excessive distributor gear wear due to high loading and absorb more horsepower than do lower pressures.

Oil Pressure Gauge

One of the best investments you can make in terms of engine support hardware is an oil pressure gauge. Mechanical gauges with a minimum 1/8 inner diameter (ID) line are preferred, because of their superior response time. This is important because you want to know if oil pressure drops to an unsafe limit as soon as possible. To help avoid a disaster when you can't directly read the gauge, tee a warning light into this system that lights when oil pressure drops to a specific level. These lights are available from aftermarket sources.

Oil Pumps

The rat's oil pump works so well that many mouse owners on a serious performance bent convert it to fit their engines. Why? Because big-block pumps have 12 teeth on each gear, spaced 30 degrees apart. This relatively close spacing provides more consistent oil pressure, and smoother pump operation when compared to a Chevy small-block oil pump. It also helps reduce the spark scatter that occurs when the distributor shaft oscillates back and forth as a result of the pump teeth meshing.

To provide an adequate volume of oil during all phases of engine operation, consider using a high-volume oil pump. These pumps have deeper

All big-block Chevy oil pumps use 12-tooth gears for smooth pump operation and minimal spark scatter. The gear on the left is pinned to the shaft to prevent it from slipping. Its non-pinned counterpart is next to it.

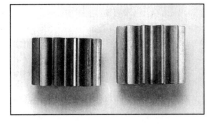

High-volume oil pumps use taller gears (right) to trap and deliver more oil than the gears used in standard pumps (left). Be careful when using a high-volume oil pump that you don't suck the oil pan dry. A 5-quart pan is the minimum size you should use with this type of pump.

bodies filled with longer (taller) gears. Because the gears are longer, they can trap more oil between their teeth and deliver it to the engine.

The additional oil provided by a high-volume oil pump helps cool the internal engine components, but you need to be careful when using one because it can suck the oil pan dry if the pan doesn't have sufficient capacity. So, stay away from a high-volume pump if your engine is equipped with a four-quart oil pan. Five-quart pans have marginal capacity for a high-volume pump, but anything larger than 5 quarts is fine.

The LS7 high-volume oil pump (p/n 3969870), originally designed for the ZL1, is probably the best big-block pump available from GM. However, the way it's currently priced, you can get the same type of pump with added anti-cavitation grooves from aftermarket sources such as Moroso for about the same price.

Anti-cavitation Pumps

At high rpm, the oil pump gears tend to pump air into the oil. This "cavitated" oil can't lubricate nearly as well as a solid stream of oil because of the air it possesses. To fight cavitation, some oil pumps have anti-cavitation grooves cut into the pump body and cover. These grooves help equalize pressure between the gears, which reduces cavitation. The grooves also reduce the power it takes to drive the oil pump.

Anti-cavitation grooves can be added to any oil pump with a grinder outfitted with a ball-shaped grinding stone. The grooves should be 0.050–0.060 inch deep and follow the pattern shown in the accompanying photo.

Mark and Gen Series Oil Pumps

Keep in mind that the factory and some aftermarket Mark series oil pumps will not directly interchange with Gen series pumps. That's because the increased height of the inner main bearing cap bolt boss on Gen series will cause interference with most Mark series pump bodies. Although this situation can be corrected by milling the offending bolt boss 0.183 inch, you may start to compromise the strength of the bearing cap. In light of this, you're better off using the appropriate pump. Most current aftermarket

The oil pump on the left can't be used on Gen series engines without reworking one of the main bearing cap bolt bosses. The pump on the right will fit either Mark or Gen series blocks, thanks to a greater distance between the pump mounting flange and the surface of the pump near the drive shaft.

The pump on the left is the GM LS7 pump. The pump on the right is Moroso's anticavitation pump. The anticavitation grooves in the top and sides of the pump body, as well as the cover, reduce the potential for pumping air into the oil at high rpm. They also cut the power required to drive the pump. You can add these grooves to your pump with a die grinder if you're so inclined.

This picture shows a Mark IV oil pump on a Gen series rear main bearing cap. Note the interference between the pump body and one of the inner cap bolts. The pump can't sit flush against the bearing cap. The best cure for this is to buy a Gen series pump.

pumps have a little longer "neck" to allow them to be used on either Mark or Gen series blocks.

Oil Pump Pickup

The position of the oil pump pickup is critical to ensuring a constant flow of oil through the engine. Consequently, you need to ensure the pickup is positioned in the pan where it has the greatest potential to receive a constant supply of oil. And where is that?

As far as depth is concerned, the pickup should be between 1/4 and 3/8 inch from the bottom of the pan. This allows the pickup to access almost all the oil that's in the pan, without it picking up any crud or debris that may be sitting on the bottom of it. The pickup also needs to be positioned where the oil will be

most of the time based on how the vehicle is used. For street and marine applications, this is the stock (center) location. For drag racing, the rear of the pan is best, and for oval track racing, placing the pickup toward the right side of the pan makes sense.

Driveshafts

In stock form, a nylon sleeve is used to connect the oil pump drive shaft to the oil pump. This is fine for normal engine service, but for high-performance applications, driveshafts with a steel sleeve are preferred for their durability, especially for the extra drag that's created by a high-volume oil pump.

Restricting Oil Flow

Currently, there's a difference of opinion as to when, or even if, you

should restrict oil flow to the top end of the engine. Typically, this has been appropriate when using roller rocker arms, because they were thought to require less oil than ball-pivot rocker arms. And this also reduced the amount of oil draining back into the oil pan, which helped reduce windage. However, some companies that produce roller rocker arms are advising against restricting oil flow because they have a detrimental effect on rocker arm life. So you need to check with the company that produced the roller rocker arms for your engine for their recommendations. You also need to consider that the majority of valve spring cooling is accomplished by the oil that washes over them. By restricting oil flow, valve spring temperature rises, shortening spring life

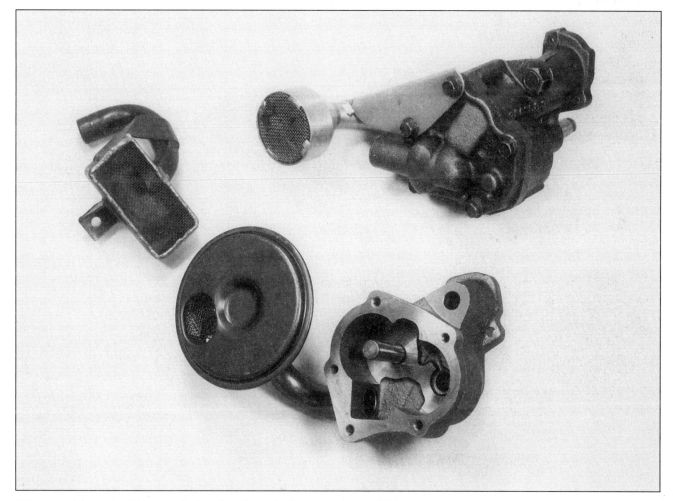

Oil pump pickups should be matched to the oil pan for best performance. This picture shows three different types. If your pump uses the large, shielded pickup in the center, don't remove the shield in an effort to get more oil into the pump. Doing so will cause a vortex in the oil, like water running down a drain, and you'll pick up lots more air.

This pickup was mated to a box-style pan used in a marine application. Marine duty is so severe, even the reinforcing bracket on this pickup is starting to crack. All high-performance engines should have the pickup tube welded to the pump body to prevent the pickup from working loose.

and increasing the potential for valve spring failure.

Oil Coolers

For optimum engine life, oil temperature should be 210–230 degrees Fahrenheit when the engine is warmed up. If the temperature is less than this, the engine can't burn off the water that occurs as a result of the combustion process. If the oil's much hotter than this, it can't cool the internal engine parts effectively.

With a high-performance engine, heat is usually the culprit that has to be dealt with most often. If engine oil temperature is beyond 230 degrees Fahrenheit, try using a synthetic oil, which can reduce oil temperature up to 20 degrees. If this isn't sufficient, you'll need to run an oil cooler.

If your engine needs a cooler, position it so it's in the direct air stream, but shielded from rocks and similar things if at all possible. Also, make sure the oil lines aren't vulnerable to attack by some road hazard or your engine can go bye-bye in a hurry. Metal-braided lines are preferred for installations where there's any chance of contact with a foreign object. And just like fuel lines, avoid using 90-degree fittings and make sure you adhere to the minimum bend radius recommendations of the hose manufacturer to ensure minimal flow restriction.

Bypass Valve

The bypass valve in the lubrication system allows oil to bypass the oil filter when engine oil pressure exceeds a certain point, as during cold weather when the engine is first started, or when the filter becomes plugged. This ensures the engine receives a supply of oil even if it hasn't been filtered. For racing applications, some people prefer to plug the bypass valve so all of the engine oil passes through the filter, all the time. This is all right provided a large capacity, high-flow racing oil filter is used.

Also, if you're installing an oil cooler and you're keeping the bypass valve, you'll need to reposition it to the rear-most oil cooler boss (above the oil filter boss) to ensure oil is routed through the cooler.

Oils

Mineral oils have come a long way since they were first used in early engines. Today's engine oils require a robust additive package to help them survive in the high-pressure, high-temperature environment of today's engines. The extreme pressure additives, primarily in the form of zinc dithiophosphate, help prevent metal-to-metal contact of highly loaded parts, such as camshaft lobes and lifter feet. And oxidation inhibitors keep the oil flowing at high temperatures, instead of allowing it to thicken into a grease-like substance.

Although conventional oil has been used successfully for many years in engines of all types, including Chevy rats, synthetic oils offer an additional margin of engine protection that cannot be matched by conventional engine oils.

Synthetic oils were first developed in the 1940s to help deal with the wide-ranging environmental and performance applications that aircraft were exposed to. Why a synthetic oil? Because it allowed the engineers to actually design and build an oil that possessed all the qualities for a specific operating environment rather than settle for the characteristics that were inherent with natural petroleum.

One of the most obvious characteristics of synthetic oils is their superior operating range when compared with conventional oils. Because the molecules in a synthetic oil are engineered to all be the same size, their operating range is typically -80 degrees Fahrenheit to more than 550 degrees Fahrenheit, versus a range of -35 to 325 degrees for conventional oils. Although the additional 45-degree range when the mercury plummets is nice, for most performance applications, it's the additional 225 degrees on the hot end of the scale that provides an important "cushion" for extreme operating conditions. And this can make the difference between engine life and death.

Synthetic oils are also "slipperier" than conventional oils, which leads to a slight increase in engine output. But this additional "slipperiness" has a downside—it prevents the engine components from bedding into one another when the engine is new. Consequently, a conventional motor oil must be used during engine break-in.

And synthetic oils are still limited by the same things as conventional oil—contamination and additive depletion. As the engine warms up, it produces a substantial amount of water. Although some of this water passes out the exhaust as water vapor, some also passes by the rings and finds its way into the crankcase, along with a dash of raw gasoline and combustion by-products. The only way to eliminate these contaminants is by changing the oil. Also, as

the engine runs, the components of the additive package that comes in the oil are used up. The only way of replacing them is by changing the oil. That's why you need to change the oil on a regular basis, as dictated by the way the engine is used, as well as its operating environment.

Assembly Checks
Oil Pump
Gear Chamfering

To ensure the edges of the gears don't dig into the pump, lightly chamfer them using a fine file or grinding point. As you're working, be careful not to scratch the mating surfaces of the gear teeth. When you've completed the chamfering, check the gear end clearance.

Checking and Adjusting Gear End Clearance

The clearance between the oil pump cover and gears should be 0.0025–0.003 inch. If it's greater than this, it will be more difficult for the pump to prime itself. If it's less than this, there won't be sufficient oil clearance.

To check gear end clearance, position the cover halfway over the gears and slip the largest feeler gauge that you can between them. If the clearance is too great, remove the gears from the pump body and sand the body on a sheet of 400-grit wet-or-dry sandpaper following a figure 8 pattern. Just make sure the sandpaper is on a flat surface, like the bed of a drill press, and use some oil to make the cutting easier. If there's not enough clearance, sand the ends of the gears using the same process.

Pickup Spacing

As was stated earlier, the oil pump pickup must be 1/4 to 3/8

inch off the bottom of the oil pan. To check for this, mount the pump on the block, then apply a strip of modeling clay about 3/8 to 1/2 inch thick on the bottom of the pickup. If the pickup only has a screen, cover it with aluminum foil before applying the clay to keep it out of the pickup. And to prevent the clay from sticking to the bottom of the oil pan, coat it with a little oil. Then install the pan gaskets and pan, and torque the pan bolts to specifications.

Now, remove the oil pan and measure the thickness of the clay at several points. If it's not within specifications, position it so it is, then check it again. When you're satisfied with the pickup's position, braze or weld it to the pump body after removing the bypass valve and spring.

Oil Pan
Crankshaft Clearance

When using a crankshaft stroke longer than 4.00 inches, you need to make sure it clears the bottom of the oil pan. To do this, install the crank into the block with the main bearings in position. Then rotate the crankshaft so the counterweights at its front are at their closest point to the bottom of the pan. Carefully lay a strip of 1/4-inch thick clay over the counterweights at this point. Then install the pan with the same type of pan gasket you plan on using and torque the pan retaining bolts to specifications.

After torquing all the pan bolts, remove them and carefully lift the pan off the block. Then measure the clay with a dial caliper or scale at several points. If clearance is less than 0.100 inch, you'll either have to modify the front of the pan to give you enough clearance or purchase another.

When purchasing a cam, your best bet is to buy an entire cam kit from the manufacturer. This ensures compatibility between all the various components and gives you a better leg to stand on if something should go wrong.
Crane Cams

CHAPTER EIGHT

CAMSHAFTS AND LIFTERS

Proper camshaft selection is key to having an engine perform the way you expect it to. It influences all the other parts and aspects of the "power path," including the fuel system, intake manifold, cylinder heads, compression ratio, and exhaust. The right cam can bring all these elements together to produce crisp throttle response, good driveability, increased performance, and in some cases, improved fuel economy.

Cam technology has grown in leaps and bounds since the first Mark IVs hit the street, so what were the hot setups over 30 years ago are now relegated to run at the rear of the pack. Sure, we still have mechan-ical and hydraulic cams, but profiles have changed dramatically. These days it's common to use a more radical cam profile on the street thanks to the blessings of the roller cam. And racing engines, which push the edge of the envelope every weekend, have some truly incredible cams from which to choose. You, too, can tap into this technological *tour de force* by using the modern cam that best fits your needs.

Four-Cycle Engine Operation

Before you can fully appreciate how cams are designed, you need to understand how air passes through the

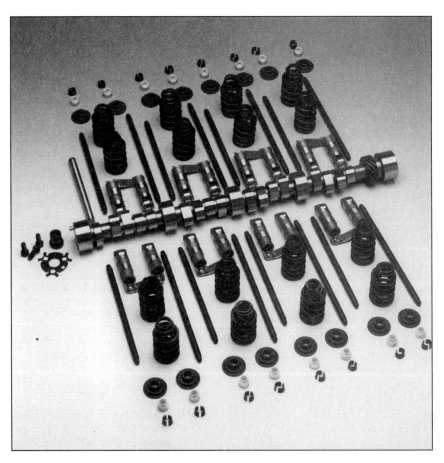

engine. Four-cycle engines, like the big-block Chevy, go through four stages (cycles) to produce power: intake, compression, power, and exhaust.

The intake stroke starts as the piston moves down the cylinder from top dead center (TDC) and the intake valve opens. Since a vacuum is created as the piston moves down the cylinder, the air/fuel mixture is pulled through the intake manifold and cylinder head port into the cylinder. After the piston reaches Bottom Dead Center (BDC), the intake valve closes and the compression stroke begins. As the piston moves up the cylinder on the compression stroke, it compresses the air/fuel mixture. When the piston reaches TDC, the spark plug ignites the mixture. As the mixture burns, it expands rapidly, pushing the piston down the cylinder for the power stroke. After the piston reaches BDC, the exhaust valve opens, and as the piston rises up the cylinder, it pushes the burned exhaust gasses out of the cylinder. Then the whole process starts again.

While this simple engine works fine at low rpm, as rpm increases, it can't take in or exhaust all the air it needs because it takes time for the air/fuel mixture to start moving. To compensate for this, we need to start opening the intake valve sooner (before the piston reaches TDC on the exhaust stroke) and start closing it later (after the piston reaches BDC on the intake stroke) to provide more time for the air/fuel mixture to flow into the cylinder. The same is true for the exhaust cycle: by opening the exhaust valve before the piston reaches BDC on the power stroke, and by closing it after the piston passes TDC on the exhaust stroke, we can pass more of the burned gasses out of the cylinder. Since most of the expansion energy of the power stroke is over by the time the piston is halfway down the cylinder, opening the exhaust valve before the piston reaches BDC has no negative effect on performance. And by keeping the exhaust valve open after TDC, we take advantage of the high velocity exhaust gasses flowing out of the cylinder to pull more of the burned gasses out of the combustion chamber.

As this process of opening and closing valves occurs, there's a point (as the piston nears TDC on the exhaust stroke, until just after TDC) where both the intake and exhaust valves are open together, referred to as overlap. Although overlap allows for some reversal of the intake and exhaust flow, it's a small handicap that's more than offset by the valves being open longer, which leads to greater power. These are the fundamentals upon which modern camshafts are designed.

Camshaft Anatomy

Camshafts primarily rely on three design principles to give them their specific performance characteristics: lift, duration, and overlap. Other factors that help fine tune a cam for a specific application are lobe separation angle, pattern type—single or dual, and lobe symmetry—symmetrical or asymmetrical.

Camshaft science is complex because factors such as duration, overlap, and lobe separation angle are all interrelated. So, changing one of these factors usually impacts the others. And this changes the performance characteristics of a cam. You need to keep this in mind as you select a camshaft.

Lift

Lift is the maximum distance the valves are lifted off their seats. Expressed in thousandths of an inch, lift is dependent on camshaft lobe height and rocker arm ratio. All stock big-block Chevys use a rocker arm ratio of 1.7:1. This means the end of the rocker arm that pushes the valve open moves 1.7 times farther than the end that is mated to the pushrod. Generally speaking, the greater the lift, the greater the power output.

The rate of lift also affects performance. The faster the valves can be lifted and lowered, the greater the flow will be with otherwise identical cams. That's because the valve is opened sooner and closed later. In turn, this provides more cylinder filling time, allowing the engine to breathe more deeply. Cams that work in this fashion, with moderate levels of duration and overlap, make good street cams because they help spread the torque curve over a greater rpm range. So, overall, you gain some top-end power without losing a significant amount of low-end torque.

Flat tappet cam profiles are more limited than roller cam profiles because their design places a higher load on the cam lobes. On the other hand, the lobes of a roller cam can be more aggressive because roller lifters decrease lobe loading.

However, no matter what type of cam is used, there are limits to the fast lift strategy. The high acceleration rates increase the loading on the valvetrain, which can cause failure. And since higher valve spring pressures have to be used to ensure the valvetrain will follow the camshaft lobe profile at high rpm, accelerated lobe and lifter wear can result, especially with flat tappet cams. As with everything else we've talked about, we need to strike a balance—in this case, between higher valve acceleration rates and the increased potential for problems.

To compare the lift rate between different cams, you'll need to map their profiles during the camshaft degreeing process. After plotting the results on a graph, you'll be able to differentiate the "fast lift" cams from the more traditional "normal lift" cams. The profile for a fast lift cam is simply flatter than a normal lift cam. And the flatter the profile, the faster the lift rate.

Duration

Duration is the period of time (in crankshaft degrees) the intake and exhaust valves are held open. The longer the valves are held open, the greater the time for clearing the burned air/fuel mixture out of the cylinder and letting the new in. And this results in more horsepower.

At low rpm, the time the valves remain open is relatively long compared to the time it takes to get the air/fuel mixture moving into and out of the cylinder. But as rpm increases, the valves are open for a relatively shorter and shorter period of time compared to the speed of the air/fuel mixture. Eventually, rpm rises to the point where the engine can't take in, combust, and exhaust gasses sufficiently. To remedy this situation, duration must be increased.

As duration increases, the engine rpm ceiling rises, as well. And increasing rpm is the way to horsepower, but only if the intake and exhaust systems are capable of moving more air, and the air/fuel ratio is changed to match the greater airflow.

Generally speaking, when you increase duration and the lobe separation angle remains the same, you also increase overlap, because the intake and exhaust valves are open together for a greater period of time. As you'll read in the next section, increased overlap reduces low speed power and torque. As a result, you want to be more conservative with duration (and overlap) when you're selecting a cam for a street engine. On the other hand, racing engines thrive on longer duration camshafts because rpm is kept significantly higher.

Duration can be measured in two ways. The first method is nonstandardized and usually begins anywhere from 0.004 to 0.006 inch of cam lift. It also takes the shape of the valve opening and closing ramps into consideration. These ramps are designed to take up clearance in the valvetrain by gently lifting and lowering the tappet as it moves from and to the base circle of the cam. This action prevents valvetrain damage because it doesn't allow valvetrain parts to bang against one another, or the valves against the valve seats. But advertised duration specifications that incorporate the opening and closing ramps can be misleading. Depending on the shape of the ramps and what lift figure is used for measurement, the duration specifications for two cam lobes with exactly the same shape can be markedly different. Consequently, when this method is used, you can't really compare one cam to another.

These days, most cam manufacturers publish duration figures based on 0.050 inch of cam lift. This is a much more accurate way of stating duration, since the ramps of the cam lobes are out of the picture at this point. It also allows comparison of specifications between different cam manufacturers—a big plus when shopping for a cam. In addition, it provides a more realistic view of cam performance, because no significant amount of airflow usually begins until 0.050 inch of cam lift is achieved, anyway.

Duration is closely related to overlap. Generally speaking, when duration is increased, overlap is increased. Likewise, when duration is decreased, overlap decreases.

Overlap

Overlap is the amount of time, expressed in crankshaft degrees, that both the intake and exhaust valves are open simultaneously. During the overlap period, the fresh air/fuel mixture is drawn past the intake valve into the cylinder thanks to the vacuum created by the piston moving down the cylinder. At the same time, the burned air/fuel mixture moves past the open exhaust valve. Since both valves are open, some of the fresh air/fuel mixture is drawn out the exhaust port as well. This "scavenging" ensures the fresh air/fuel charge is undiluted by the burned exhaust gasses. It's also good for creating horsepower, as well as higher exhaust emissions.

Cams with lots of overlap allow the burned air/fuel mixture to travel back past the intake valve, diluting the fresh air/fuel mixture in the intake manifold. In turn, this causes the engine to run roughly at idle and decreases low-rpm power. This is why you don't want a cam with lots of overlap for street machines or pleasure boats. On the other hand, too little overlap ensures good driveability, but it also ensures high rpm power will disappear. So once again, you have to compromise.

Overlap impacts engine compression as well. As discussed in previous chapters, two forms of compression exist in an engine: static and dynamic.

Static compression ratio compares the volume above the piston when it's at the bottom of its stroke to the volume above the piston when it's at the top of its stroke *while the engine is at rest*. So, for example, if the volume above the piston when it's at the bottom of its stroke is nine times greater than when it's at the top of its stroke, the compression ratio is 9:1. Static compression ratio is what's quoted on an engine specification sheet.

The dynamic compression ratio is the measured compression ratio in the cylinder *when the engine is running*. How can this be different than static compression ratio? Because it takes into account the effects of valve timing. Using our previous example, we

know that the valves must open earlier than TDC or BDC, and close later, for an engine to run at anything above a mere idle. The later the intake valve stays open after the piston reaches BDC, or the sooner the exhaust valve opens before the piston reaches BDC, the lower dynamic compression ratio will be because some of the compression (cylinder pressure) will bleed off past the open valves.

This means that as valve timing increases, static compression ratio should increase as well to compensate for the compression loss that longer valve timing brings with it. If static compression isn't increased, performance will drop off. The degree to which it drops is proportional to the decrease in dynamic compression ratio.

Dynamic compression is also affected by exhaust valve timing. The sooner the exhaust valve is opened, the greater the loss of compression. However, this isn't as much of a problem with the exhaust timing as it is with the intake timing, since the lion's share of energy that is exerted on the piston during the power stroke is dissipated by the time the piston is halfway down the cylinder.

High performance street engines on a diet of 90-94 octane pump gas (depending upon altitude) should have a dynamic compression ratio between 140 and 180 psi when the engine is cranking. If dynamic compression is below 140 psi, you'll be short on power. If it's over 180 psi, you'll probably need to run some sort of octane booster to prevent detonation. You'll also need to ensure the carb is jetted toward the rich side and total ignition timing is adjusted accordingly. Bracket racing engines typically have a cranking pressure of 200–220 psi. For all-out racing engines, you want as much dynamic compression as you can get—on the order of 250 psi during engine cranking.

Dynamic compression is most easily checked during engine cranking than when the engine is running because it provides a broader compression range to work with. For example, a street engine that's supposed to have 140 to 180 psi when cranking may have only 35 to 45 psi when the engine is actually running. And while few gauges are accurate enough to display subtle changes within the 10 psi window when an engine is running, most can easily give more accurate readings within the 40 psi window afforded by a cranking pressure test.

And don't forget about computer simulation. A program like Performance Trend's Engine Analyzer can calculate both cranking and dynamic compression if you so desire, allowing you to check and "adjust" these values as you see fit *before* the engine components are even purchased, much less assembled. This can save you lots of time and money.

In addition to throttle response, overlap also affects engine vacuum, fuel economy, and exhaust emissions. The longer the overlap period, the lower engine vacuum and fuel economy will be. Also exhaust emissions will be higher. With all this in mind, you're better to err on the side of too little overlap than too much for street and marine applications.

Lobe Separation Angle

Lobe separation angle refers to spacing between the centerline of the intake and exhaust lobes, expressed in camshaft degrees. Take a careful look at the nearby photo that illustrates lobe separation angle (or lobe centerline angle as it's sometimes called). If this angle is reduced, it has the effect of increasing overlap, because both intake and exhaust valves are open together for a longer period of time.

Wide lobe separation angles produce a smoother idle and a broader power range, but provide less torque. Narrow lobe separation angles are just the opposite—they give a rough idle and a narrower power range for the sake of more

torque. Generally, lobe separation angles for a big-block Chevy range from 102 to 116 degrees.

Engine size affects lobe separation angle selection because the larger the engine, the more torque it produces. Therefore, you can use a cam with less lobe separation angle on a larger engine and still have an abundance of torque.

Because there are so many variables that need to be taken into consideration when selecting a lobe separation angle that works best for your particular parts, vehicle and gearing combo, you need to talk to a technical adviser at one of the cam companies before deciding on the best approach for your particular situation.

Single Pattern

Camshafts can have single or dual patterns. A single pattern cam has identical lift and duration values for both intake and exhaust lobes. This is how most cams used to be manufactured. However, it's been found that by optimizing the shape of the intake and exhaust lobes for their respective jobs, a performance increase can be realized. And this design feature can be found in dual pattern camshafts.

Dual Pattern

Almost invariably, big-block Chevys like dual-pattern cams. A dual-pattern cam can be identified quickly by the different lift and duration periods for the intake and exhaust lobes. Using different lift and duration specifications for the intake and exhaust lobes allows camshaft designers to tailor the lobes to work with their particular

set of limitations. For example, big-block factory production cylinder heads have relatively high flowing intake ports (except "peanut" port heads), but the exhaust ports flow much less. By increasing the lift, lift rate, or duration of the exhaust lobes, the exhaust flow can be better balanced relative to the intake flow. And this provides greater power and torque.

Symmetrical and Asymmetrical Lobes

Camshafts can have symmetrical or asymmetrical lobes. Symmetrical lobes have the same profile on their opening side as their closing side. Asymmetrical cam lobes use a more aggressive shape on their opening side compared to symmetrical cam lobes. This helps open the valve quicker for greater torque. The closing side has a less aggressive shape that gently lowers the valve to its seat, increasing valvetrain durability.

Although keeping the exhaust valve open for as long as possible will bring more power, if you hold it open too long, the speed at which it will need to close will affect durability. So the camshaft manufacturer has to balance the exhaust valve closing rate against valvetrain longevity. The key thing to remember here is that your rat prefers a diet of asymmetrical cam lobes, with a Ford or Mopar on the side.

Camshaft Designs

Four different types of camshaft designs are currently available: mechanical flat tappet, hydraulic flat tappet, mechanical roller, and hydraulic roller. The flat tappet designs and roller designs each have particular strengths and weaknesses that must be considered when selecting a cam.

Flat tappet cams use tappets (lifters) whose bottoms are nearly flat and slide over the cam lobes. Roller cams use a wheel on the bottom of each tappet, which rolls over the cam lobe.

Mechanical Flat-Tappet Cams

Mechanical cams offer three advantages over hydraulic cams: more stable valve motion at high rpm, faster rpm rise, and limited

Lobe separation angle—the amount of offset between the intake and exhaust lobes—has a significant effect on where in the rpm band power is produced.

adjustability of engine performance characteristics. With a mechanical cam, if you increase valve lash, camshaft duration effectively drops, making a radical cam easier to live with. By decreasing valve lash, camshaft duration effectively rises, making the cam more radical.

According to Crane Cams, for each 0.001-inch change in valve lash, camshaft duration is altered by about three degrees. But there are limits. If lash is increased too far, the valve will hit its seat hard as it closes, causing potential valvetrain durability problems. Crane suggests limiting this "adjustment" to a maximum of 0.004 inch beyond its recommended valve lash settings.

Decreasing lash softens bottom-end torque while providing better top-end performance. When a rat is nested in a vehicle with a traction problem, this can be an advantage as it prevents the tires from going up in smoke from a dead stop. The problem with decreasing valve lash is, that beyond a certain point, the valves may not seat solidly against the head, which can lead to burned valves. Another consideration is that by decreasing valve lash, the valves move closer to the piston. So you need to check this clearance if the valve-to-piston clearance was near the minimum 0.100 inch when the engine was assembled.

Drag racing engines can have their valve lash decreased by as much as 0.010 inch. Because they're run only a few minutes at a time, these engines have only a slim chance of burning valves. Street and marine engines are a different story. Since they're expected to last tens of thousands of miles (or thousands of hours), valve lash for these engines shouldn't be reduced more than 0.004 inch or the valves may die prematurely.

Hydraulic Cams

A hydraulic cam is almost identical to a mechanical cam except that it uses hydraulically operated lifters to maintain zero valve lash.

Hydraulic cams make a lot of sense for street and marine applications because they offer noiseless valve operation and require no periodic valve adjustments. The only real disadvantage is that during high rpm operation the lifters may "pump-up," preventing the valves from fully closing until engine rpm drops.

However, there is a way you can raise the limit at which hydraulic lifter pump-up occurs. As you lash each valve, simply tighten the rocker nut just 1/4 turn after all the valve-train lash is taken up. This slight "preloading" keeps the pushrod seat in the lifter near the top of its travel, which can add 200–300 rpm before the lifter pumps up.

If the rules in your racing class dictate that hydraulic lifters are required, you can raise the rpm range at which lifter pump-up occurs even further by using just 0.002–0.003-inch preload on the valvetrain. But this brings a problem because with this little preload, pressure within the lifter can rise to around 500 pounds or so. To prevent this pressure from blowing the "guts" out of the lifter, you'll need to replace the standard snaps rings with Tru-Arc snap rings. Tru-Arc snap rings are available at local machine supply companies.

Roller Cams

As their name implies, roller cams use a roller to follow the cam lobe profile. This provides two advantages over a flat tappet cam: less friction and more optimal lobe profiles. Use of a roller instead of a sliding flat tappet gives cam designers more latitude to design more aggressive cam lobe profiles without worrying nearly so much about lobe and lifter durability.

To limit hydraulic lifter pump-up, you can adjust the valve lash as explained in the text. However, when you do this, the potential for the wire retaining clip at the top of a standard lifter coming out increases. To prevent this from happening, buy lifters that use a snap ring to retain the lifter internals, such as these from Lunati. Alternately, you can replace the wire retainer with a Tru Arc type.

In turn, when the valves are held open longer, power increases, and holding the valves open longer requires the nose of the cam lobes be flattened somewhat. Although this design would wipe out a flat tappet cam in no time, it was made possible by using a wheel on the bottom side of the roller. In addition to allowing cam lobe profiles that simply weren't workable with a flat tappet cam, the roller significantly lowers friction and allows higher valve spring pressures to be used. This translates into faster engine acceleration, and when properly setup with the right components, engine speeds of up to 8,500 rpm or more are possible. Also, roller cams have a power band that is typically 500 rpm wider than a flat tappet cam because of their lobe profiles, and they have a broader torque curve, as well.

The downside to roller cams is that they cost money—considerably more when compared to flat tappet cams. However, a mechanical roller cam is the best way to go in a serious racing engine, and a hydraulic roller cam is an excellent choice for street and marine applications. Just be sure to match it to the other engine components, as well as vehicle gearing (or prop pitch), and weight. And keep in

Study this photo carefully. The roller cam on the left with its nearly straight ramps belongs in a maximum effort race car or boat. Ramps like these require frequent valve train inspection and regular valve spring replacement. The flat tappet cam in the middle represents what's in the majority of street and marine applications. The roller cam on the right has ramps with less severe angles than the cam on the left, making it acceptable for street use. *Crane Cams*

All engines benefit from the use of a thrust button on the front of the cam because it keeps ignition timing more accurate. Available in either aluminum (left) or a needle bearing design (right), they require that a stamped timing chain cover be reinforced to help limit movement. Reinforcement of aluminum timing chain covers isn't usually necessary because of their increased rigidity.

the lifter bores aren't absolutely square to the cam bearing bores, the lifters apply a lateral force to the camshaft lobes. Depending upon which way the lifter bores are misaligned, the camshaft will be pushed forward or backward in the block when the engine is under a load, and the cam will move in the opposite direction when the load is removed. This causes the cam to rub against the timing chain cover and the camshaft timing gear to rub against the front of the block. It also causes the ignition timing to change if the engine uses a camshaft-driven distributor. A thrust bearing on both the front and back sides of the cam sprocket will prevent this "cam walk" from occurring. To

billet steel drive gear is matched with the stock distributor driven gear, rapid (driven) gear wear will result because the gear metals are incompatible with one another. To prevent this, the distributor must be fitted with an aluminum/bronze driven gear. Also, keep in mind that some camshaft manufacturers offer roller cams with a cast-iron distributor drive gear. This type of gear is compatible with the driven gear used on stock distributors, so you don't have to worry about excessive gear wear.

By the same token, if you plan on running a mechanical fuel pump with a roller cam, you'll need a fuel pump pushrod with an aluminum/bronze tip to minimize wear.

Small Base Circle Cams

As you increase crankshaft stroke, you increase the potential for the rods to give the cam the kiss of death. Longer stroke cranks bring the rods closer to the cam. And if the rods are relatively bulky, like aluminum rods, chances are they're going to contact the cam. In some instances, you can grind the rod slightly in the area of interference, but sometimes you can't. Although you could remedy this situation by using rods with slimmer big ends, from a cost standpoint, you're usually better off using a cam with a smaller base circle.

These cams have the base circle ground to a smaller size but keep the original lobe profiles. This allows more clearance for the connecting rods and keeps the performance characteristics the same, but does change valvetrain geometry. And by making the base circle smaller the radius of the cam lobe will be smaller, as well. Depending upon how much smaller the base circle is, cam lobe loading will rise proportionally. If you go far enough, the lobes on a flat tappet cam will die prematurely. To get around this problem, you'll have to use a roller cam.

Gen V and Gen VI engines have their own peculiarities when it comes to using a camshaft with a smaller-than-stock base circle diameter. If you need to go this route to provide clearance for a stroker crank, you'll need to modify the Gen V or VI heads for the Mark IV adjustable

High performance engines require a premium timing chain set to ensure accurate camshaft and ignition timing. Roller-cammed engines require a camshaft gear with a thrust bearing on their back side, as well as a thrust button on their front, to limit camshaft end play. This Cloyes Hex-A-Just has these features and allows easy adjustment of camshaft timing.

mind that when you purchase a roller cam, most manufacturers insist that you purchase their roller lifters, as well, to ensure compatibility between the lifters and the cam lobes. If you don't do this and the camshaft fails, the warranty is usually voided.

Unlike a flat tappet cam, the lobes on a roller cam have no taper (both mechanical and hydraulic). If

accommodate the rear thrust bearing, the back side of the camshaft sprocket must be designed with a recess or be machined.

You also need to consider distributor drive gear compatibility if you want to use a roller cam. Most roller cams have a billet steel distributor drive gear because that's what the cam needs to be made from to survive the high lobe loading. However, when a

rocker arms. See Chapter 10, *Cylinder Heads*, for details on this procedure.

Cam Compatibility

Without question, the camshaft you choose must be compatible with the other components in the engine's power path. The basic premise of camshaft selection is to mate the engine's torque curve to the way you plan on using the vehicle. If you do, you'll find magic in them thar lobes. If not, automotive mediocrity is just a crank of the starter away.

As you consider the various camshafts, keep the intended use of the engine in mind. Towing, street, street high performance, racing, marine, and marine high performance all have their own special requirements that impact camshaft selection. Relatively minor changes in cam duration (5-10 degrees at 0.050-inch lift) and lift (0.050-0.075 inch) can net relatively large gains.

For general guidelines on how much duration will work in a particular application, read the accompanying "Cam Duration and Application" chart. Just remember, components such as supercharging, turbocharging, and use of nitrous oxide, can change these recommendations.

Cams must be matched to a specific rpm range to get the most from them. Short duration cams with low valve lift provide crisp throttle response and decent fuel economy. Long duration cams with lots of overlap and lift are great for producing big horsepower numbers when matched with the proper components. But unless you're racing, you'll have to pick a cam that has some characteristics of both of these types of cams. And therein lies the rub—will you have enough or will you have too much? Only careful selection and planning will get your bumpstick in the right ballpark.

One strong consideration when choosing a cam is the maximum engine rpm at which you'd like to run the engine. Larger horsepower numbers often come with increasing rpm. However, as engine rpm increases, engine life drops. An engine that sees a maximum of about 5,500 rpm will last about twice as long as one that tops out at 7,000 rpm. Engines that hit 8,000 rpm on a

regular basis are really only suitable for racing because they wear parts out relatively frequently.

So if your car or truck is a daily driver that you depend on to get you back and forth to work, you're probably better off staying somewhere within the 5,500-6,000-rpm range. Torque is what really provides acceleration, not horsepower. Consequently, if you can fatten up the torque curve between 2,000 and 5,000-rpm, a street-driven engine will be more satisfying and provide better driveability in the process.

The fuel system (carburetion or fuel injection), intake manifold, cylinder heads, and exhaust system must also be considered during camshaft selection. Medium-size carburetors (750-850 cfm), dual plane intake manifolds, oval port heads, and headers with 2-inch diameter primary tubes all work well with a street high-performance camshaft.

On the other hand, drag racing engines fitted in light vehicles (3,000 pounds or less) with large carburetors (950+ cfm), single plane manifolds, rectangular port heads, and 2 1/8-inch header primary tubes cry out for a cam with at least 260 degrees of duration and a lobe separation angle of 106-108 degrees.

Engine size affects camshaft selection as well. A cam that idles rougher and acts more radical in a smaller engine, like a 396, will idle smoother and act less radical in a larger engine when operated in the same rpm range. That is because the flow velocity through a smaller engine is less than in a larger one.

For example, let's take a 396 and a 454 that are in the same state of tune. Let's say the airflow through the 396 is 200 cfm and the 454 flows 250 cfm. Let's also state that a particular cam improves airflow through the engine by 50 cfm. Now let's determine the percentage improvement of airflow in each engine. Divide the 50 cfm provided by the cam by the 200 cfm airflow of the 396 and the result is 25 percent ($50 \div 200 = .25$). So the cam increases airflow through the 396 by 25 percent. When you follow the same formula for the 454, you find the cam increased airflow only 20 percent ($50 \div 250 = .20$). Comparing the 25 percent improvement of

the 396 to the 20 percent improvement of the 454, you can begin to understand why a particular cam acts more radical in a smaller engine than in a larger one.

Vehicle weight, transmission type (automatic or manual), transmission ratios, and drive axle ratio also affect camshaft selection.

Heavier vehicles should use a cam with less than 250 degrees of duration, otherwise too much low-end torque will be lost and driveability will suffer if the vehicle sees street duty. And automatic transmissions need to be fitted with high-rpm stall torque converters to take advantage of more radical camshafts. More radical cams don't pose as great a problem for manual transmission-equipped vehicles because engine rpm can be raised before engaging the clutch, which prevents a weak start.

If you prefer not to switch to a high stall converter, choose a cam with high lift (0.500-0.600 inch) and short duration (230-250 degrees) so the engine makes maximum low- and mid- rpm torque. The same goes for vehicles equipped with a manual transmission that has one or two overdrive ratios because they impose an extra load on the engine. Overdrive ratios snuff out the performance advantage of a hot cam at most legal highway speeds, as will a numerically low axle ratio.

If your ride is on the light side, uses a manual transmission, and has a numerically high axle ratio, you can get by with just about any type of cam, but you're still limited by the use of the vehicle. If you're going to be driving on the street, you'll have to control your impulse to buy a really radical cam because it'll make your car or truck undriveable under most circumstances. However, if you're going racing, the sky (or rules) is the limit *if* you have all the other engine pieces that work with that particular cam.

And if you want to install a cam in a street-driven engine that must meet emission standards, you'll need to use one that's certified to pass emissions or has an Executive Order (EO) exemption.

How do you know when a cam is right for you? You won't until after you've considered what your goals are, how you want to use your vehicle,

CAMSHAFT SELECTION CHECKLIST

Land Vehicles	Marine Use
• Engine bore and stroke	• Engine bore and stroke
• Engine displacement	• Engine displacement
• Type of heads (oval or rectangular port, closed or open chamber)	• Type of heads (oval or rectangular port, closed or open chamber)
• Valve size (intake and exhaust)	• Valve size (intake and exhaust)
• Rocker arm ratio	• Rocker arm ratio
• Carburetor size or fuel injector flow rate	• Carburetor size or fuel injector flow rate
• Compression ratio	• Compression ratio
• Vehicle weight	• Trim devices
• Transmission type (automatic or manual)	• Hull design & weight
• Rear axle ratio	• Drive type (jet, stern, V-drive, inboard)
• Tire size	• Prop specifications (pitch & # of blades)
• Exhaust sizing & configuration	• Exhaust system
• Intended engine use	• Air intake temperature
	• Gearset ratios (if applicable)

1965 and 1966 Mark engines require a cam with a grooved rear bearing journal for proper engine oil flow. Cams with nongrooved journals are used in 1967 and later engines. However, they can be modified to work in 1965 and 1966 engines as well.

the performance characteristics of the other types of parts that you'll be using, and the vehicle's weight and gearing. Also take a look at the nearby "Camshaft Selection Checklist." This checklist provides you with questions that need to be answered to ensure you're picking the right cam.

Also, keep in mind that most cams cannot be used in Gen V and VI engines unless the cylinder heads are converted to adjustable-style rocker arms. Refer to Chapter 10, *Cylinder Heads,* for details on this modification.

One last item. Before you buy that killer cam, check what diameter valve springs are required for it. Factory big-block heads use valves springs with an outside diameter of 1.487 inch. Valve springs with a diameter greater than 1.550 inch will require machining of the spring seats on the cylinder head, and this will add to your costs.

Interchangeability

Nearly all of the Mark IV, Gen V, and Gen VI camshafts will interchange between engines. The exceptions to this rule are
- 1965-66 cams
- Cams for Throttle Body Injected (TBI) and Port Fuel Injected (PFI) engines

Mark IVs produced in 1965 and 1966 had a 3/16-inch wide by 7/64-inch deep groove machined into the rearmost camshaft journal to allow oil to flow to the lifters. If this groove is missing, the engine will fail due to a lack of lubrication. Conversely, if

you want to use a 1965 or 1966 cam in a later block, you'll need to have a special bearing installed at the rear of the block to prevent a significant internal oil leak.

Camshaft Drive Systems

A camshaft drive system consists of the camshaft sprocket, crankshaft sprocket, and a medium to connect the two—either a chain, belt, or gears. Whatever type of system is used, its main purpose in life is to keep the camshaft properly phased to the crankshaft. This is as important to power production as it is to engine longevity. Once any appreciable slack is introduced into this system, the

CAM DURATION AND APPLICATION CHART

Duration @ 0.050in. lift (in crankshaft°)	Street & Strip	Drag Racing	Oval Track Racing	Boats
Up to 230°	Good idle and torque. Heavy car with automatic transmission.	(Not normally used)	High torque. Heavy car with small engine and low compression.	Mild modified. Pleasure and fishing.
230°-250°	Heavy car with large engine.	(Not normally used)	Heavy car with small engine. Hobby class.	Pleasure and mild racing with small engine.
250°-260°	Middleweight car with large engine. Marginally streetable.	High torque. Super Stock.	Stocks, Modifieds, Sportsmen and Short track cars.	Fast sport runabouts. Super light cruisers with large engines. Combination super pleasure & racing.
260°-270°	Pro Street Light car with large engine.	Super Stock with large engine. Heavy car with limited carburetion.	Light car with large engine. Short and long tracks. Wide power range.	Marathon racing. Small or large boat with large engine. Ski boats. Hydroplanes. Racing runabouts.
270°-285°	(Never used.)	Modified Production.	Super long track. Super speedway.	Super closed course racing. Light boat with large engine. Drag boats. Supercharged gas.
285°-300°	(Never used.)			Super drag boat. Supercharged fuel & alcohol

Chart courtesy Crane Cams

The lifter on the left has seen better days, as evidenced by the marking on its foot. It should be replaced with a new lifter like the one on the right. Remember, never use old lifters on a new cam or the cam will fail in a short time. Lightly sanding the feet of new lifters with 600-grit wet-or-dry sandpaper makes them more compatible with the camshaft lobes.

camshaft has to play catch up with the crankshaft as the throttle is opened and closed. In turn, the opening and closing of the valves occurs later than it should, providing less than optimum timing for power and torque.

Secondary functions of the cam drive system are to drive the distributor and oil pump. And just like the intake and exhaust valves, once appreciable slack occurs in the cam drive system, ignition timing moves from the optimum as well.

Camshaft drive systems for Chevy's rat take the form of the traditional chaindrive or the more exotic belt or gear drives. Each has their advantages and disadvantages.

First and foremost, the cam drive in a high-performance engine must be able to keep the camshaft accurately timed to the crankshaft. Proper timing ensures peak performance from a given camshaft. With cam-driven distributors, it also ensures ignition timing will remain as set. If the ignition timing is set so that maximum cylinder pressure is obtained, any additional advancement will cause engine-damaging detonation. Conversely, any decrease in timing will cost you horsepower. Either way you lose.

Timing Chains

Timing chain sets are the most common means of linking the camshaft to the crankshaft, and for good reason—they're relatively inexpensive and usually quite durable. However, just like a chain on a motorcycle, the sideplates on a timing chain stretch. The degree to which they stretch is dependent upon the material used for the plates, as well as how the plates are processed (heat treating, etc.) The greater the stretch, the lesser the durability and the more inaccurate camshaft timing becomes. The best chains use hardened side plates and rollers manufactured from high-strength steel.

Side plate and pin strength is important, especially if you opt to use any type of rev limiter. Since rev limiters cut the spark to one or more cylinders to prevent over-revving the engine, the timing chain has to contend with some pretty wild back-and-forth motion as the crankshaft accelerates and decelerates rapidly. This can result in the chain snapping and the outstanding balance on your Visa escalating wildly to pay for new valves, pistons, or even a whole new engine. Consequently, a high-quality timing chain set is essential in these applications.

Traditional chain drives can run from the inexpensive to moderately priced. The Morse chains are at the low-end of the performance (and cost) spectrum. These chains are quiet in operation and can last tens of thousands of miles. Some even use a nylon coating on the camshaft sprocket to reduce noise even further. However, their cast-iron sprockets, high internal friction, and nonadjustability make them an inappropriate choice for high-performance work.

Moving up the performance ladder are the cheaper "roller" timing chains. These chains use a single or double set of rollers and are usually paired with cast-iron sprockets, although some use the more desirable hardened cast-iron or steel sprockets. Unlike true roller chains whose rollers actually rotate to reduce friction, the rollers used on the cheaper roller chains are stationary. So instead of rolling when they meet the cam or crank sprockets, they slide into and out of them, keeping friction at a relatively high level. Crankshaft sprockets included with this type of timing chain set may have more than one keyway to allow for adjustment of camshaft timing. This type of timing chain setup strikes a balance in cost and performance between the Morse timing chain offerings and the true roller.

This billet timing chain set has a crank sprocket that allows you to advance or retard camshaft timing up to eight degrees. *Crane Cams*

The next level of performance is provided by timing chain sets that use rollers that actually rotate. These types of timing chains are the most effective at reducing roller-induced friction. Typically, they also use high-quality materials and construction for enhanced durability. Cloyes, Crane, Competition Cams, Lunati and others offer these types of high- quality timing chain sets.

The best timing chain sets use the roller timing chain and billet steel camshaft and crankshaft sprockets. Billet steel is the strongest material and can best deal with high valve spring loads. These types of timing chain sets also usually have provisions for a thrust bearing on the backside of the cam sprocket, which is necessary (along with a thrust bearing or button) to eliminate camshaft end play, and is especially critical when using a roller cam.

Although hardened cast-iron sprockets are just as durable with a

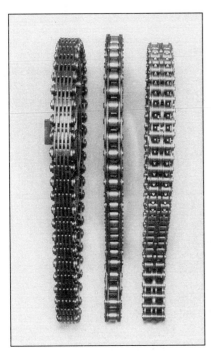

These are the three basic timing chains available from the factory (left to right): morse, single roller, and double roller. If you need a timing chain, you can get a quality timing chain set from the aftermarket for less money than these factory pieces. And if you opt for a true roller chain, you'll pick up power as well, because none of the factory chains use true rollers.

roller timing chain as a billet sprocket, they're not as well balanced as billet sprockets due to the greater machining that billet sprockets undergo.

Another consideration is align-honing. If your block has been align honed, you'll need to use a timing chain set with slightly larger sprocket(s) to compensate for the shorter distance between the camshaft and crankshaft that resulted from the align honing. Typically, if this is the first time the block has been align honed, the set will need to be 0.005 inch shorter. These "shorter" timing chain sets are available from Cloyes and Competition Cams. Each subsequent align hone will reduce this dimension by another 0.005 inch until you reach the maximum of 0.015 inch.

Timing Adjustments

Some of the more specialized timing chain and gear sets have more than one keyway in the crankshaft sprocket. These keyways allow for fine tuning of a particular camshaft's power characteristics by providing you a way to advance or retard the camshaft. In a like fashion, some of the camshaft sprockets have ways to advance or retard camshaft timing, as well.

These can prove helpful if, for example, your engine puts out too much low-end torque and sends the tires up in smoke. Retarding the cam will soften up the low-end power delivery. Conversely, if you'd like a little more bottom-end grunt, you'll need to advance cam timing. How much depends on a number of factors, but is found through trial and error. For more information on this subject, refer to the "Comparing Specifications" section, near the end of this chapter.

Gear Drives

Gear drives use two or more

Camshaft timing can also be adjusted by using a crankshaft timing chain sprocket with numerous keyways.

gears to connect the camshaft to the crankshaft. Chevrolet has used gear drives on some of its heavy-duty trucks and in some marine applications quite successfully. However, when it comes to a high-performance engine, using a gear drive is a good news/bad news situation.

The good news is that gear drives do a good job of keeping the cam accurately timed to the crank. Also, they hold up quite well when combined with a rev limiter. The bad news is that because the gears effectively couple the crankshaft solidly to the cam, they pass along more vibration to the cam than either a chain or a belt. And this can induce some strange harmonics into the cam and valve-train at high rpm. In turn, this results in less power and decreases valve-train durability.

Belt Drives

Jesel belt drives are becoming more and more popular these days. This system consists of a 25 millimeters-wide cogged belt with matching sprockets. The biggest benefit of a belt drive over a chain or gear drive is its ability to damp high-frequency vibration. Because the belt is relatively soft, it dampens high-frequency vibrations that

Gear drives provide accurate camshaft timing but can pass along some strange vibrations into the cam and valvetrain that can reduce power and valvetrain life.

could otherwise upset camshaft operation. And this can lead to higher rpm horsepower–about 10 ponies worth, according to Jesel.

In addition to the horsepower advantage, this system eliminates the need to remove the front cover when removing or replacing the cam. Belt drives are also much quieter than chain or gear drives, and are run dry, without any lubrication. Drag racers like this set-up because the camshaft can be easily advanced or retarded without having to pull the damper and timing chain cover off.

Assembly Checks

As you're assembling your engine, there are certain checks and adjustments you need to make to ensure the engine lives a long, strong, and happy life. Those outlined below cover most of the operations related to camshafts.

Timing Chain Set Preparation

Timing chain sets have everything they need as they come from the factory. However, there are a few things you can do to ensure your timing chain will live a long and happy life.

As the chain comes from the factory, it's coated with a paraffin-based wax that feels relatively dry to the touch. To increase chain longevity, liberally coat it with some fresh engine oil before you install it. Work from the inside out as this will put the centrifugal force of the chain as it rotates to work for you, providing better lubrication of the chain. If you don't plan on starting the engine within a day or two, substitute some engine assembly lube (or GM Engine Oil Supplement) for the oil. The assembly lube will stay in place much longer than motor oil and has a higher percentage of anti-wear additives.

Once you've installed the sprockets and chain, the chain should have a "snug" side-to-side play of about 1/8 inch on its slack side. If it's less than this, the chain will wear prematurely. To remedy this problem, you can try using another timing chain, which can be purchased separately. If this doesn't work, you'll need another timing gear set.

Timing chain gear alignment must be within 0.010 inch to prevent excessive timing chain wear.

During engine mock-up, check the clearance between the backside of the chain and the block. It should be a minimum of 0.050 inch. If it isn't, you'll need to use another timing chain set.

You also need to ensure that the camshaft and crankshaft sprockets are aligned with each other to prevent excessive timing chain wear. To check this, push the cam to the rear of the block, lay a straight edge across the sprockets (with the timing chain removed), then slip a feeler gauge under the straight edge. A maximum of 0.010-inch misalignment is allowed. If it's more than this, you'll need to use a Torrington bearing behind the sprocket to compensate, or shim the Torrington bearing, if one is already being used.

For engines that will be run above 6,000 rpm for extended periods of time, such as in endurance racing, you'll need to check the run-out of the camshaft drive gear because excessive run-out will cause the timing chain to wear prematurely. To check run-out, install the gear on the cam and torque the retaining bolts to specifications. Then by positioning the tip of a dial indicator on the front of the gear as close as possible to the outside edge (without touching the teeth) and rotating the cam 360 degrees, you can determine if runout is acceptable. If it's more than 0.005 inch, make sure the camshaft sprocket is fully seated and the front of the cam is square to bearing journal.

Camshaft Degreeing

Camshaft degreeing compares the timing of the valve opening and closing events of the camshaft as installed

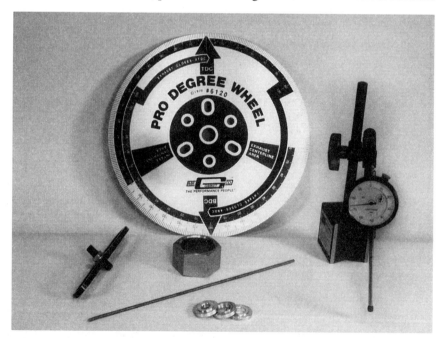

These are the things you'll need to degree the cam. Although degreeing isn't totally necessary, it ensures optimum camshaft performance. The crankshaft nut in the center is optional for this process.

in the engine with the lift and duration figures listed on the specification card that accompanies the cam. Why would you need to degree a cam? Because of a potential stack-up of machining tolerances or markings that could cause camshaft timing to be off considerably. The cam gear locating dowel, the dowel hole in the cam gear, the keyway in the crankshaft gear, and the timing marks on the cam and crank gears are all potential problem areas.

Although camshaft degreeing isn't absolutely necessary, you'll want to degree the cam to ensure the best engine performance.

To degree the cam, you'll need a number of tools, including
- piston stop
- degree wheel
- 6-inch length of coat hanger
- dial indicator and stand
- crankshaft socket tool or equivalent

The degreeing process I'll outline here is the "duration at 0.050-inch lift" method. In addition to checking symmetrical cam lobes, this process allows accurate checking of asymmetrical lobes, as well. Although you could use the more traditional "centerline method," it's less accurate when checking asymmetrical cams because the centerline on these cams could be two to six degrees away from the point of maximum lift.

Begin the process by bolting the degree wheel to the nose of the crankshaft then snugging the retaining bolt. Next, grind one end of the coat hanger to a point, then bend a loop in the opposite end so you can mount it to the block. With the hanger mounted in a suitable location, bend it so it extends over the front of the degree wheel to act as a pointer. And be sure the pointer is totally stationary to prevent erroneous readings.

Finding Top Dead Center (TDC)

Now you need to find the true location of top dead center (TDC). Take your time here because the degreeing process depends on accurately locating TDC. Since the piston moves almost imperceptibly when it's near TDC, you really can't use a dial indicator to check for it. Instead, you need to use the positive stop method of finding TDC. A tool

for performing this procedure bolts to the deck of the block and uses a bolt that reaches down the cylinder about 1/2 inch. Ready-made positive stops are available inexpensively from the aftermarket.

Before you install the piston stop, rotate the crankshaft until the piston in cylinder #1 appears to be at TDC. To rotate the crankshaft easily, screw a couple of flywheel bolts into the back of the crank and wedge a long prybar or similar device between the bolts. Whatever you do, don't use the bolt that secures the degree wheel or the wheel may slip as you're working, sending all your efforts out the window.

While keeping the piston at approximately TDC, rotate the

Use of a piston stop is the only real way of determining top dead center for camshaft degreeing. Although they can be fabricated, they're readily available for $10 to $15 from aftermarket sources.

degree wheel so its TDC marking is aligned with the pointer. Then rotate the crankshaft so the degree wheel moves counter-clockwise when viewed head-on. Rotate it far enough to allow you to bolt the positive stop to the deck without its center bolt touching the piston. Just be sure the positive stop is snug so it doesn't move during the degreeing process.

Now rotate the crankshaft (from the rear) until the piston just touches the stop bolt. Note the reading on the wheel, then rotate the crankshaft in the opposite direction until the piston touches the stop bolt once again. Look at the degree wheel once again, then add this figure to the first reading and divide the result by two. For example, if the first reading was 48 and the second was 40, add them

together (48 + 40 = 88), then divide the result by two (88 ÷ 2 = 44). So, in this case, 44 degrees is the halfway point, which is also TDC.

Now without allowing the crankshaft to turn, loosen the degree wheel and rotate it to the halfway point. Lock the degree wheel in this position then carefully rotate the crankshaft back and forth. If you've found true TDC, the degree wheel will indicate the halfway point (44 degrees for our example) each time. If not, repeat the process. When you've found and set the piston at true TDC, carefully loosen the degree wheel and rotate it until the TDC (zero) mark is aligned with the pointer.

To be sure the wheel is in the proper position, carefully rotate the crankshaft back and forth until it touches the piston stop. The wheel should read zero in both directions. If not, split the difference in readings and check for true TDC once again. When you've found TDC and zeroed the degree wheel, remove the positive stop from the cylinder deck.

Mounting the Dial Indicator

At this point, mount the dial indicator so you can check the intake and exhaust lobes for cylinder #1. The indicator must be securely mounted to ensure accurate results. Since the most accurate results are taken off the top of the lifter, Chevy big-blocks have a problem in that the lifter bores are too close to the side of the cylinder case to allow room for mounting the indicator tip against the top of the lifters. To get around this, you'll need a dial indicator extension to ensure the indicator plunger is directly in line with the lifter. If it's off by any substantial amount, it will skate to the side, introducing some margin of error. Also, for checking purposes, it's best to use a very light lubricant on the cam lobe, lifter foot or roller, and on the side of the lifter body. This will reduce the chance for false readings.

With the dial indicator securely mounted, slowly rotate the crankshaft clockwise (when viewed from the front) until the intake lifter is riding on the base circle of the camshaft, directly opposite the camshaft lobe.

A dial indicator extension is required for degreeing a big-block Chevy. When setting the indicator up, be sure the indicator plunger is parallel to the lifter travel to avoid false readings.

Then set the indicator to zero. Verify the zero reading by rotating the crankshaft clockwise at least five times and watching that the dial indicator always returns to zero when the lifter is on the base circle of the camshaft. If it doesn't, make sure the indicator is mounted solidly. Also check that the lifter moves smoothly and freely in its bore. If it doesn't, correct the problem before continuing. A coating of light oil on the side of the lifter body usually does the trick. If not, light honing of the lifter bore with a brake cylinder hone should fix it.

Base Circle Runout

As you're checking that the dial indicator is zeroed, pay close attention to the indicator needle as it passes over the camshaft base circle. A variance of 0.002 inch or more indicates the grinding machines used to produce the cam weren't maintained properly, causing the cam to be ground off-center. In turn, this excessive base circle runout will cause hydraulic lifters to "pump-up" prematurely. The only remedy for this situation is to return the cam and buy a high-quality cam to take its place. If base circle runout is less than 0.002 inch, you'll know you have a high-quality cam.

Comparing Specifications

After ensuring base circle runout is acceptable, slowly rotate the crankshaft clockwise until the dial indicator reads 0.050 inch. Check the reading on the degree wheel and write it down. If you go past the point at which you want to take a reading, don't turn the crankshaft counterclockwise to backup. If you do, all the slack in the timing chain and gears, will be taken up and you'll get some pretty far out readings. Instead, continue rotating the crank clockwise until you reach the point you missed. Then continue rotating the crankshaft until maximum lift is indicated and write this reading down.

Finish by rotating the crankshaft until the dial indicator reads 0.050 inch again. Write this wheel reading down, as well. Now you should have three readings, the first at 0.050 inch lift on the opening side of the lobe, the second at maximum lobe lift, and the third at 0.050 inch on the closing side of the lobe. Compare these numbers to the numbers on the cam specification card that came with your cam. If they're within 1 degree of each other, the camshaft is installed in the proper "straight up" position.

Follow this same procedure to check the exhaust lobe.

What do you do if the cam isn't correctly timed to the crankshaft? It depends on whether the camshaft is retarded or advanced. Viewed from the front of the block, all land-driven and most marine-bound Chevy rats have a clockwise rotating camshaft. This means to advance the cam, it will need to be rotated farther clockwise. Conversely, retarding the cam requires that it be rotated counter-clockwise.

In some instances, it may be preferrable to advance or retard the camshaft timing from the "straight up" position. Advancing the camshaft helps increase low-rpm torque, because the intake valve closes sooner. In turn, this increases cylinder pressure, which helps increase torque. The downside is that high-rpm power may drop. Retarding the cam has the opposite effect. Because the intake valve closes later, more of the air/fuel charge is pulled into the cylinder, increasing high-rpm power. However, the later closing of the intake valve bleeds off some cylinder pressure, reducing low-rpm torque. At least two degrees of advance or retard is necessary to actually feel a change. Eight degrees often causes overall camshaft performance to suffer.

You also need to consider that as you advance or retard a camshaft, valve-to-piston clearance decreases. When you advance the cam, the intake valve moves closer to the piston. As you retard the cam, the exhaust valve moves closer toward the piston. Consquently, if valve-to-piston clearance is at or near the minimum, you increase the chance of the valves contacting the pistons if you advance or retard the camshaft. In this situation, the only way to be sure valve-to-piston clearance is sufficient is to measure it.

The method used to advance and retard the cam is dependent upon the timing chain set or gear set that you're using. Most high-performance timing chain sets have crankshaft sprockets with three or more keyways. These keyways are cut at different points from one another relative to the sprocket teeth. Depending upon which keyway you use, camshaft timing will be advanced, straight up, or retarded. Other timing chain sets use an adjustable camshaft sprocket. This type of sprocket has an oversize dowel hole that allows the use of eccentric bushings to advance or retard the camshaft, as necessary.

Pre-Assembly Lubrication

Before you install the camshaft for the last time, clean it with liquid soap and hot water, then blow it dry. Don't wipe it with anything, since you may leave some lint or other residue behind. With the cam clean and dry, lubricate it. Proper lubrication of the camshaft lobes is absolutely critical to camshaft life due to the high loading of the lifters against the lobes. To combat this loading during the critical break-in period, you must liberally coat both the camshaft lobes and the feet of all the lifters with a moly lubricant when using a flat tappet cam. Most camshaft manufacturers offer this type of lubricant under their own brand name, such as Crane Super Moly Lube, Lunati Moly Lube, and so on. Since the loading of roller cams is much less severe, all that's needed is a coating of engine assembly lube on the lobes and lifters.

For added assurance, pour a can of GM EOS into the crankcase when filling the engine with oil. EOS (engine oil supplement) contains zinc dithiophosphate, a strong anti-wear additive that helps fight excessive engine wear. And as far as engine oil goes, don't even think about using a synthetic oil until you've put at least 5,000 miles or so on the engine. Synthetic oils won't let the parts bed into each other the way conventional oils do, and that's the whole purpose of the break-in period.

Valvetrain Adjustments
Mechanical Cams

Since hydraulic cams operate without any clearance in the valvetrain, they don't use a lash adjustment. Valve lash is the clearance between the ends of the rocker arms and the tips of the valve stems. The amount of valve lash is dependent upon the shape and height of the clearance ramps on the camshaft lobes, as well as the material used for the cylinder heads and block.

Mechanical cams should be lashed when the engine is hot to allow for expansion of the valves and valvetrain. This presents a dilemma if you've just assembled the engine, since you have to lash the valves before you start the engine, but you have to run the engine before you can lash the valves. How can you get around this problem? By scientific guesstimation.

Metals expand when heated. And aluminum expands more than cast iron. Three likely scenarios exist when building an engine: cast-iron heads and block; aluminum heads and cast-iron block; and aluminum heads and block. To roughly compensate for the different levels of expansion in these situations, follow these guidelines offered by Crane Cams:

- Cast-iron heads and block—add 0.002 inch to the recommended lash
- Aluminum heads and cast-iron block—subtract 0.006 inch from the recommended lash
- Aluminum heads and block—subtract 0.012 inch from the recommended lash

These recommendations will put you in the proverbial ballpark so you can start and run the engine. After the engine has reached operating temperature, set the lash to the recommended hot lash setting(s).

Lash Adjustment

Before you can properly lash each valve, the lifter for that valve must be on the base circle of the camshaft. You can ensure this is the case by closely watching the valves as you rotate the crankshaft in a clockwise direction by hand. When an intake valve is almost closed, adjust the lash of the exhaust valve on that same cylinder. When the exhaust valve begins to open, adjust the lash of the intake valve for that same cylinder. Because of valve timing, this method will ensure each lifter is on the base circle of the cam while you're adjusting valve lash.

Tuning

As we talked about earlier, mechanical cams for our favorite rat can be "tuned" with a simple valve lash adjustment. By decreasing valve lash, the camshaft becomes more aggressive because of the net increase in valve lift and duration. Increasing valve lash can tone down a racy cam because valve lift and duration drops.

But you can't just go hog wild. If you decrease valve lash more than 0.008 inch, the valves may not close completely, which can cause them to burn. On the other hand, if valve lash is increased more than 0.004 inch, the extra slack in the valvetrain can cause it to hammer itself apart.

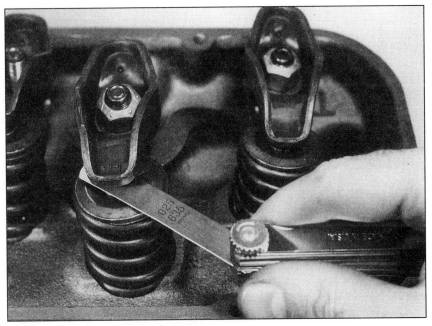

Valve lash can be used to "adjust" the performance of mechanical cam. Tighten the lash and the cam becomes more radical; loosen the lash and the cam becomes more docile. But you can't go too far either way without encountering problems. Refer to the text in this chapter for details.

Valvetrain components must be carefully selected and assembled for maximum performance. Stud girdles help prevent rocker stud flexing when high-valve spring pressures and high-lift cams are used. They also extend valvetrain life.

CHAPTER NINE

VALVETRAIN

The big-block Chevy's valvetrain, pushrods, rocker arms, valve springs, valve spring retainers, and valves are critical to power production and engine longevity. Careful selection and assembly of these components will enhance engine power and durability.

Anything you can do to lighten the valvetrain is better, no matter what the rpm range of the engine is. It lightens the loading on the valvetrain, increasing its longevity. But lighter components cost more money, so for most street high-performance applications, cost needs to be balanced against the benefits of lower weight.

As long as the engine isn't spun much past 6,000 rpm, the stock valvetrain will be all right. However, if you cam, carb, and gear the engine to spin higher than this, you'll want to lighten the valvetrain to reduce loading. Aluminum roller rocker arms are the best place to start, because, in

addition to lightening the valvetrain, they also reduce friction significantly, as well as minimize flexing. If you want to use a lightweight steel rocker arm, consider the Pro Magnum Rocker Arms offered by Comp Cams. These rocker arms are very strong and are 5 percent lighter at the valve stem tip than aluminum rocker arms.

Pushrods

Pushrods need to be matched to the specific application in terms of maximum valve spring pressure and rocker arm geometry.

Pushrods need to be strong enough to minimize flexing under the pressure exerted by the valve spring when the valve is fully open. If they flex too much, power will be lost because the pushrods won't fully transfer the motion of the cam profile to the valve.

The more radical the cam, the higher the valve spring pressure needs

to be to ensure the lifters follow the cam lobes at high rpm. In turn, this requires the pushrods be stronger to prevent them from flexing. This is more true for flat tappet cams than roller cams, because the camshaft lobes on a flat tappet cam have more severe acceleration and deceleration ramps than their more rounded counterparts on a roller cam.

Typically, pushrods are made of 1010 steel or 4130 chrome moly steel. Pushrods made of 1010 steel are fine for engines with less than 380 pounds of open valve spring pressure. For open valve spring pressures greater than this, you'll need to use 4130 chrome moly pushrods.

Weight is another concern. Not only does increasing pushrod diameter increase weight, but the greater the diameter, the greater the amount of oil that it carries. And this adds to the weight situation. Although it's usually best to have the lightest pushrods (and valvetrain) possible, lightness must be balanced against durability for certain applications.

Proper rocker arm geometry is critical, as well. Pushrods need to be of a certain length that when the valve is at half-lift, the valve tip end of the rocker arm is directly in the middle of the valve stem. If it isn't, valve guide wear will increase due to side loading of the valve stem. And if the rocker arm geometry is off far enough, the rocker arm can end up riding on the valve spring retainer, forcing the retainer sideways with potentially disastrous results.

Block height plays into rocker arm geometry, too. If you're using one of the tall deck blocks, you'll need longer pushrods to ensure proper rocker arm geometry.

No matter what the situation, the proper length pushrods are those that put the rocker arm in the middle of the valve stem at half camshaft lift. To determine what length pushrods are needed, refer to the "Rocker Arm Geometry" section near the end of this chapter.

Recommendations

Three different diameter pushrods are available for the big-block Chevy: 5/16 inch, 3/8 inch, and 7/16 inch. If your engine has the 5/16-inch diameter pushrods and you plan to do anything more than a stock rebuild, dump them in favor of their 3/8-inch diameter siblings.

The 3/8-inch diameter factory pushrods possess sufficient strength for high-performance street and marine applications that require open valve spring pressures of less than 320 pounds. Aftermarket chrome moly 3/8-inch diameter pushrods are good for valve spring pressures up to about 400 pounds.

Two versions of the 7/16-inch diameter pushrod exist: standard duty and high-performance. The standard duty version is made from 1010 case-hardened steel and is good for high-performance street applications using 360 to 380 pounds of open valve spring pressure. The high-performance version is made from chrome moly tubing, which has greater strength and rigidity than the 1010 case-hardened steel version. This pushrod is suitable for all street and racing applications where valvetrain weight isn't a major factor.

However, for short-deck engines, 7/16-inch diameter pushrods are quite heavy and get even heavier when they're filled with oil. Instead of using these heavier pushrods, consider lightening the valvetrain, which, in turn, allows you to run lighter valve spring pressures. This will allow you to use a strong, 3/8-inch diameter pushrod, saving even more valvetrain weight.

Pushrod Guide Plates

Pushrod guide plates used with Chevy big-blocks help stabilize the valvetrain by guiding the pushrod on a specific path, instead of relying on the rocker arm to locate the pushrod. To be effective, they must match the outside diameter of the pushrods. Since pushrod guide plates are stamped, they tend to have a rough surface in the pushrod slot. Removing this roughness with a fine tooth file or sanding cone in a die grinder will help extend pushrod life. Work in the direction of pushrod movement to prevent making a surface that may abrade the pushrod.

Rocker Arms

Rocker arms for the big-block Chevy come in a number of designs. All of these designs attempt to capitalize on four basic design elements: ratio, friction, strength, and durability.

Ratio

Stock big-block rockers have a 1.70:1 ratio, so the valve end of the rocker arm moves 0.170 inch for every 0.100 inch of movement on the pushrod side. A higher ratio, like 1.80:1, will cause the valve to move 0.010 inch further than 1.70:1 rockers with the same 0.100 inch of pushrod movement.

Higher rocker arm ratios effectively increase the opening and closing rates of the camshaft. This is most beneficial for mild cams, with decreasing benefits for more radical cams, because the additional opening and closing speed that a higher rocker arm ratio provides is built into the cam lobe profile. Higher rocker arm ratios provide more "lift under the curve," which means that although the time the valves are open in crankshaft degrees remains the same, the distance that the valves remain open is proportionally greater. Consequently, power is greater. But the other characteristics of the cam remain the same, providing the best of both worlds.

As rocker arm ratio is increased, so is the loading on the valve guides and valve springs. High rocker arm ratios tend to push the valve to the side of the guide, increasing wear on both the guide and the valve stem, increasing friction and sapping horsepower. If you opt to use higher ratio rocker arms, be aware that coil bind may become a problem since the valve spring is compressed more.

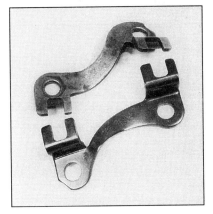

Pushrod guideplates must be matched to the outside diameter of the pushrods being used to be effective.

79

Grooved rocker balls allow greater oil flow to the highly loaded area of a stamped steel rocker arm compared to the stock, nongrooved balls.

When using a cam with a lift of 0.500–0.600 inch, you need to use long-slot rocker arms to prevent interference with the rocker arm stud. Factory long-slot rocker arms can be identified by the H, L, or M on their valve stem end. If camshaft lift is greater than about 0.600-inch lift, you'll need to use roller rocker arms. See the text for more details.

Rocker studs must be larger in diameter to deal with higher valve spring pressures. The stud on the left is 3/8 inch in diameter and is acceptable for mild performance applications, but the 7/16-inch-diameter stud in the center is much stronger and can be used with much higher spring pressure before it deflects significantly. The stud on the right has longer threads to engage more material in an aluminum cylinder head. It also has a more generous radius when it meets the hex for greater strength.

Also, the valves may come too close to or even touch the tops of the pistons. Accordingly, these things need to be checked before you assemble the engine for the last time.

Stock big-block rockers are stamped out of steel, which makes them easy to manufacture and quite durable. However, the production stamping process doesn't consistently produce rocker arms with a 1.7:1 ratio. Some will have a lesser ratio and some may have more. This really isn't a problem for a run-of-the-mill production engine where maximum performance isn't much of a concern. But when maximum performance is a concern, ballpark rocker arm ratios just won't do.

Rocker arms with accurate ratios, along with other features, such as roller tips, are available from the aftermarket for slightly more than you'd pay for GM rocker arms.

Slot Length

Stock rocker arms have a slot in their bottom which provides clearance for the rocker arm stud as the rocker arm moves up and down. When the rocker arm is fully up or down, the clearance between the slot and the rocker arm stud is at its minimum. With a stock lift cam, this clearance is sufficient. However, if you switch to a high lift cam while retaining the stock rocker arms, the rocker arms could contact the studs. And this could result in bent studs or pushrods. This is when long slot rocker arms are required.

Both GM and aftermarket suppliers offer "long slot" rockers arms, but their lift limit is typically 0.600

inch. If camshaft lift is higher than 0.600 inch, you'll need to use roller rocker arms. Valve spring pressure is another consideration: Once valve spring pressure exceeds 350 pounds, ball-pivot rocker arms become overloaded, and roller rocker arms must be used in their place.

Mark IV production rocker arms will work with cams that produce up to 0.560-inch lift. Service design Mark IV and aftermarket

long-slot rocker arms provide extra clearance around the rocker arm stud and will allow the use of cams with up to 0.600-inch lift. They can be identified by the letter "H" or "L" on their top side above the valve stem end. Production Gen V and VI nonadjustable rocker arms will work with cams up to 0.520-inch lift. Long-slot rocker arms are also available for Gen V and Gen VIs, as part number 12523976. Cams with up to 0.560-inch lift can be used with these rocker arms.

Friction, Strength, and Durability

To combat friction, rocker arms use one or more design features such as roller tips and needle bearings. To gain strength and durability, they can be made from cast or forged (extruded) aluminum, steel, or stainless steel. Each has its place when building a Chevy big-block.

Roller Rocker Arms

As a rocker arm moves up and down, its ends swing in an arc. This motion causes the flat end of a stock rocker arm to scrub across the top of the valve stem. It also tends to rock the valve stem side-to-side in the valve guide. Both of these actions increase friction significantly. And as valve lift increases, the rocker arms swing in a larger arc, which adds to the problem.

Roller tip rocker arms use a hardened steel roller to reduce this friction significantly. And anytime you can reduce friction, you free up valuable horsepower.

To reduce rocker arm friction even more, you'll want to use "roller rockers." According to Crane Cams,

Roller tip rocker arms are a good step in reducing valvetrain friction and freeing up some horsepower. *Crane Cams*

Roller rocker arms, while expensive, are suitable for use in street machines. They'll even reduce friction enough to free up 15 to 20 horsepower from your rat.

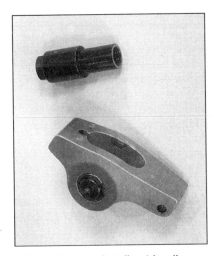

When using a stud girdle with roller rocker arms, special stepped nuts are required to provide a surface with which to clamp a stud girdle to.

this type of rocker arm works so well that on Chevrolet big blocks, it's worth about 15 to 20 horsepower. Two types of roller rockers are available. The less expensive units use a die cast body, which helps reduce machining costs. These rockers strike a balance in cost and features between stamped steel roller tipped rockers and the more expensive roller rockers that feature a forged (extruded) aluminum body for maximum strength.

Roller rockers are suitable for use in all street, marine, and racing engines. Extruded rockers are preferred over cast, but either are preferred over nonroller rockers. Generally speaking, cast aluminum rockers have smaller and fewer bearings than their extruded counterparts, but they're are also less expensive. On the other hand, extruded rockers are the strongest type of aluminum rocker arm, but are more expensive than cast. Cast aluminum rockers will handle up to about 550 pounds of open valve spring pressure, where extruded aluminum rockers will handle whatever valve spring pressure you can throw at them.

If you opt to use roller rockers, keep in mind that they're significantly larger than stamped steel rockers, so they'll require tall valve covers. You'll also need to make sure they won't touch the valve spring retainer as the valve fully opens and closes.

Interchangeability

Forget about interchanging rocker arm assemblies between Mark IV and Gen V/Gen VI engines. Gen V and VIs rocker studs are 1/8 inch larger in diameter than those used in Mark IVs and the rocker arm slots are correspondingly wider. Besides, Gen V rocker arms use a net lash adjustment—torque the rocker stud nut to a specific torque and that's it, the valve lash "adjustment" is complete.

The net lash system makes engine assembly quicker, but it

Vacuum-cast roller rocker arms aren't as strong as extruded billet rocker arms, but they offer significantly less friction than stamped steel rocker arms. *Crane Cams*

This picture illustrates the difference in load bearing capacity between Mark IV rocker arm assemblies (left) and Gen V rocker arm assemblies (right). The Mark IV's rocker arm and ball has a much greater surface area, and therefore load capacity, than the Gen series.

Gen series engines can use cams up to 0.520-inch lift if outfitted with the rocker stud and nut shown on the left. They're available from GM dealers as part numbers 10198929 and 10198930, respectively. The aftermarket stud on the right allows the use of Mark IV adjustable rocker arms on Gen series heads.

Tall rocker covers are required when using some types of roller rocker arms and when using stud girdles.

being loaded by opening or closing valves help support those that are. The jury is still out on whether or not stud girdles help increase horsepower, but they do add substantially to valvetrain life. Stud girdles are required when valve spring pressure rises above 350 pounds, and with aluminum heads when a mechanical cam with a rpm potential over 7,000 rpm is used.

If you plan on using stud girdles, you'll need taller rocker arm covers to clear the girdles.

Valve Springs

A camshaft is only as good as the valve springs it's mated with. Valve springs that are too weak will limit engine rpm by allowing the valves to "float." Valve springs that are too strong will generate unnecessary friction between the lifters and camshaft lobes, causing rapid lobe wear. To avoid either scenario, valve

limits the type of cam a Gen V or VI can use because of its nonadjustability. To overcome this problem, you can simply screw in a set of 3/8-inch diameter rocker arm studs, which are available from the aftermarket. Or, if you're using valve spring open pressures over 350 pounds, have your local machine shop drill and tap the Gen V head to accept 7/16-inch diameter factory rocker arm studs.

Alternately, Crane offers a 7/16-inch diameter stud to convert Gen V and VI heads to adjustable

rocker arms. Available as part number 99152-16, these studs have a 3/8-16 lower thread and must be used with their respective factory guide plates. These studs are recommended for use where valve spring open pressure is less than 480 pounds. Comp Cams offers a similar stud, as does Lunati.

Stud Girdles

A stud girdle helps prevent movement of individual rocker arm studs by mechanically tying them all together, so the studs that are not

springs have to be matched to the profiles of the camshaft lobes.

Valve float usually occurs when valve seat pressure is insufficient. Instead of holding the valve tightly against its seat when it's closing, the valve bounces off the seat. From the driver's seat, valve float causes a perceptible loss in engine power and changes the exhaust note from smooth to ragged. Inside the engine, valve float can, under extreme circumstances, cause severe engine damage.

It's also interesting to note that once the valves have been floated, the

Dampers (center) are used in all valve springs to change their natural resonant frequency. This reduces the potential for valve float and other problems. Some springs rely on flat wound dampers, like the one shown here, or use double or triple coils to provide proper damping.

rpm at which it happens again will drop. This vicious cycle will continue until corrections are made to prevent the valve float, or the engine eats a valve.

Valve springs that provide excessive spring pressure are more of a problem with a flat tappet cam, because the action between the lobes and the lifters is a sliding motion that can round the lobes. This generates greater loads than do roller lifters on their respective lobes.

Materials

Due to higher valvetrain pressures and speeds, modern valve springs are made from some pretty exotic alloys such as chrome silicon, H-11 steel, and Pacaloy.

Chrome silicon is a good choice for high-performance street, marine, and racing applications where maximum high-speed endurance isn't required. If it is, you'll want to use valve springs made of H-11 steel.

H-11 steel (also known as Vasco Jet) comes from the aerospace industry, where the best and purest materials are required to prevent catastrophic failures. H-11 valve springs are alloyed with other materials like molybdenum, nickel, and vanadium to increase their resistance to temperature and fatigue. Consequently, these springs are a good choice for highly stressed street applications, as well as most racing applications.

Valve springs made from Pacaloy are the latest trend. This material is claimed to maintain higher seat loads (300+ pounds) up to five times longer than other valve spring materials. Because of the very

high seat and open pressures (650–950 pounds) they offer, Pacaloy springs are best suited to roller-cammed drag race rats.

Temperature

Temperature is a valve spring's biggest enemy. As the springs are compressed, friction within the spring climbs. It's this internal friction that elevates spring temperature. This rise in temperature is moderated by oil splashing off the rocker arms. Use of a high-volume oil pump will add to the amount of oil available to cool the valve springs. However, under certain conditions like off-shore racing, oil splash from the rocker arms just isn't sufficient to cool the springs. In these circumstances, additional measures like adding an engine oil cooler or using coated valve springs or oil spray bars is warranted.

Selection

The biggest rule of valve spring selection is to choose a spring with just enough tension to get the job done and no more. The easiest way to do this is to buy the springs recommended by the camshaft manufacturer. However, the recommendations made in the cam catalogs may not be optimal for your situation. Why is that? Because a cam that produces maximum power at 7,000 rpm in a 396 may reach its power peak at 6,000 rpm in a 454 because of the increased airflow in the larger engine. And this disparity grows as engine displacement increases.

Since the 454 won't need to be wound as tight as the 396, the valve springs don't need to possess the higher closed and open pressures required with the 396. With reduced pressure, you've effectively increased cam lobe and lifter life. In turn, this reduces internal friction, allowing more horsepower to reach the flywheel. Reduced pressure also decreases spring temperature, extending spring life.

Camshaft type also impacts spring selection. Flat tappet cams will only tolerate valve spring pressures up to about 400 to 425 pounds. Beyond that limit, lobe and lifter life drop dramatically. If the flat tappet cam you're thinking about

requires valve spring pressures near this limit, you should seriously consider using a roller cam. Roller cams tolerate higher valve spring pressures much better, and lifter and lobe life will be significantly greater than with a flat tappet cam. And keep in mind that higher the valve spring pressures require stiffer rocker arm studs that will better resist flexing.

How do you determine valve spring rates? Coil springs are rated by how much pressure it takes to compress them 1 inch. So, if it takes 175 pounds to compress the spring 1 inch, the spring is rated at 175 pound-inches. If the valve springs you're considering don't have a spring rate listed, it can be easily calculated.

For example, let's say a valve spring exerts a pressure of 110 pounds at an installed height of 1.688 inch. When the valve spring is compressed to a height of 1.208 inch, the open pressure is 320 pounds. Begin by subtracting the installed pressure from the open pressure (320 - 110 = 210). Next, calculate the distance the spring moved by subtracting the compressed height from the installed height (1.688 - 1.208 = 0.480). To calculate spring rate, simply divide spring pressure (210) by the distance it moved (0.480). In this example, the spring rate works out to 437.5 pounds-inches (210 ÷ 0.480 = 437.5). Use of this formula will allow you to select the best spring rate for your application.

The more radical the camshaft profile, the greater the spring pressure required to keep the valvetrain adequately preloaded. When this limit surpasses what can be achieved by increasing coil diameter, the outside diameter of the spring must be increased. And when this happens, the spring seats on the cylinder heads may also need to be enlarged.

Factory big-block heads use valves springs with an outside diameter of 1.487 inch. Valve springs with a diameter greater than about 1.550 inch will require machining of the spring seats on the cylinder head.

Valve spring installed height is critical to achieving advertised spring closed and open pressures. Differences in the valve spring seat height due to variations in cylinder head castings, incorrect valve seat machining, and valve and seat grinding can cause variations in valve spring closed and open pressures. To achieve equal pressures from all the valve springs, valve spring shims are usually required. Available in thicknesses ranging from 0.015 to 0.060 inch, their inside and outside diameters must be matched to the inside and outside diameter of the valve springs being used.

Although you can set springs heights to their installed specification and hope for the best (spring tension in "matched" valve spring sets can vary by up to 10 percent), if you have access to a spring tester, you can shim each valve spring so it produces the closed pressure required by the particular camshaft. Here's the formula:

Spring rate x shim thickness = change in seat pressure.

Using the numbers from our example above, if the spring rate is 437.5 pounds, using a .060-inch thick shim would increase seat pressure by 26.25 pounds (437.5 x 0.060 = 26.25). Conversely, removing a 0.060-inch thick shim would reduce valve spring pressure 26.25 pounds. When you're juggling shim thicknesses to increase seat pressure, you also have to consider that each shim used reduces the distance the valve

To prevent the valve spring from moving around on the head, a valve spring seat should be used. Positioned underneath the valve stem seal, spring seats are required on aluminum heads to prevent head damage.

spring can be compressed before the coils start to bind. So this needs to be taken into consideration, as well.

Lower spring seats are designed to keep the valve spring from dancing around on the heads. They're also required for aluminum heads to prevent the ends of the valve springs from digging into the soft aluminum. If any shims are needed to establish proper valve spring installed height, they're fitted underneath the spring seats. Since the inside diameter of spring seat is smaller than the outside diameter of a guide-mounted valve stem seal, the shims and seat must be installed before installing the valve stem seal.

Valve Spring Retainers and Locks

Valve spring retainers have been made from three different materials: steel, aluminum, and titanium. Of these three, steel and titanium are the materials of choice. Aluminum retainers used to be readily available, but their inferior fatigue resistance compared to steel or titanium retainers makes them a less desireable choice. Consequently, few companies still offer them for Chevy rats.

Steel retainers are the most cost-effective choice for engines run below 8,000 rpm. Their weight disadvantage is overshadowed by their strength, fatigue resistance, and substantially cheaper cost compared to titanium retainers. Above 8,000 rpm, titanium retainers are the way to fly. With considerably less mass than steel and

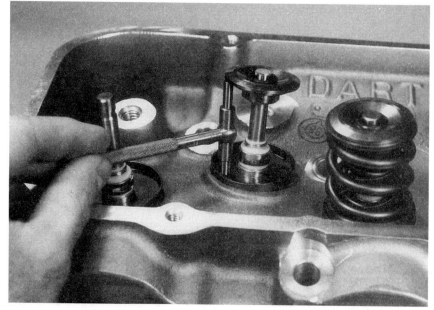

Valve spring installed height is important to achieving the correct valve closed pressure. If the distance is too great, use spring shims to close the distance. If the distance is too short, a dished retainer or longer valves can be used.

It seems as though each company has its own viewpoint as to what type of valve stem locks work best for a particular situation. In this photo, you can see the stock 7-degree locks on the left, and the beefier 10-degree locks on the right.

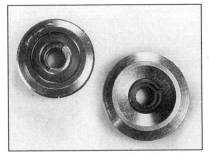

Valve spring retainers must fit the outside diameter of the valve springs to prevent performance and durability problems. The valve stem lock in the retainer on the right is relieved to accept a lash cap.

For engines that rev beyond 8,000 rpm, titanium retainers are the way to go. They're very light, strong, and considerably more expensive than steel retainers. *Lunati*

higher strength, titanium lessens the load on the valvetrain, raising valvetrain limiting speed. When you combine the high spring pressures used with roller cams with high engine speeds, the strength of the retainer is of paramount importance.

Retainers must also fit the valve springs being used. The outside

diameter of each step on the retainer must match the inside diameter of the spring package being used. A sloppy fit here will cause the retainer to fail.

The other part of the equation is the valve stem locks. Produced in 7- and 10-degree designs, they must be matched to the lock angle manufactured in the retainer. Valve stem locks were manufactured first with a 7-degree angle. Although these proved reliable for production and some racing engines, the higher spring pressures required with the more radical roller cams necessitated a stronger retainer/valve stem lock combination. The result was the 10-degree locks. Due to their greater angle, 10-degree locks do a better job of distributing valve spring loads over the surface of the retainer, reducing the chances of the locks pulling through the retainer. If valve spring open pressures are above 360 pounds or engine speed exceeds 7,500 rpm, you'll want to check into these locks.

However, there's another school of thought that says 7-degree locks provide more clamping power on the valve stem where 10-degree degree locks put an inordinate amount of stress on the keeper groove. Crane and Manley both offer heavy-duty 7-degree locks and retainers that have significantly more load bearing ability than the ordinary 7-degree lock and retainer set-up. So you'll want to check into these, too.

As you're selecting retainers, there are a couple of other things to keep in mind—spring height and lash caps. In some cases, in order to obtain the proper valve spring installed height, you may need to use a dished or shallow retainer. As their name implies, the surface on which the valve spring(s) ride are either higher or lower than the stock location. And this can help provide the necessary clearance for establishing the correct valve spring installed height. These types of retainers are available from aftermarket suppliers such as Crane and Comp Cams.

Likewise, if rocker arm geometry is such that the rocker arm will ride low enough on the rocker arm stud to contact the retainer, you should

Valve lash caps are required to prevent rapid wear of the valve stem tips on titanium valves. They're also used to correct valvetrain geometry. Whatever the case, the valve spring retainers must have a step in their tops to accept them. *Lunati*

consider the use of lash caps. Lash caps are small, cup-shaped discs that fit over the ends of the valves stems to effectively lengthen the valve stems. Made of heat-treated steel, lash caps can also be used to extend the life of the tips of stainless steel valves and are required with titanium valves. Some retainers have a relief in the top sides that prevent any interference between the lash cap and the retainer, while others don't. So check to be sure before you buy.

Valve Stem Seals

Valve stem seals for Chevy big-blocks come in two basic styles: umbrella type and guide-mounted. The umbrella type rides on the valve stem and will provide good service if all you're doing is a stock rebuild. Guide-mounted seals are secured to the top of the valve guide and provide better oil control than umbrella type seals. And since they're not moving up and down with the valve, they don't impose a penalty on valvetrain weight. In light of these advantages, they're the seals to use for high-performance applications.

Other than sealing considerations, you also need to know if the outside diameter of the seals you're contemplating buying will clear the innermost valve spring or damper. Seal height is another thing to think about. High lift cams can sometimes cause the valve spring retainers to touch the tops of the seals at full lift. If this is a problem, you'll need to have the tops of the valve guides trimmed or use a shorter seal.

Valves

When it comes to selecting valves, you have to choose the head diameter, valve stem diameter, length, and material that are appropriate for your particular use.

Head Diameter

Larger valves will bring more flow if the ports are sized to support the valve size increase. Fortunately, this is true for both factory oval port and rectangular port heads.

Two different diameter intake and exhaust valves have been available on production big-block heads: 2.06- and 2.19-inch intake valves, and 1.72- and 1.88-inch exhaust

valves. With few exceptions, the smaller valves were fitted to the "peanut" port and oval port heads, while the larger valves were used in rectangular port heads.

To increase the breathing of oval port heads while adding another 15 horsepower or so, 2.19/1.88-inch valves can be substituted for the stock 2.06/1.72-inch pieces. Your local machine shop can perform this operation very easily. Alternately, you could use valves with undercut stems. This type of valve increases flow at low valve lifts, providing extra power without the added expense of machine work.

Stem Diameter

Selection of valve stem diameter is dependent on engine use. For endurance applications, and that includes street as well as racing engines, 3/8-inch diameter valve stems with an 11/32-inch undercut are preferred. The undercut helps flow below valve lifts of 0.300 inch—an area where street engines can benefit most, especially if they're outfitted with street-oriented cams. Unfortunately for marine applications, the extra performance of undercut valve stems is outweighed by trade-offs in durability, so they shouldn't be used. Valves made with Inconel are the best bet for marine applications (as well as turbocharged engines) due to their excellent durability. On the other hand, valves with 5/16-inch diame-

ter undercut valve stems should only be considered for racing engines where endurance isn't a priority.

Length

Valve length is something that's more or less selected for you when you buy your cylinder heads. Intake and exhaust ports with relatively stock dimensions require stock length valves. Raised ports usually require a corresponding increase in valve length, depending upon how the valve spring pockets in the heads are cut. However, in some instances, you can use a shorter valve than what is normally called for if you want to retain more material under the valve springs for durability. Longer valves may also be required if valvetrain geometry is incorrect.

Material

There are numerous materials available to manufacture valves with, some better than others for certain applications. Let the nearby chart guide you toward what to use for your specific needs.

Valve Float

With all this talk about valves, you need to know about their arch enemy—valve float. Valve float can be heard as the exhaust note goes from smooth to ragged at high rpm. You can also feel the engine lose power. Valve float can destroy the valves and engine quickly if not detected and remedied, and each time it occurs, the rpm at which it occurs next time drops.

When valve float occurs, the valves go into a type of antigravity mode, rotating, unloading the retainers and valve stem locks, pounding into their seats, or not seating when they're supposed to. All the things you don't want your valves to do and the signs are visible on the valves.

Valve float is usually caused by inadequate valve spring pressure and can present itself in three ways on the valves: unusual wear of the valve stem tip, valve stem lock groove, or the valve head. Valve float is also visible on the valve springs. If valve float has occurred, the top and bottom of each coil will be marked from contacting one another as the springs try to jump off their seats.

The "extra" cut on the backside of the exhaust valve (left) helps increase flow. The intake valve (right) doesn't have this cut.

Valve head shape can effect compression ratio. The thicker and flatter the head, the higher the compression ratio. But don't choose valves based on the shape of their heads. Instead, purchase them based on how the engine will be used, plus valve stem diameter and shape.

This photo illustrates the difference in valve stem lengths. The taller valve on the right is required for heads with raised ports. The valve on the right also uses a larger head than the one on the left—2.30 inches vs. 2.19 inches.

VALVE SELECTION GUIDELINES

Valve Type	Application			
	Stock & Mild Street Performance	High-Performance Street/Strip	Engine Operation Over 8000RPM	Offshore Powerboat & High Performance Marine
Stock Replacement	Acceptable			
Undercut Stem Stainless Steel	Preferred			
Race Flo & Race Master	Extra Insurance	Acceptable		
Severe Duty		Preferred		Required Intake
Turbo Tuff				Acceptable Exhaust
Extreme Duty INCONEL		Preferred w/ Restricted Carb.	Top Fuel Funny Car Exhaust Only	Preferred Exhaust
Titanium			Required	Race Only

Chart courtesy Manley Performance Products

If the camshaft profile isn't causing this problem and valve spring seat pressure is all right, lightening of the valvetrain may be in order. Maybe the most cost-effective solution is to use lighter retainers and valve locks. If your engine is using stainless steel valves, switch to valves with thinner stems if engine operating conditions permit, or use titanium valves.

You might also try using a better set of valve springs to better control the closing of the valves. And in this same vein, stronger pushrods could help, as well.

Component Preparation
Valve Springs

Begin valve spring prep by removing the burrs from the ends of each coil with 400-grit sandpaper. This will eliminate stress risers and will also prevent the spring from cutting into the retainer. For these same reasons, radius the edges of the coils where they were ground, then polish them. A rubber-based abrasive wheel chucked into a Dremel grinder works well for polishing.

Dampers are important, too. If the springs use a damper, remove them, radius all their sharp edges, then reinstall them. Radiusing the edges of the damper will help prevent stress risers.

Pre-Assembly Checks
Valve-to-Piston Clearance

Valve-to-piston clearance should be checked when a high lift cam, higher rocker arm ratios, stroker crank, longer rods, or pistons with higher compression or a different compression height are used. The only true way of checking valve-to-piston clearance is with the engine dummied up with the crankshaft and camshaft in place, the connecting rod and piston (rings aren't necessary) for cylinder #1 attached to the crankshaft, and the timing chain and gears set up the way you're going to use them.

One way to check this clearance by substituting low tension valve springs (such as those made by Crane, Isky, or Tavia) in place of the stock springs. This method will allow you to check how far the valves can travel before touching the pistons.

To begin, install the low tension springs on the head for cylinder #1. Then install the head gasket you're going to use on the block, along with the head and torque the head bolts to specifications. With the rocker arms removed, rotate the crankshaft slowly until the piston is at the top of its stroke. Measure the distance between the underside of the valve spring retainer and the spring seat with the valve closed. Then slowly push the valve down until it contacts

the top of the piston and take another measurement.

The difference in measurements between the valve closed and touching the piston equals the valve opening range. Subtract 0.100 inch from this calculation to allow a margin of error for valve float. The remainder should be greater than total valve lift. If it isn't, you'll need to use a thicker head gasket or have the pistons machined for adequate clearance.

Rocker Arm Geometry

Engine modifications such as aftermarket rocker arms, excessive cylinder head milling, decking of the block, and using a smaller base circle camshaft or aftermarket cylinder heads can affect the relationship between mating parts of the valvetrain.

This Manley pushrod length checker can make short work of determining what pushrod length to use for proper valvetrain geometry. *Manley*

ABOVE AND OPPOSITE: Proper rocker arm geometry reduces valve guide wear, as well as the potential for valvetrain damage. Rocker arm geometry is correct when the rocker arm tip is in the middle of the valve when the valve is at half lift (right photo). If it's positioned before or after the middle (as shown above), your engine and Visa card will be in trouble.

If the geometry between these parts gets out of whack, bad things can happen, like accelerated valve guide wear and broken parts.

How do you know when rocker arm geometry is right? By checking the position of the rocker arm where it touches the valve stem tip. If the geometry is right, the tip of the rocker arm should be in the middle of the valve stem when the valve is half open. Other than measuring valve lift to ensure the valve is halfway open, this is an eyeball check. If the rocker arm tip isn't in the middle of the valve stem tip, shorter or longer pushrods are required. Most camshaft manufacturers offer an adjustable length pushrod to help you determine how long your pushrods should be.

Rocker Arm-to-Stud Clearance

If you're using a cam that has a higher-than-stock valve lift along with slotted rocker arms, you'll need to check the clearance between the rocker arm and rocker stud. High-lift cams can cause the slot in the rocker arm to hit the stud as the rocker arm is at or near maximum lift. If the clearance is okay, you should be able to slip the end of a large paper clip (about 0.060 inch) between the stud and the rocker arm slot when the rocker arm is at maximum lift and the valve is fully closed. If this isn't the case, you'll have to lengthen the slot with a grinding stone or buy long-slot rocker arms or roller rocker arms.

Rocker Arm-to-Valve Spring Check

Another clearance check should be made between the underside of the rocker arm and the valve spring/retainer. A large diameter valve spring and retainer can sometimes contact the rocker arm as the valve moves through its travel. Minimum clearance here should be .030 inch, which can be checked with a wire-type feeler gauge.

Although you can notch the underside of a rocker arm for clearance, keep in mind that notching the underside of a cast rocker arm weakens it more than a forged rocker arm.

Coil Bind

Coil bind occurs when the coils of the valve spring are pushed against one another. This is usually a result of having a camshaft lift or rocker arm ratio that's too high for

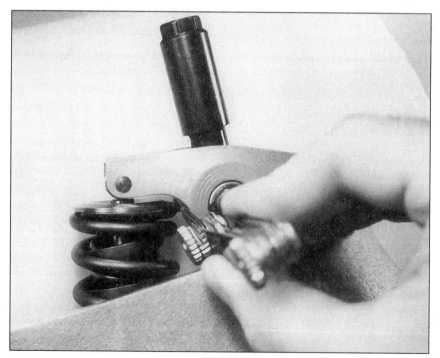

To prevent immediate problems when the engine is started, a minimum 0.030-inch clearance between the rocker arm and valve spring/retainer is required. A wire-type spark plug gauge can help you check this clearance.

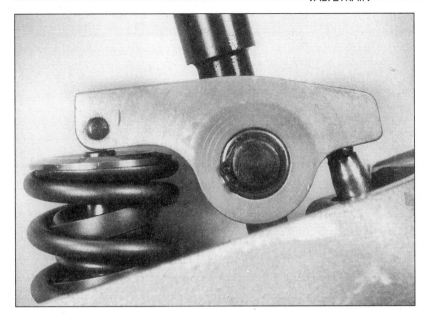

the springs being used. Coil bind quickly fatigues the spring and leads to breakage. To check for coil bind, slowly turn the crankshaft until the valve is at maximum lift, then try to slip a 0.060-inch feeler gauge between the coils.

If you can't, you'll have to use dished retainers, which will typically provide another 0.050 inch of clearance, at the cost of decreased spring tension. If this doesn't

work, you'll need to buy a different set of valve springs.

Valve Spring Retainer-to-Guide Clearance

Whenever you deep-six the stock cam, rocker arms, valves or retainers, you need to check the clearance between the valve spring retainers and the top of the valve guides (or valve stem seals). This job is made easier if you substitute light check-

ing springs for the valve springs that you'll be using when the engine is together. It also helps if you have dial calipers or a dial indicator that is capable of measuring total valve lift.

To check retainer-to-guide clearance, simply push the valve down an amount equal to total valve lift. While holding the valve at this point, slip some feeler gauges that together total 0.075 inch between the retainer and the top of the guide (or valve stem seal). If the feeler gauge combo won't fit, try using another type of valve stem seal. Speed Pro seals are shorter than Perfect Circle seals. If this won't provide sufficient clearance, you'll have to shorten the valve guides, but only do this as a last resort, because it can cause guide durability and valve sealing problems.

Stud Girdles

When installing a stud girdle, make sure the rocker arm nuts with the longest shoulders are positioned on the exhaust valve rocker studs. Otherwise, the stud girdle won't fit properly. The rocker arm nuts should clear the interior of the rocker arms throughout the range of rocker arm motion. Also, hand tighten each girdle retaining bolt a little at a time until they are all snug against the retainer. Then tighten the bolts in three passes until the torque specification is reached.

When installing a stud girdle, you also need to ensure the rocker arms don't contact them at full lift. If they do, pull the girdle up to gain sufficient clearance.

Coil bind must be checked when the valve is at full lift. A minimum of 0.060 inch is necessary to prevent valve spring breakage. If it's insufficient, dished retainers or other valve springs are needed.

Your choice of cylinder heads must complement the other components in your engine's "power path." The upper Dart head has sewer-pipe size ports for an alky engine, while the lower Dart head is prepped for mere 572 cubic inch and larger gas-swilling rats.

CHAPTER TEN

CYLINDER HEADS

Selection of the proper cylinder heads is key to making the most of the fuel system, camshaft, pistons, and headers stuffed into or stacked onto your Chevy rat. Like these other components, the cylinder heads must be picked with the intended use of the engine foremost in mind. Gaseous gobs of horsepower belted out by huge ports and valves only serve to kill the rewarding low-end power so necessary in hometown stoplight shuffles. So don't rush out and buy the latest go-fast heads without doing some considerable soul-searching. If you know what heads best complement the other power producing components in your engine, you'll be well on your way to being a happy camper.

Port design, combustion chamber design, and combustion chamber size are what differentiates Chevy big-block cylinder heads from one another. These factors need to be considered carefully to get the most from your engine.

Port Design

Three types of ports have been used on rats: peanut, oval, and rectangular.

Peanut Port

Peanut ports are the newest addition to the family of cast-iron big-block heads. Based on the oval port heads, they use smaller ports and valves for crisp throttle response and lots of low-end torque. This makes them best-suited to RV and towing vehicles where engine speed doesn't rise above 4,500 rpm.

Oval Port

Oval port heads are the best choice for street applications that won't see more than 6,500 rpm. Since hydraulic cams run out of breath in the 6,500 rpm neighborhood, oval port heads and hydraulic cams make fantastic dancing partners. The great thing about oval ports is they keep the velocity of the

Port volume has a significant effect on engine breathing and must complement the intake manifold, camshaft, and exhaust system. The Dart 360-cc head (top) has drainpipe size ports that require a racing engine with at least 572 cubic inches or so to be useful. The center-most head is a standard factory rectangular port offering with 325-cc intake ports, which are most suitable for a hot street/strip engine. The lower head is factory oval port unit with 260-cc intake ports. These heads provide crisp throttle response and can support over 600 streetable horsepower.

Casting numbers are usually found on the top side of the head above the intake ports. The number 14097088 identifies this head as a Gen V HO unit.

air/fuel mixture fairly high. The resulting thorough blend of air and fuel promotes crisp throttle response and low emissions. Although oval port heads use conservatively sized 2.06-inch diameter intake valves and 1.72-inch diameter exhaust valves, they can be replaced easily with 2.19-inch and 1.88-inch units, respectively, at the machine shop. When properly prepared, these heads can

Here's a side-by-side comparison of closed and open chamber heads. The head on the left uses a closed chamber design and 2.06/1.72-inch intake and exhaust valves. The head in the center is a high-performance version of the first head, featuring 2.19/1.88-inch intake and exhaust valves and is made of aluminum. The Dart 360-cc head on the right has heart-shaped open chambers with 2.30/1.88-inch intake and exhaust valves. The laid-back area around the exhaust valves helps increase breathing.

supply enough fuel and air to support 625 horsepower. And some aftermarket versions are good for 700-plus horsepower.

All factory oval port heads were produced in cast iron, and most were of the closed chamber design. To get into a semi-open chamber design, you'll want to get your hands on casting numbers 336781, 346236, 353049, 3993820, or 3999241, which all have 113-cc combustion chambers. An alternative is using oval port heads from aftermarket suppliers, like Brodix, Dart, Edelbrock, or World Products. Their heads use either a semi-open or open chamber design, and most are made from aluminum.

Rectangular Port

From semi-race street applications to moderate competition use, look no farther than the factory rectangular port heads. Using 280 to 325-cc intake ports coupled with 2.19-inch intake and 1.88-inch exhaust valves, these heads are good to about 8,000 rpm. However, you'll need high numerical gearing (3.73:1 or higher) to keep these heads in the fat part of their power band. With some careful pocket porting and port matching, these heads with open chambers will flow sufficiently

to support 700 horsepower. If this doesn't move your molecules fast enough, 750–775 horsepower is possible with extensive port work.

Available in both cast iron and aluminum, rectangular port heads with the most desirable features (118-cc open chambers with 2.19/1.88-inch valves) are casting numbers 3946074, 3994026, 6258723, 6272990, and 14096188. If you're looking to buy factory heads over the counter, ask for 6260482 for Mark IV blocks or 14096801 for Gen V blocks.

If your needs or desires take you beyond the horsepower level provided by factory rectangular port heads, you'll need to look to the aftermarket. Brodix, Dart, Edelbrock, and World Products all offer cylinder heads that are described more completely later in this chapter.

Combustion Chamber Design

Most big-block Chevy cylinder heads use either a closed- or open-chamber design. Closed chamber heads have a bathtub-shaped combustion chamber, whereas open chamber heads take one side of the "tub" and extend it toward the spark plug. Each design has a direct bearing on the type of pistons that can be used. Engines equipped with closed chamber heads require closed-chamber domed pistons to prevent contact with the cylinder heads—open-chamber pistons cannot be used. Open-chamber heads allow the use of either open- or closed-chamber domed pistons. Flat-top and dished pistons can be used with either type of head.

Open-chamber heads produce more power than closed-chamber heads because of the way they complement the combustion process. As the piston approaches top dead center (TDC) on the compression stroke, the spark plug ignites the air/fuel mixture. The fuel molecules closest to the spark plug ignite first, producing a flame. This flame front spreads to the other side of the combustion chamber, igniting the fuel molecules as it goes.

With closed-chamber heads, a significant amount of the air/fuel mixture in the combustion chamber isn't ignited because it's underneath and behind the spark plug, hidden by the combustion chamber. This cuts power and increases exhaust emissions. Open-chamber heads have combustion chambers that are open in this area so the air/fuel mixture directly around the spark plug can be ignited. With more complete combustion, power is increased and emissions are lowered.

Some late-1960s to early-1970s heads split the difference in shape between the closed and open chamber designs, as well as their advantages and disadvantages. Appropriately enough, these heads are called semi-open chamber heads.

Combustion Chamber Size

Eight sizes of combustion chambers have been used with factory heads. Closed chamber heads have volumes of 97, 98, 101, or 107 cc. Semi-open chamber heads sport combustion chamber volumes of 109, 112, or 113 cc. Open chamber heads have chamber volumes of 118 cc.

Although closed chamber heads work fine for street high-performance and marine applications, open chamber heads are the best choice, even in spite of the lower compression ratio they bring.

Mark Series Versus Gen Series

Factory big-block heads are either of the Mark IV or Gen V/VI design. Mark IV heads were installed on all big-blocks produced from 1965 to 1990. In 1991, Chevrolet changed the design of the big block as we knew it, appearing as the Gen V. As part of the redesign, the rocker arms were changed from an adjustable style to what's called "net lash" to save adjustment time during production engine assembly.

Instead of using a rocker arm stud that allowed valve lash adjustments, a shouldered stud was employed. This shoulder is at a pre-calculated height so that when the rocker arm nut is torqued to a specific value, the valvetrain is properly adjusted. If you want to put out some serious horsepower with valve lifts over 0.560 inch, you'll need to change the rocker arm assemblies and studs to the Mark IV type. Two types of studs are available to do this.

For valve spring open pressures below 480 pounds, aftermarket sources, such as Crane, offer 7/16-inch diameter studs with 3/8-inch diameter threads that fit the stock, threaded holes in the Gen V heads. These studs must be used with the Gen V pushrod guideplates. For valve spring open pressures over 480 pounds, the stock rocker stud holes must be drilled and tapped to accept the standard 7/16-inch diameter rocker arms studs from a Mark IV head. Both of these studs use the Mark IV rocker arm assemblies.

Another difference with production Gen V heads is that their coolant passages are tear-drop-shaped versus the round holes used with Mark IV heads and blocks. Because of this difference, the potential for a coolant leak is pretty high if you mix Gen V and Mark IV heads and blocks. Sallee Chevrolet in Milton-Freewater, Oregon, among others, offers a plug and gasket kit that allows the use of Mark IV heads on Gen V blocks. Although these kits are controversial, all of the people I asked about them have used them with good results.

Factory High Performance Heads

Aside from the factory production heads mentioned earlier, GM Performance Parts offers three high-performance Bow Tie heads in their "Signature Series" that are applicable to street and marine high-performance applications, as well as lower-level racing. Beyond these, the symmetrical port Bow Tie heads and Pontiac Super Duty heads are available for high-level racing classes, such as Pro Stock. These heads are available in various machined states, as well as raw castings for those individuals who want to modify them in their own way.

These Chevy symmetrical port heads are designed specifically for 500 cubic-inch Pro Stock Racing engines. They use intake runners raised 0.950 inch and exhaust ports raised 1.150 inches from their stock locations along with 72-cc combustion chambers to wake up sleeping giants. Each port is the same length to aid in even fuel mixture distribution whereas on most other heads, they're different lengths.

Gen V HO heads, like this one, use open chambers and 2.19/1.88-inch valves. The area around the valves are unshrouded at the factory. Note the triangular shape of the coolant passages.

Bow Tie Head Part Number 12363399

These oval port heads work well in both street and marine high-performance applications providing strong midrange punch with an abundance of torque. Besides being made from 356-T6 aluminum alloy, they also feature

- Semi-open 110-cc combustion chambers
- 290-cc intake ports
- 110-cc exhaust ports
- Semi-finished 2.19-inch intake and 1.88-inch exhaust valve seats
- Semi-finished bronze valve guides
- Exhaust crossover passage
- Heli-coiled rocker stud and exhaust flange bolt holes
- CNC machined intake ports and exhaust port bowls
- Compatible with standard intake and exhaust manifolds
- Compatible with all blocks
- Accessory bolt bosses
- For 396–502 cubic-inch engines

Bow Tie Head Part Number 12363410

These rectangular port heads are made from 356-T6 aluminum alloy and are engineered for street and water high-performance rats where strong power is required betweeen 3,500 and 7,000 rpm. Some of their other features include

- 118-cc open-style combustion chambers
- 315-cc long and 300-cc short intake ports
- 110-cc exhaust ports
- Semi-finished 2.19-inch intake and 1.88-inch exhaust valve seats

- Semi-finished bronze valve guides
- Exhaust crossover passage
- Heli-coiled rocker stud and exhaust flange bolt holes
- Compatible with standard intake and exhaust manifolds
- Compatible with all blocks
- Accessory bolt bosses

Bow Tie Head Part Number 12363425

These racing heads are made of 356-T6 aluminum and offer a measurable performance improvement over production castings. The "W" port exhaust runners and large port volumes lend these heads to large displacement racing engines. They also offer

- 105-cc open-style combustion chambers
- 380-cc intake ports
- Intake ports raised 0.100 inch
- Exhaust ports raised 0.750 inch
- Semi-finished 2.19-inch intake and 1.88-inch exhaust valve seats
- Semi-finished bronze valve guides
- Valve cover rails raised 0.250 inch
- Reinforced rocker stud bosses
- Two auxiliary head gasket bolt holes
- Compatible with all blocks

Also note that these heads require longer-than-stock head bolts for the exhaust port side, as well as valves that are 0.200 inch longer than stock.

Aftermarket Cylinder Heads

Cylinder head technology has evolved dramatically within the last few years, courtesy of computer-aided design (CAD) and computer-aided manufacturing (CAM). Consequently, the number of companies engineering and supplying cylinder heads has risen as well.

Some companies have developed cylinder heads to work as part of a package to enhance their induction systems, although they could be used with other components, as well. Other companies have concentrated on bringing cylinder heads to market that work with any number of aftermarket components. The route that's best for you depends on what you want the final product to be and your level of experience. Buying cylinder heads as part of a package is easier for novices and experienced people alike, whenever you want an engine that runs well without any extra "engineering." On the other hand, mixing cylinder heads with other components can take more

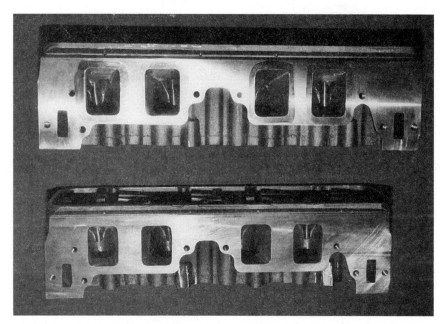

This is the intake side of the Dart heads shown earlier. Notice how much larger the ports on the alky head (top) are compared to the gas heads (bottom). This increase in size is necessary for flow, because alcohol has only 60 percent of the energy of gasoline.

time, but you'll probably learn more along the way, and may discover some additional power.

There are various circumstances that dictate the use of aftermarket heads, including reconditioning cost, application, and compression ratio.

When reconditioning heads for a high-performance engine, things like Magnafluxing, hot tanking, seat and guide replacement or upgrading, new valves, valve springs, retainers, seals, and milling are often what's required for best performance. However, by the time you pay for all these parts and services, you're not that far price-wise from a comparable pair of new, aftermarket heads. Typically, aftermarket heads have better ports and are adaptable to all Mark IV, Gen V, and Gen VI blocks, so you gain some power and versatility, as well.

The specific application also impacts the decision to stay with factory production heads or move to aftermarket heads. Street and marine engines up to 540 cubic inches with compression ratios below 9.5:1 that run at low rpm work just fine with factory oval port or rectangular heads. Hot street and race motors above 509 cubic inches benefit significantly with aftermarket high-performance heads, such as the Dart 320. Aftermarket high-performance heads with larger ports work best on engines above 560 cubic inches.

Compression ratio is another matter. Sometimes the traditional 118–119-cc open chamber heads have too much volume to provide the compression ratio you desire without resorting to high-dome pistons. And high-dome pistons interfere with flame front travel, reducing horsepower. If this is your case, and you're not going into Pro Stock racing, there are a number of aftermarket heads with combustion chamber volumes in the mid-90-cc range after angle milling. This will provide a wide variety of compression ratios from which to choose.

Cylinder Head Features
Aluminum Versus Cast Iron

Differing points of view exist regarding the compression ratio capability of cylinder heads. Some manufacturers and builders believe that aluminum heads can tolerate 1/2 to 3/4 of a point more compression than their cast-iron counterparts due to the superior heat dissipation properties of aluminum. There's another camp of manufacturers and builders (albeit significantly smaller) that say you can't compare the compression ratio tolerance of aluminum and cast-iron heads because the exact same head isn't manufactured in aluminum and cast iron for a real apples-to-apples comparison. That may be true. However, experience shows that aluminum heads will allow a bump in compression ratio over cast-iron heads, regardless of the fact that they're not the same exact design.

Admittedly, some of the benefit of the compression increase will be lost to the cooling system, due to the greater heat dissipation of aluminum, but you still wind up with a net increase in power. Scott Shafiroff believes that a street engine with a true 10.5:1 compression ratio is achievable provided you use aluminum heads with the combustion chamber modifications outlined in the "Cylinder Head Modifications" section use 94 octane fuel and have the right cam and ignition timing.

Deck Thickness

Contrary to what you may have heard, deck thickness isn't a reliable indicator of cylinder head durability. If the heads are cast from a more pure material, their decks don't need to be as thick as decks using a less pure or inferior material. Heat is what produces power. By using thin decks, more horsepower reaches the flywheel because less heat is absorbed by the head.

On the other hand, thick decks made of high-quality material provide you with the option of angle milling or machining to achieve the compression you require.

Raised Ports

In the never ending quest for more airflow, the intake and exhaust ports on some aftermarket heads are "raised" (taller) than their counterparts on a factory-stock cylinder head. This increases airflow through the port substantially. In some cases, however, raised ports may also require special intake and exhaust systems.

"Rolled Over" Valves

Valves that are "rolled over" are changed from their stock angles (26 degrees intake, 17 degrees exhaust) to angles that better complement airflow through the head. If the "rollover" is severe enough without relocating the rocker arm studs, shaft-type rocker arms may be required.

Brodix Heads

Brodix offers six different types of aluminum cylinder heads for Chevy rats, each tailored to a specific application.

All Brodix heads share these features:

- Competition three-angle valve job
- Valve bowls blended
- Intake ports matched to Fel-Pro FP 52465 gasket
- 10-degree steel valve stem retainers and locks
- Solid phosphorus bronze valve guides
- Recommended spark plug starting point: Autolite 52 (gas) 51 (alcohol)
- Fit all Mark IV, Gen V, and Gen VI blocks

Torque values and machining formulas for Brodix heads are as follows:

- Head bolts: 70 pound-feet
- Rocker studs: 40–45 pound-feet
- Flat milling: remove 0.0050 inch per cc
- Angle milling: remove 0.0066 inch per cc

BB-1 OEFI

The BB-1 OEFI heads are Brodix's offering for strong running street machines. Featuring high-velocity oval ports, these heads produce lots of torque and are just right for street and strip machines making use of a hydraulic cam, pump gas, and displacing 468–482 cubic inches. These heads feature:

- 258-cc intake ports
- 2.250-inch intake valves
- 1.880-inch exhaust valves
- 119-cc combustion chambers
- D-shaped exhaust ports,

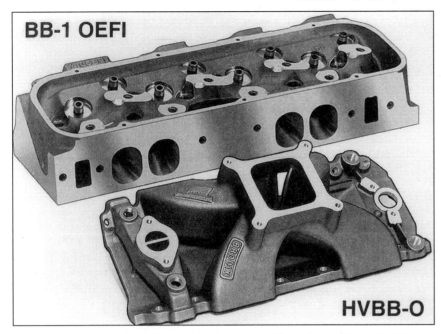

The Brodix BB-1 OEFI head uses oval intake ports and is engineered for 468–482-cubic-inch street engines. These heads produce torque in the rpm range most often used on the street. *Brodix*

raised 0.600 inch
- Stated CFM flow at 0.700 inch lift: 273 intake, 225 exhaust
- RPM range: 3,000–6,500
- Uses standard pistons, pushrod lengths, intake manifolds, valve covers, and exhaust flange bolt patterns

Due to the raised exhaust ports, longer head bolts or studs are required.

BB-1

The BB-1 head is a rectangular-port cousin of the BB-1 OEFI head. The relatively small intake ports provide good velocity. In turn, this makes them suitable for a number of applications where torque and throttle response are important, such as street and marine use, as well as oval track and dirt modified racing. The preferred engine displacement for these heads ranges from 427 to 482 cubic inches. Besides good torque and throttle response, these heads offer:

- 280-cc intake ports
- 2.250-inch intake valves
- 1.880-inch exhaust valves
- 119-cc combustion chamber
- D-shaped exhaust ports, raised 0.600 inch
- Stated CFM flow at 0.700 inch lift: 303 intake, 225 exhaust
- RPM range: 3,000–7,000
- Uses standard pistons, pushrod lengths, intake manifolds, valve covers, and exhaust flange bolt patterns

Like its cousin, the BB-1 heads require longer bolts or studs along the exhaust ports. Also, if an increase in compression ratio is desired, these heads can be angle-milled to a combustion chamber volume of 108 cc or angle-machined to a volume of 98 cc. With some minor port work, Brodix states these heads will flow 347 cfm on the intake side and 269 cfm on the exhausts at .700-inch lift.

BB-2

Moving up the performance ladder, we come to the BB-2 head. Recommended for 427–509-cubic-inch engines with a minimum 12:1 compression ratio, these heads can be milled for a Jesel rocker shaft system. They can also be angle-milled to obtain a combustion chamber volume of 108 cc or angle-machined to 98 cc. Other features include

- 305-cc intake ports
- 2.250-inch intake valves
- 1.880-inch exhaust valves
- 119-cc combustion chamber
- D-shaped exhaust ports, raised 0.600 inch
- Stated CFM flow at 0.700-inch lift: 320 intake, 225 exhaust
- RPM range: 3,500–7,300 rpm
- Uses standard pistons, pushrod lengths, intake manifolds, and valve covers

Like other Brodix heads, the BB-2s require longer head bolts or studs for the exhaust sides. They also require 0.250-inch longer-than-stock intake valves.

This Brodix BB-1 is appropriate for 427–454-cubic-inch engines that turn 6,800 rpm or less. It's basically a rectangular port version of the BB-1 OEFI head. *Brodix*

BB-2X

The BB-2X is a serious racing head that works best if used with a light car or large engine (482–572 cubic inches). Closely related to the BB-2 heads, they share most of their features with the following differences

- 2.30-inch intake valves
- 340-cc intake ports
- Stated CFM flow at 0.700-inch lift: 323 intake, 225 exhaust
- RPM range: 3,500–7,500 rpm

BB-3

The Brodix BB-3 heads have the largest intake ports of all the conventional big-block heads Brodix offers. With their huge ports, they're recommended for 540–605-inch racing engines. If necessary, they can be angle-milled for a 110-cc combustion chamber volume, but cannot be angle-machined. Also, the exhaust valve has been moved 0.030 inch away from the intake valve. Other features include

- 2.30-inch intake valves
- 1.88-inch exhaust valves
- 370-cc intake ports
- Stated CFM flow at 0.700 inch lift: 372 intake, 278 exhaust
- RPM range: 3,500–7,500
- Uses standard intake manifolds, rocker arms, and valve covers

Note that a Jesel rocker shaft system is not recommended for these heads. These heads also require longer head bolts or studs for the exhaust sides and 0.250-inch longer-than-stock intake valves.

BB-4

The BB-4s are engineered for bracket racing engines displacing 468-572 cubic inches with a minimum 13:1 compression ratio and turning at least 7,000 rpm. Both intake and exhaust ports are raised and the valves are "rolled over"—all to enhance airflow. Other features include

- 2.30-inch intake valves
- 1.90-inch exhaust valves
- 340-cc intake ports
- 134-cc combustion chambers
- Stated CFM flow at 0.700 inch lift: 361 intake, 252 exhaust
- RPM range: 3,500–7,500

When using a short-deck block, a tall-deck intake manifold is required for these heads, as are special guide plates or pedestal rocker arms. If necessary, the BB-4s can be angle-milled for a combustion chamber volume in the mid-90-cc range.

BB-5

The BB-5 is Brodix's latest and deepest foray into the high-performance market. Designed by Sonny Leonard and manufactured by Brodix, these heads are for radical street and competition engines. Using Sonny's combustion chamber and intake port design, coupled with the exhaust port configuration from Brodix's BB-4 head, increased performance significantly. Although this head is loosely based on the Brodix BB-4 head, it has a number of additional features including:

- 108-cc combustion chambers
- 381-cc intake ports
- 272-cc exhaust ports
- 2.30-inch intake and 1.88-inch exhaust valves with a two-degree rollover
- Exhaust rocker pads raised 0.200 inch
- Intake valve spring seats raised 0.100 inch
- Valve guides machined for 0.500 inch valve stem seals

Also note that these heads require bolts or studs that are 0.150-inch longer than stock on the exhaust port side. They also need head bolts with a shank that's slightly larger than stock (15/32 inch versus 7/16 inch). Sonny Leonard can CNC port these heads so the intake port volume increases to 427 cc and the exhaust port volume comes in at an even 300 cc.

Because of their flow capability, the BB-5 heads are intended for use on engines displacing 600+ cubic inches. However, in their out-of-the-box state, they can be used on 540- and 572-inch engines provided the engine is in a light vehicle, such as a dragster. If you so desire, these heads will accept 2.35-inch diameter intake valves with 1.900-inch diameter exhaust valves, or 2.300-inch intakes with 1.940-inch exhausts.

Dart

Dart heads are designed for a variety of applications, from street cars to race cars to high-performance marine applications. All are made from 355-T6 aluminum alloy.

Oval Port Heads

For all you street and bracket racers, as well as high-performance boaters, Dart has an oval port head just for you. With 265-cc intake ports and valves that have been rolled over two degrees for improved breathing characteristics, these heads can produce over 700 horsepower on a 454–468-cubic-inch rat. A close relative of the 320-cc and 360-cc heads covered below, these heads also feature

- Reinforced rocker arm bosses
- Integral valve guides with bronze liners
- Ductile iron valve seats
- Blocked heat risers
- Available CNC machined

Be aware that these heads use intake valves that are 0.250-inch longer than stock and require extra-long head bolts for the exhaust side. Dart recommends these heads for engines 468 cubic inches and smaller

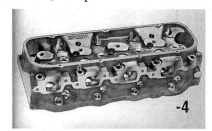

The Brodix BB-4 head is intended for 468–572-cubic-inch racing engines with a minimum 13:1 compression ratio. *Brodix*

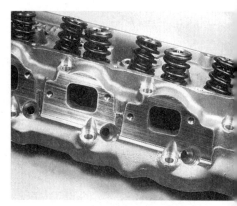

The exhaust port flow of stock heads can be inadequate for some racing situations. Specialized heads, like these Dart 360-cc heads, provide significantly greater flow than reworked, factory rectangular port heads.

that turn less than 7,500 rpm installed in vehicles that weigh over 3200 pounds.

320 and 360-cc Heads

As their name implies, Dart's 320-cc and 360-cc rectangular port heads have intake port volumes of 320 cc and 360 cc, respectively, and are designed for hot street and marine applications, as well as professional racing.

These heads come in two versions, regular and bolt-on. The regular versions are racing heads with 140-cc as-cast combustion chambers. So, unless you're supercharging or turbocharging your big-block, the decks will need to be angle-milled to get combustion chamber volume down to a manageable level.

The 320-cc and 360-cc bolt-on heads typically use 2.25- or 2.30-inch diameter intake valves and 1.88-inch exhaust valves. Their other features include

- 140-cc open-style combustion chambers (as cast)
- 2.30 inch intake and 1.88 inch exhaust valves with a two-degree rollover
- Uses standard rocker arms and guideplates
- Raised exhaust ports

Dart recommends the 320-cc heads for engines ranging in size from 468–509 inches turning 6,500–8,000 rpm. A manual transmission or automatic transmission with a high-stall converter should be used, and vehicle weight should range from 2,500 to 3,400 pounds. These race heads can be used with nitrous oxide.

The 360-cc heads are for engines displacing 525 cubic inches or more, revving to 8,000 rpm and beyond. These drag race heads require a manual or clutchless transmission and a vehicle weight of less than 2,500 pounds. The ports on these heads enable the use of alcohol, as well as nitrous oxide.

Big Chief

Big Chief heads feature shaft-mounted rocker arms and are best suited for Pro Stock engines. However, some Pro Street engines can use these heads to good effect provided they're properly carbed, cammed, and geared. A unique feature of the rocker arms is that three different types are used on a single head. While the exhaust rocker arms are all the same, two different types of rocker arms are used for the intake valves to accommodate the offset intake ports in the cylinder head.

Edelbrock

Edelbrock offers three types of street and marine high-performance heads with their Performer and Performer RPM series, as well as three racing heads in their Victor series. All of these heads are made from 356-T6 aluminum alloy.

Performer and Performer RPM 454-O

These oval-port heads produce lots of low-rpm torque and throttle response with outstanding horsepower potential. When combined with Edelbrock's Performer RPM Power Package and a 9.5:1 compression ratio, these heads will support over 540 horsepower. Other features include:

- Semi-open 110-cc combustion chambers
- 290-cc intake ports
- 110-cc exhaust ports
- 2.19-inch intake valves
- 1.88-inch exhaust valves
- 11/32-inch-diameter valve stems
- Exhaust crossover passage
- Heli-coiled rocker stud and exhaust flange bolt holes
- Valve springs capable of 0.700-inch lift
- CNC port-matched intake and exhaust runners
- Compatible with standard intake and exhaust manifolds
- Compatible with all blocks
- Accessory bolt bosses
- For 396–502- cubic inch engines
- 50-state legal

By taking a careful look at this photo, you'll see the three different rocker arms used on Big Chief heads. These rocker arms run on rocker shafts due to the revised valve positioning of these heads.

This is a cross-section of Edelbrock's 6045 oval-port head. It uses large, 290-cc runners to provide a boost in performance compared to factory oval-port heads, yet still retains more velocity than rectangular-port heads.

Edelbrock's 6045 oval-port head uses 110-cc semi-open combustion chambers. The angled area below the spark plug hole "opens up" the combustion chamber to a greater area of the piston for greater combustion efficiency compared to closed-chamber heads.

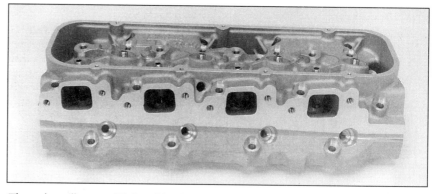

These shots illustrate Edelbrock's Victor Race Head, #7760. It uses exhaust ports that are raised 0.750 inch from the stock location to aid exhaust flow. The decks are 9/16-inch thick for strength and use 115-cc open-style combustion chambers.

Performer RPM 454-R

The *R* in this name signifies rectangular port heads and all the airflow that comes with them. Designed for street high-performance rats turning 3,500–7,000 rpm, these heads use open chambers and high-velocity ports for maximum street performance. Some of their other features include:

• 118-cc open-style combustion chambers
• 315-cc long and 300-cc short intake ports
• 110-cc exhaust ports
• 2.19-inch intake and 1.88-inch exhaust valves
• 11/32-inch-diameter valve stems
• Exhaust crossover passage
• Heli-coiled rocker stud and exhaust flange bolt holes
• Valve springs capable of 0.700-inch lift
• Compatible with standard intake and exhaust manifolds
• Compatible with all blocks
• Accessory bolt bosses

Victor Jr. CNC Race Heads

These rectangular port heads are the CNC-ported versions of the Performer RPM 454-R heads, described above. Capable of 700+ horsepower on a 468-cubic-inch engine with a 12.5:1 compression ratio, these heads use CNC-machined intake and exhaust ports to best advantage. They also include:

• Fully CNC-machined combustion chambers
• 325-cc intake ports
• 110-cc exhaust ports

• 2.25-inch intake and 1.88-inch exhaust valves
• 11/32-inch-diameter valve stems
• Compatible with standard intake and exhaust manifolds
• Compatible with all blocks
• Accessory bolt bosses

Victor Race and CNC Race Heads

Engineered for high-rpm or large-displacement rats, these rectangular-port heads will accommodate all standard location rectangular-port Victor series intake manifolds. The unported heads will support more than 800 horsepower, while the CNC race-ready heads will handle over 850 horsepower. Other features include:

• 115-cc open-style combustion chambers (race)
• 120-cc open-style combustion chambers, fully CNC-machined
• 370-cc intake ports
• Intake ports raised 0.100 inch
• Exhaust ports raised 0.750 inch
• Valve cover rails raised

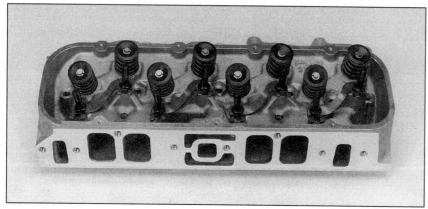

This port-side shot of Edelbrock's 6055 head shows its 315-cc rectangular ports and exhaust gas crossover—an important consideration for cold weather driveability.

0.250 inch
- Reinforced rocker stud bosses
- Two auxiliary head gasket bolt holes
- Compatible with all blocks
- Accessory bolt bosses

Note that the race heads require professional preparation, and the CNC Race Heads are sold without valve springs or retainers.

World Products

World Products' cylinder heads for big-block Chevys are unique in the aftermarket, because they're the only heads made of cast iron. Offered in both oval- and rectangular-port varieties, these "Merlin" heads provide a number of features including:

- 119-cc combustion chambers
- 295-cc intake ports (oval port heads)
- 340-cc intake ports (rectangular port heads)
- Raised exhaust ports
- Reinforced rocker stud bosses
- Chambers can be angle-milled to 100 cc

Merlin heads from World Products use D-shaped exhaust ports to achieve significant exhaust flow.

Cylinder Head Modifications
Valve Job

Next to using the appropriate heads for your engine, precision reconditioning of heads is the most cost-effective route to power production, relative to cylinder heads.

Cylinder head reconditioning begins with the valve guides, because they're the base from which the valve seats are ground. And well-machined valve seats are critical to power production in a big-block Chevy.

Valve Guides

Chevy big-block factory-production heads use cast-iron valve guides. From a production standpoint, these make good sense because they're fairly durable and are inexpensive to manufacture. However, if the valve guides need work, don't waste your money on having them knurled. All knurling does is cause the guide to be tighter in some spots than in others. After a few hours of running the engine, valve guide clearance is back to where it was before knurling, and all chances of well-sealing valves go right out the window.

However, the addition of a bronze (actually silica-bronze) sleeve to the inside diameter of the guide will allow the guide to be machined to a tolerance of just 0.0002–0.0003-inch greater than the valve stem diameter because of the differences in the metals. With less lateral movement, valve face-to-seat sealing is improved, and since bronze guides wear less than cast-iron guides, valve sealing stays better, longer.

Another important point is that bronze guides help dissipate the heat from the valve stem more readily than cast iron, adding to valve life. silica-bronze guides can be installed by your local machine shop.

Valve Seat Widths and Angles

Seat widths and blending are most important to engine performance and durability. The seat is the only place where the valve can transfer its heat to the cooling system. The greater the seat area, the greater the cooling. If the seat is too narrow, the valve will burn. This is especially critical for exhaust valves due to their higher operating temperature. Seat width also impacts durability. Narrow seats increase flow but the narrower the seat, the shorter its life. Consequently, the valve seat width has to fit the use of the engine—street, marine, or race.

Typical valve seat widths for street engines are 0.080 inch, while marine engines require 0.100-inch wide seats, due to their strenuous life. Race engines can get by with 0.060-inch-wide valve seats because they're rebuilt on a frequent basis and their seat cuts are very precise. The extra precision eliminates the need for extra seat width just to ensure a seal.

A good three-angle cut on the valves and seats works best for most street high performance and marine applications. The top cut is made at 45 degrees and is what the valve face contacts. Below this, two other cuts are made, typically at 60 and 70 degrees, depending upon the head. These cuts improve airflow past the valve.

Both the top and bottom cuts need to be blended for optimum performance. The top cut should be blended into the combustion chamber. The bottom "cut" is actually a radius that should be blended into the port throat.

Lapping the valves after they and their seats have been cut provides the opportunity to check valve sealing around their entire perimeter. If they're sealing well, no paste should be visible on the seat. Lapping also allows you to check that the seat extends to the very edge of the valve. Otherwise, the advantage of using the full diameter of the valve is lost. Although lapping is typically performed on racing engines, it's an extra edge you can get for your street or marine engine for maybe an hour's worth of time.

Valve Upsizing

The way you plan on using your vehicle should be considered when choosing particular valve sizes. Smaller valves, like the 2.06/1.72-inch intake and exhaust combinations are well-suited to commuting, as well as a moderate level of high-performance street use. Pocket porting of factory oval port heads with these valves will provide even stronger street performance with excellent driveability, because the velocity of the air/fuel mixture is kept high.

To increase the breathing of oval port heads while adding another 15 horsepower or so, 2.19/1.88-inch valves can be substituted for the stock 2.06/1.72-inch pieces at your local machine shop. Alternately, you could use valves with undercut stems. This type of valve increases flow at valve lifts below 0.300 inch, providing extra power without the added expense of machine work. Or you could combine the larger valves with the undercut feature for even

A good selection of sanding cones is essential for cylinder head porting work. Carbide burrs can also be used, but they take out a lot of material in a hurry, so you need to be careful when using them. Although these sanding cone kits are nice, if you live near an abrasive supply store, you can "make" your own kit for much less.

greater benefits. Cylinder heads using 2.19-inch diameter intake valves can be upgraded to 2.30-inch units using this same process.

In addition to increasing flow by virtue of their larger diameters, larger valves also help flow if the valves they're replacing have sunk into the head. By not sitting so deeply into the port throat, they need to move less to provide an equal amount of airflow. They'll also decrease combustion chamber volume slightly, which provides a slight bump in compression ratio.

Porting

There are some things you can do to unleash more power from practically any head, including pocket porting, lightly reworking the short side radius of the ports, and matching the ports to the intake manifold and headers. All of these modifications, especially pocket porting, will provide you with a real world power increase.

Beyond this, especially for serious racing applications where power output is critical and the heads are *really* big bucks, you're better off enlisting the aid of a reputable, experienced professional. Not only do the pros have their own little "tricks" they perform based on years of expe-

rience, they'll also have access to an airflow bench and maybe even a dyno. This allows them to test the modifications they make to ensure they're increasing the airflow through the ports and to what extent. This is critical, because sometimes what seems like a natural impediment to airflow, like a bump on the bottom of the port floor, actually increases airflow.

If your heads require more than what you can do on your own to be competitive, you should consider moving up to a set of heads that flow better right out-of-the-box than yours would with lots of professional help. This can be cheaper, and if even

When matching intake ports, blend them about 3/4 inch into the port to ease the transition. In this photo, you can see the pocket porting directly above the valve seat.

more power is needed, the better heads will be more able to support it. Just remember, if you're using your car for more than Saturday night drag races, as you move up to heads with larger intake ports, you'll be giving up some driveability because port velocity will drop. So you may want to think twice if your car, truck, or boat is used daily.

And before you resort to having the exhaust ports worked for more airflow, be aware that it's not the only way you can improve the performance of stock heads. MPG Head Service offers specially designed exhaust port plates that increase flow by changing the shape of the port floor, kind of like "C" port heads. They also increase low- to mid-rpm torque to the tune of about 25 pound-feet.

Pocket Porting

Pocket porting provides a lot of bang for the buck and is useful for street, marine, and mildly tuned racing engines.

As you would expect, as a valve opens, the area between the underside of the valve and the valve seat increases. In turn, flow past the valve increases. However, when valve lift is equal to one-fourth of the valve diameter, the valve no longer limits maximum breathing, the area of the port throat does. This is why pocket porting is so effective.

Pocket porting consists of blending the sharp edges underneath the valve seats (left after the machining process) into the port. By simply blending these edges, you improve airflow through the ports markedly. Best of all, you can do this on your own with a die grinder and some sanding cones. It's easy to see where the machining stops and your blending should begin underneath the intake port seat.

This is what the pocket porting should look like once it's completed. Note how the blending extends into the valve bowl but stops short of the valve guide.

After a three-angle valve job, the throat of a port is cut to open the area below the valve seat. This area is where most of the porting work pays off. This cut is then blended into the port bowl, as well as the short side radius. The whole idea is to remove the sharp edges underneath the valve (other than the valve seat) to promote airflow.

Short Side Radius

The short side radius of the ports (where the port floor turns to meet the port throat) is another area where an amateur can do some good. By carefully increasing this radius enough just to smooth the transition of air into the valve bowl, airflow will increase.

Port Matching

Matching the shapes of the intake ports in the head with those of the intake manifold can help the engine produce some extra power, provided it's done right. For detailed information on port matching, refer to Chapter 11, *Induction Systems*.

Combustion Chamber Modifications

Practically every cylinder head produced will benefit from pocket porting, as well as from unshrouding the valves and a light cleanup and polishing of the combustion chambers.

Valve Unshrouding

Unshrouding the valves is a relatively easy way of increasing engine performance. Even though the valves in a big-block Chevy move away from the sides of the combustion chamber as they open, "laying back" the chamber in the area of the valves, will provide an increase in airflow.

Big-block Chevys with open chamber heads respond well to having the rounded edge of the combustion chambers matched to the cylinder head gasket, especially the smaller-bore engines, like 454s. Also, "laying back" the combustion chamber in the area of the exhaust valve pays dividends, as well. In this process, you take the edge of the combustion chamber that's below the exhaust valve (near the center of the cylinder bore) and lessen the angle at which it meets the combustion chamber. This helps unshroud the exhaust valve, providing better breathing.

Although these changes reduce compression ratio slightly, they still increase power and torque throughout the rev range. For best results, the tops of the cylinder bores should be "laid back" in a similar fashion so

This is a "birds-eye" view of how the valves are oriented to the combustion chamber looking from the bottom of the cylinder upward. By "laying back" the chamber and the bore, you unshroud the valves and make more power. The relationship between bore size and valve sizes dictates how much material needs to be removed.

For best power output, the combustion chamber and tops of the cylinders should almost match the head gasket. This unshrouds the valves for maximum breathing. These chambers need to be "laid back" to the gasket.

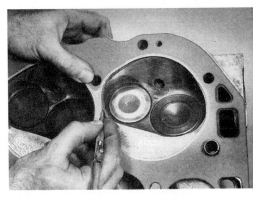

Before you begin scribing, install the dowels from the block into the head to ensure the gasket is properly registered (see lower right of head). Then carefully scribe the outline of the gasket, but don't go beyond the bottom of the chamber where it bisects the cylinder bore.

they complement the changes to the cylinder heads. Refer to Chapter 2, *Cylinder Blocks*, for details on this part of the process.

To "lay back" the chambers, clean the decks of both heads with carburetor or brake cleaner then coat the area around each combustion chamber with machinist's blue or a black magic marker. Now take the dowels from the deck of the block and slip them into their respective positions in the head. With top side of the head gasket you're going to use facing the cylinder head, slip it over the dowels to ensure it's properly registered. Now use a scribe to trace the pattern of the head gasket onto the head along the outside of the combustion chamber.

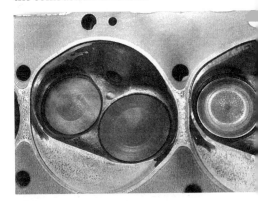

When "laying back" the chamber, you'll typically need to remove more material on the exhaust valve side of the chamber than the intake side. This is how the chamber should look after the initial matching. Follow this up by CC'ing, then polishing the chamber.

With your "pattern" in place, remove the head gasket and carefully blend the side of the combustion chambers to within about 0.025–0.030 inch of your scribed lines. There's no need to go all the way to the line, and you don't want to take the chance of going beyond the line or the head gasket will hang over into the bore.

After this process is complete, it's the perfect time to "CC" the combustion chambers, if you're so inclined. If not, polish and blend the chambers as detailed later.

CC'ing

CC'ing the combustion chambers in your head will provide you with two basic benefits: It will help you accurately calculate compression ratio; plus it will show you the volume of each chamber so you can equalize them. Equal-size combustion chambers are essential to getting the most performance out of an engine, because it helps ensure each cylinder is doing equal work. If you plan on "laying back" the chambers, as described earlier, do that first so you won't have to CC the chambers a second time.

To CC the heads, you'll need a burette, a 1/2-inch thick piece of clear plexiglass 6 inches square, 2 quarts of windshield washer fluid, a small amount of grease, and food coloring. CC'ing kits that contain all the necessary hardware are available from a number of aftermarket sources.

Before CC'ing the combustion chamber

• Make sure all valve work has been completed
• Slip the valves you plan on using into place (and seal them with a little grease)
• Lay back the chambers (if desired)
• Complete all chamber smoothing and polishing
• Install and torque the spark plugs you plan on using to specifications

Also, prepare the plexiglass by drilling a 1/4-inch-diameter hole near its center, about 1 inch from one edge. This hole will be used to direct the washer fluid into the combustion chamber.

To start, lay the head on the bench so that the combustion chambers are facing you and one edge of the cham-

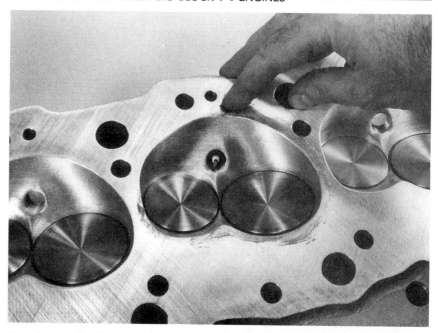
Prep the chamber for CC'ing by installing the valves and spark plugs you plan on using. Then apply a light coating of grease around the perimeter of the chamber.

bers is about 1/2-inch higher than the other. This will help purge any trapped air as you're filling the chambers with the windshield washer fluid.

After the valves and valve seats have been reconditioned (if necessary) and otherwise prepared, wipe a thin film of grease across their sealing surfaces and slip them into place, pushing them against their seats. In a similar fashion, wipe a film of grease around the combustion chamber you want to check and press the plexiglass onto it. Be sure to position the fill hole in the plexiglass right next to the topmost edge of the combustion chamber.

Now fill the burette with the washer fluid, then open the petcock and drain the burette until it reads exactly zero. Without disturbing the plexiglass, position the tip of the burette into the fill hole and open the petcock. As the chamber fills, the level in the burette will drop. If you're using a burette that's 100 cc's or smaller, close the petcock when it reaches the end of its graduated limit or you won't be able to accurately determine how much washer fluid you've dispensed into the combustion chamber. Then refill the burette as you did earlier and continue filling the chamber. When the washer fluid level in the chamber reaches the bottom of the fill

hole, close the petcock. Add all your readings, and the result is the combustion chamber volume. Then perform this same operation for the remaining seven chambers.

If the variation between all the chambers is 0.3 cc or less, the chambers are pretty much equal and need no further work. However, if the variation is greater than this, or you simply want all the chambers exactly equal, determine which is the largest, then carefully grind away the other chambers until they all have the same volume. Don't work too much in any one area and check your work frequently so you don't take too much material out of the other chambers.

When you've finished equalizing the combustion chambers, you can proceed to polishing them. However, if the chambers are too large to provide you with the compression ratio you desire, you can use a thinner head gasket or have the heads milled.

Polishing

Scott Shafiroff calls his chamber modifications "marine chambers." Basically, this entails removing and blending all the sharp edges in the combustion chamber, especially the area between the intake and exhaust valves. Polishing the chamber is a good idea, as well. Together, these

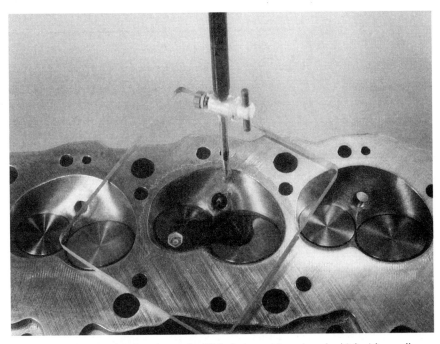

Place the plate over the chamber so its fill hole is positioned at the high side to allow air to escape. Press the plate firmly into place, then fill the chamber with the fluid. Windshield washer fluid works pretty well if you don't feel like coloring some alcohol. Measure the amount of fluid carefully.

techniques help reduce the potential for detonation, allowing you to run a little more ignition timing, which, in turn, provides greater power. This is especially critical on street and marine engines where you're trying to run a true 9.5 or 10:1 compression ratio using 93-94 octane gas. If you plan on blending and polishing the combustion chambers, do so after unshrouding the valves (if this appeals to you).

Smoothing and polishing of the combustion chambers when all the other chamber work is done will help reduce the tendency for premature detonation. And if all the cylinders have the same detonation point, you'll make more power than if the detonation point in just one cylinder was significantly lower. Why? Because you won't be limited by your weakest link.

For example, let's say an edge of one combustion chamber was sharp while all the others weren't. Under a load, this sharp edge would get hot enough to initiate combustion on its own, and this would cause detonation. To prevent this detonation, you would need to dial the ignition timing back. But this decreases cylinder pressure in not just the problem cylinder, but all the cylinders. And with decreased cylinder pressure, power drops off.

Another benefit of polishing the chamber is heat rejection. In order to produce power, you need to produce heat. By polishing the chamber, you've removed all the small surface irregularities that help dissipate heat. Since there's less surface area to absorb the heat, more heat stays in the cylinder.

To polish the chambers, you'll need some 180-grit sanding cones, some rubber-backed polishing cones, and a die grinder or similar tool. With a pair of scrap intake and exhaust valves in place to prevent damaging the valve seats, smooth the chambers with the 180-grit sanding cones. Pay particular attention to where the spark plug hole meets the chamber. Often, a small section of plug thread will hang into the chamber. Any small mass of metal that protrudes into the combustion chamber is a great place for detonation to start. So make sure it's removed and gently radius the edges around the hole. For the same reason, chamfer the edges of the chamber. After the entire surface of the chamber has been smoothed, polish it with the polishing cone.

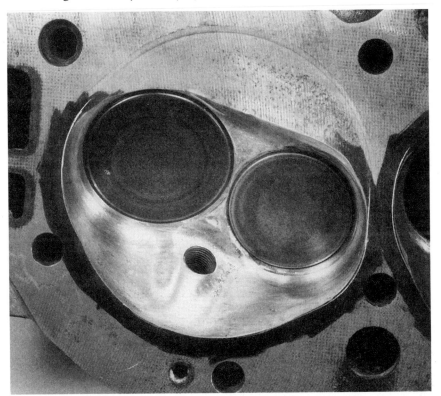

Polishing the combustion chambers reduces the potential for premature detonation, which allows greater ignition timing and more power.

103

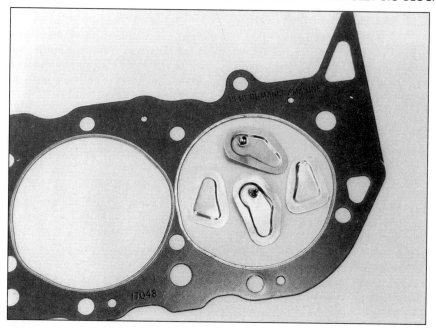

This head gasket and plugs are part of a kit to adapt Mark IV heads to Gen V blocks. Available from Sallee Chevrolet and other suppliers, it works well, but isn't necessary with Gen VI blocks.

Milling
Flat Milling

Flat milling positions the head perpendicular to the cutting tool. As the tool passes over the surface of the head, it removes a few thousandths of material. Typically, flat milling is used to remove cylinder head warpage, as well as to reduce combustion chamber volume when required.

Angle Milling

Angle milling is a process where the head is positioned at an angle in the milling machine so that more material is taken from the exhaust port side of the head than the intake port side. This does two things: It reduces combustion chamber volume, and, in effect, raises the roof of the intake port. Like a good porting job, this straightens the flow path to the back side of the intake valve, which helps increase power. It's not without its share of problems, however. The angle of the valve reliefs to the valves can be skewed, pushrod clearance to the head can be a problem, and the cylinder head bolt seats may need to be spot-faced to work with the new head bolt angle.

Angle Machining

Angle machining does the same thing that angle milling does—the difference is that angle machining takes the material off the head before the bolt holes are machined. This prevents the head bolts from binding in the head, which is a typical problem after angle milling. It also allows more material to be taken off the head, because the bolt hole alignment can be established after the angle machining is complete.

Head Gaskets

If the block and heads are made of cast iron, either shim or composition head gaskets can be used, because the cast-iron heads will expand at about the same rate as the block. Aluminum heads require head gaskets with a graphite or teflon coating to allow the head slide on them without causing a leak. Also note that if you're building an engine that's going to be used in saltwater, the head gasket core must be made of stainless steel to prevent it from corroding.

To seal properly, steel shim head gaskets must be coated with head gasket sealer, or be sprayed with aluminum paint. On the other hand, composition gaskets should never be coated with anything. They're designed to be installed as is.

When purchasing head gaskets, your best bet is to buy premium head gaskets, such as those offered by Fel-Pro and other quality manufacturers—especially if you're using aluminum heads on a cast-iron block.

Torquing Head Bolts

For any head gasket to do its job, the head bolts must be properly torqued. The clamping load provided by the head bolts ensures the gasket has sufficient pressure to prevent leakage of combustion pressure, coolant, and oil. Like every other bolt in the engine, head bolts must be stretched into their elastic range to ensure a sufficient clamp load and to prevent them from loosening.

Bolt torque readings are calculated acknowledging a certain amount of friction between the threads in the block and those on the bolt, as well as the friction between the underside of the bolt head and the block. If the head bolt threads in the block aren't free of contaminants—such as old sealer, corrosion and burrs—bolt friction will rise proportionally to the amount of crud it has to fight against. So, while you've torqued the bolt to specifications, it really isn't stretched into its elastic range because the friction level between the mating threads is too high. Consequently, the clamp load on the head gasket is below what it really should be, and the gasket fails.

To address this situation, thoroughly clean the threaded holes in the block. Running a tap through the holes until you're able to thread the bolts into the holes by hand will ensure thread friction is near its minimum.

Just prior to installing the head bolts, coat their threads with sealer if they're in contact with the cooling system. This will prevent coolant from finding its way up the bolt threads and into the engine. Use of hardened washers under the bolt heads helps spread the bolt load more evenly, ensuring a more accurate torque and helps prevent head cracking. When using aluminum heads this is especially critical.

K&N air filters use gauze and wire mesh to straighten the airflow before it reaches the carburetor or throttle body. This decreases power-robbing turbulence. *K&N*

CHAPTER ELEVEN

INDUCTION SYSTEMS

Proper selection and tuning of induction system components is critical to engine performance. The air filter, carburetor or fuel injection system, and intake manifold must be matched to the engine in terms of air and fuel flow capacity for the engine to run at its maximum potential. Not only must these induction system components complement one another, they must also complement the cylinder heads, camshaft, and exhaust system used.

Air Filtration

What's better for performance? Not using an air filter or using one? If you said the latter, you'd be right. Contrary to what some people believe, using a high-efficiency air filter can actually increase horsepower. And that says nothing of the increased engine longevity that comes with it.

How can an air filter increase horsepower? By straightening the air before it flows through the carburetor or fuel injection system. Think of it as a pre-cylinder head porting trick. As the air passes through the filter, its path is straightened by the woven mesh and wire grid. Since straight air moves faster than turbulent air, airflow is increased.

Filter Types

Basically, three types of air filters are available: paper, foam, and gauze. Paper filters work fairly well and they're inexpensive, but they're also quite restrictive. Foam filters must be treated with oil to capture the small particles floating in the air that the engine would otherwise ingest. Unlike paper filters, they'll also pass water without closing off and choking the engine. And when they get dirty, airflow through them decreases significantly.

Gauze filters are the domain of K&N Engineering. These filters use a cotton gauze mesh that must be treated with a special oil to trap airborne contaminants. Unlike foam filters, gauze filters can accumulate a 1/8- to 1/4-inch thick layer of gunk on their exterior before airflow drops enough to warrant cleaning.

Of the three types of filters, independent tests have shown that K&N air filters flow the most air by a significant margin. Since increased inlet airflow can lead to significant power gains, K&N filters are the type I'll discuss here.

Sizing

Air filters need to be sized for the environment the vehicle will be used in, engine displacement, and rpm capability. To determine how much total effective area the filter should have, multiply the engine displacement in cubic inches by the maximum rpm you plan to run the engine at and divide the result by 20,839.

Total Effective
Filtering Area = $\dfrac{\text{cid x maximum rpm}}{20{,}839}$
Required

For example, let's say your engine displaces 468 cubic inches and will redline at 7,200 rpm. The formula would look like this:

$\dfrac{468 \times 7{,}200}{20{,}839} = \dfrac{3{,}369{,}600}{20{,}839} = 161.697\,\text{sq in}$

So your engine would require about 162 square inches of effective filtering area. Now you need to determine the area of the filter you plan on using. To do this, take the diameter of the filter and multiply it by pi (3.14159), then multiply this result by the height of the filter.

Total filtering Area = Filter Diameter x 3.14159 x Filter Height Area

So, if the filter you wanted to use was 14 inches in diameter and was 4 inches high, the formula would look like this:

14 x 3.14159 x 4 = 175.929 sq in

However, this isn't the total effective filtering area, because part of

this area is taken by the seals. To compensate for this, take the filter area and multiply it by 0.80. The result is the total effective filtering area.

Total Filtering Area x 0.80 = Total *Effective* Filtering Area
Plugging our numbers into the formula:
175.929 x 0.80 = 140.74 sq in
Total *effective*
filtering area

So, we have a shortfall of about 21 square inches of effective filtering area (162 - 141 = 21). To make this up, you could select a filter that's larger in diameter, or taller, or both. If you're thinking of going taller, you'll have to consider if you'll have sufficient underhood clearance.

If you don't have sufficient clearance and you don't want to use a larger diameter filter, you could use a low profile (drop base) air cleaner housing. This type of housing is stepped to move the air filter closer to the engine and will work all right, as long as the air cleaner lid stays at least 2 inches above the carburetor venturis. If it's any closer than this, it will restrict the airflow to the carburetor.

Also, keep in mind that K&N's airflow bench has shown that airflow through four-barrel carbureted engines is highest when air filter diameter is four to five times greater than its height. So for a 3-inch-high filter, filter diameter should fall between 14 and 17 inches. But this doesn't hold true for fuel injection systems equipped with a throttle body. These systems work better when the air is straight before it enters the throttle body. So, in these situations, an air filter that's two to four times taller than its diameter is called for.

Engine operation off-road requires an air filter that has one to two times more surface area than called for in the sizing formula to allow for the build-up of dirt.

Stubstacks

In keeping with the need to gently bend the airflow as it meets the carburetor, K&N offers a short velocity stack called the "Stubstack." This molded piece streamlines the edges of the carburetor air horn that normally would cause turbulence. By reducing this turbulence, airflow through the carbure-

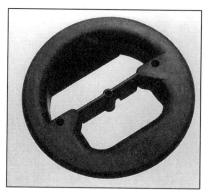

K&N Stubstacks, like the one shown here, reduce the turbulence of the air as it enters the carburetor, thereby increasing carburetor airflow. They're available for Holley, Edelbrock Square Bore, and Carter carburetors. *K&N*

tor can increase significantly, up to 40 cfm. This increase in airflow also allows you confidently choose a carburetor that's slightly on the small side (based on your airflow calculations) so you can increase throttle response and fuel economy for your street-driven car or truck while reaping the benefits of more top-end power.

If your engine is over-carbureted, you probably won't feel any difference. On the other hand, if your engine is appropriately carbed (or especially undercarbed) the performance increase will be significant. It can also prove helpful if the racing class you're in dictates carburetor size.

Stubstacks are offered for squarebore Holley (4150, 4160, Dominator) and Edelbrock Performer Series carburetors. Stubstacks aren't offered for QuadraJet carburetors because their equalized flow around the air horn doesn't work well with the unequal draw of the Q-jet's small primary and large secondary venturis. Furthermore, Stubstacks only work effectively with K&N air filters and air filter housings.

Carburetors

Holley and QuadraJet carburetors have been the carburetors of choice when the factory issued carbureted big blocks—and for good reason. Each of these carburetors offer good performance and impressive throttle response.

Selecting a Carburetor

To select the right carburetor for your engine, you need to know its airflow requirement in cubic feet per minute (cfm). You also need to know how the secondary valves are operated and what type of acceleration pump system is used. All of these things impact engine performance, responsiveness, and driveability.

Determining Carburetor Size

Carburetors are selected primarily based on their airflow capacities. Too little airflow restricts horsepower and torque. Too much airflow hurts low- and mid-rpm power and throttle response. Consequently, airflow capacity must be matched to engine size and maximum engine rpm. However, this doesn't account for other things that can affect airflow including:

• Type of air cleaner and intake manifold used
• Cylinder head port size and shape
• Combustion chamber size and shape
• Piston dome size and shape
• Intake and exhaust valve sizes
• Camshaft duration and lift
• Whether the engine uses headers or not
• Exhaust system configuration

All of these items affect the actual airflow through the engine.

Maximum engine rpm is used to calculate theoretical air capacity. When speaking big-block Chevys, this ranges from about 5,500 rpm for engines outfitted with peanut port heads to about 7,200 rpm for street engines using rectangular port heads with 2.19/1.88-inch intake and exhaust valves and headers.

By using numbers that best describe your engine, you can determine theoretical air capacity using the following formula:

$$CFM = \frac{\text{maximum rpm x displacement}}{3,456}$$

As an example, let's say you estimate maximum engine rpm to be 6,200 and your engine displaces 468 cubic inches. Plugging these figures into the formula would give you the following equation:

$$CFM = \frac{6,200 \times 468}{3,456} = 840 \text{ cfm}$$

This number of 840 represents the theoretical airflow for an engine running at 100 percent efficiency. Unfortunately, engines used in street and nonracing marine applications can't flow all that air due to the less than optimal tuning of their induction, camshaft, and exhaust systems, as mentioned earlier. To account for these inefficiencies, a factor called volumetric efficiency (VE) is used.

Volumetric efficiency is the difference between theoretical and actual airflow through an engine and is highest at peak engine torque. High-performance engines with a good exhaust system and ported heads typically have a VE of about 85 to 90 percent. Bracket race and circle track engines have a VE of 90 to 95 percent, while an all-out racing engine has a VE of 98 to 112 percent, based on its state of tune and number of carburetors. Those equipped with one four-barrel carb have a VE that varies from 98 to 105 percent, while those using two four-barrel carbs can have a VE of between 100 and 112 percent.

Homing in on carburetor size, if our hypothetical 468 is used for street duty, its VE is probably around 85 percent (0.85). Using this 0.85 VE factor would result in the following equation:

$$CFM = \frac{6,200 \times 468 \times 0.85}{3,456} = 714 \text{ cfm}$$

So our hypothetical 468 requires a carb that flows 714 cfm. The problem is carburetors are produced only in particular sizes (600, 650, 700, and so on). In this case, two carb sizes come close: 700 and 750 cfm. In contrast to the bigger is better theory, it's usually best to err to the smaller side when it comes to carburetion. Smaller venturis increase velocity of the air entering the engine, which helps keep the fuel mixed with the air. This ensures good throttle response and driveability. Consequently, you're better off opting for the 700 instead of the 750. To gain some airflow (on the order of 20–25 cfm) you could use a K&N Stubstack, which won't detract from bottom end response but will help on the top end.

As always, there are exceptions to the "smaller is better" rule. Engines used for racing can get away with the larger carburetor because driveability is usually secondary to wide open throttle (WOT) performance. Also, lightweight street vehicles (under 3,000 pounds) with high numerical axle ratios (3.73:1 or higher) and a manual transmission (or an automatic transmission with a high-stall torque converter) could work very well with the larger carb. Heavy vehicles (over 4,000 pounds) with automatic transmissions and low numerical axle ratios (3.08:1 or smaller) will work best with the smaller carburetor. So, always keep the intended use of the vehicle in mind.

After determining what size carburetor is required, you need to consider how the secondary valves are operated because this has a great impact on driveability. Open them too slowly or too quickly and performance suffers. Secondaries can be controlled either by vacuum or mechanically.

Vacuum Secondaries

As air passes through the primary venturis, it creates a vacuum. The further the throttle is opened, the greater the volume of air that passes through the venturis. In turn, this increases the amount of vacuum. It's this vacuum that's used to operate vacuum secondaries. Carburetors with vacuum secondaries are preferred for the street because the secondary valves open only in response to engine load. This produces a strong signal at the venturis allowing a larger than normal carburetor to be used with the benefit of more high-rpm power. How much larger? Somewhere in the range of 10 and 15 percent.

If you plan on using two four-barrel carburetors, you can increase the airflow limit by another 30 to 45 percent because of the stronger signal provided by eight venturis instead of four. This means you could use two 600 cfm carbs with vacuum secondaries and still have strong throttle response with a fantastic top-end rush. Alternately, you could use four two-barrel carburetors, which would provide even greater throttle response, due in part to the shorter and straighter intake runners used with these manifolds.

Mechanical Secondaries

For competition engines, there's no substitute for mechanical secondaries. They provide better control of engine rpm since they are directly linked to the primary throttle valves. So when the throttle is opened, both primary and secondary valves open at the same rate. Although this is a benefit in a racing situation, it can cause a problem at low speeds on the street because if the throttle is opened completely, too much air will be fed to the engine. The result is poorer acceleration than if the throttle was opened slowly, which is why vacuum secondaries are preferred for the street. However, this problem can be partially compensated for by using a "double-pumper" carburetor.

Single- and Double-Pumpers

When you open the throttle on a regular four-barrel carburetor, an accelerator pump adds an extra "shot" of fuel to the primary venturis. This extra fuel prevents a momentary loss of power. Double-pumper carbs use an accelerator pump for both the primary and secondary venturis. This type of design compensates for the extra air drawn into the cylinders when the secondary throttle valves are yanked open via a mechanical linkage.

As you can imagine, fuel mileage with this type of carburetor drops significantly if you're constantly opening and closing the throttle.

Marine Carburetors

Marine carburetors are similar to automotive carburetors, but are designed and manufactured to prevent the possibility of an explosion. And this effort focuses on preventing fuel from exiting the carburetor.

The main criteria that a marine carburetor must meet is that if a carburetor should flood, only 0.5-cc of fuel is allowed to escape in 30 seconds. And to prevent the potential for a fire in the event of a backfire, no gasket is used between the airhorn flange and the flame arrestor.

The fuel bowl vent tubes and throttle shafts receive special attention, as well. To prevent fuel from exiting the carburetor if flooding should occur, the vent tubes are bent inward toward the venturis in a "J"

shape. This routes any fuel that comes out of the vent tubes back into the engine. The throttle shafts are designed for the same response: to prevent fuel from leaking out the ends of the throttle shafts during a flooded engine condition, the throttle shafts are grooved to channel the fuel back into the intake manifold.

All of these steps are taken to prevent gasoline or gasoline fumes from accumulating, which, in turn, prevents fires and explosions. So, unless you're in a hurry to meet your maker, *never* use an automotive carburetor in a marine application.

Aftermarket Carburetors
Holley 4150/4160

The 4150/4160 line of carburetors have seemingly been with us since the advent of high-performance street vehicles, and rightfully so. Their performance has been legendary and their modular design provides an amazing amount of versatility when it comes to performance modifications.

Using their famous square bore design (four throttle plates of the same diameter), these Holleys range in size from 390 to 850 cfm. These carburetors are designed for street performance and come in two styles of float systems, side or center pivot. The center-pivot floats are preferred because they provide the best fuel

control whether the vehicle is turning right or left.

While 4150 models have separate metering blocks for the primary and secondary circuits, 4160 models only use a metering block for the primary circuit. The secondary circuit is handled by a plate that uses nonreplaceable fuel metering restrictions.

Holley 4165/4175

Holley 4165 and 4175 model carburetors were designed as a replacement for Rochester QuadraJet carburetors, and therefore share the same spread-bore throttle valve pattern. Looking like their 4150/4160 cousins, the 4165/4175 series Holleys share only jets, power valves, floats, needles and seats, and some other miscellaneous hardware. Everything else is unique to the 4165/4175 family.

The 4165 model uses mechanical secondaries and flows either 650 or 800 cfm. It also features a double-pumper accelerator pump design and "reverse" idle screws (turn the screws in to richen the mixture; back them out to lean it). High-performance models use the center-pivot float design, while the standard models make do with side-pivot floats.

The 4175 model has vacuum secondaries and flows 650 cfm. Along with the reverse idle screw adjustment used on the 4165, the

This Holley 4150 flows 750 cfm and is designed for competition use. It features mechanical secondaries, dual 30-cc accelerator pumps, and a four-corner idle system. *Holley*

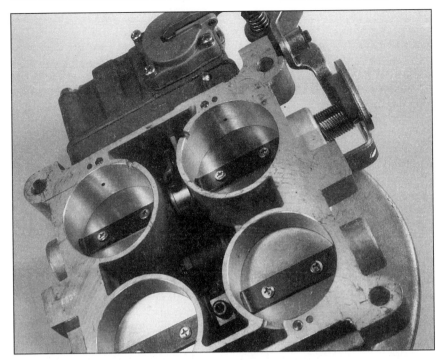

High-performance Holley carburetors designed for use with high-overlap cams use a "four corner" idle system. This allows each carburetor bore to be adjusted individually so the engine can idle. Here you can see the bleed holes below the throttle blades.

Holley's Pro-Series HP line of carburetors are designed to eliminate the need for having a carburetor re-engineered by a professional carburetor shop. *Holley*

4175 also uses a single accelerator pump and side-pivot floats.

Since the 4165/4175 family was developed as a bolt-on replacement for emissions-regulated applications, it remains a good choice for emissions-sensitive areas throughout the country.

Holley 4010/4011

Holley 4010 and 4011 carburetors are designed and manufactured for street-performance applications with a strong slant on cosmetic appearance. Available with vacuum or mechanical

When it comes to serious racing carburetors, Holley Dominators are one of the few games in town. Available in one streetable size (750 cfm) and two racing-sizes (1,050 and 1,150 cfm), these carburetors have mechanical secondaries and a strong racing heritage.

secondaries, these carburetors range in airflow from 600 to 750 cfm for the square-bore 4010 design, while the cfm rating for the spread-bore 4011 model ranges from 650 to 800 cfm.

Although these carburetors differ from the 4150/4160 models in that the float bowls are integral with the throttle body, they share the same jets, power valves, pump diaphragms, and brackets. Consequently, they have a lot of "tunability" for specific applications.

Holley 4500

The 4500 model carburetor, better known as the Dominator, probably comes immediately to mind when you think of a racing carburetor. And true to their Dominator name, they've helped win more than their fair share of races.

Available in 750-, 1,050-, and 1,150-cfm versions, there's a Dominator sized to fit your needs. All Dominators use dual-feed float bowls with center-pivot floats, four-corner idle system, and mechanical secondaries, along with dual accelerator pumps.

Holley Pro-Series HP

In 1997, Holley released its Pro-Series HP line of competition carbure-

tors. Drawing on its racing experience, Holley incorporated a number of improvements to this latest line of carburetors. What's most visible, upon first inspection is the newly designed main body with specially contoured venturi entry angles and symmetrical venturi bores. What's most obviously invisible is the choke tower—it's gone.

These changes reduce the obstacles the air has to overcome, thereby reducing turbulence, which adds to airflow. They've also decided to use a double-step design in the booster venturi. These steps strengthen the vacuum signal, resulting in improved throttle response.

Most of the Pro Series HP carburetors also use a four-corner idle system, which allows you to adjust the idle mixture for all four venturis, not just the primaries. And this can be very useful when trying to set the idle on an engine fitted with a long duration cam. Available in both vacuum-secondary and progressive, mechanical-secondary versions, there's a size to fit most big-blocks.

Two 750-cfm Pro Series carburetors are offered for mildly warmed-over big blocks. Part number 0-80528 uses progressive mechanical secondaries, along with dual 30-cc accelerator pumps, and features distributor, intake manifold, and PCV ports. Part number 0-80529 also has these ports, but uses vacuum secondaries and a single 30-cc accelerator pump. Both models are designed for street/strip duty.

Other big-block-appropriate models range in capacity from 830 to 1,000 cfm. These competition-only models vary in their capability to handle gasoline or alcohol, and some use annular booster venturis to increase engine response.

Marine Applications

For marine applications, Holley offers a number of carburetors with vacuum secondaries as well as mechanical secondaries. A number of these carburetors have what Holley calls "universal marine calibration" which means that they'll work in a number of different applications. Based on the 4150/4160 family, these carburetors range in airflow from 600 to 850 cfm. For the big dogs, a 1,050 cfm Dominator carburetor with racing calibration, 50-cc accelerator pumps, and dual fuel inlets are available as part number 0-80340.

Edelbrock

Edelbrock markets performance carburetors based on both Carter and Rochester QuadraJet designs. Some of these carburetors are street legal, while others are not.

The Carter-based carburetors are a square bore design and typically offer two vacuum ports (ported and manifold), unique mechanical secondaries that open in response to engine load, and GM-style throttle linkage.

The two rat-appropriate models are offered in 600- and 750-cfm sizes.

Carter-based 600- and 750-cfm carburetors specifically engineered for marine applications are also offered. These units will fit the induction needs of most water-bound rats used for pleasure boating.

Two distinct types of Performer Q-Jet carburetors are available from Edelbrock: Performer and Performer RPM. The two Performer models (750 cfm and 795 cfm) work with the stock intake manifolds and are street-legal in all 50 states. They're compatible with EGR systems and include vacuum take-offs for both ported and full vacuum needs. The lone Performer RPM model is calibrated for high-performance use but is not emissions legal. With an airflow of 850 cfm and a 0.149-inch needle and seat assembly, it has the ability to support over 500 horsepower. To enhance its compatibility with long duration, high-lift camshafts, it utilizes slotted idle mixture screws and large idle discharge ports.

Tuning Holley Carburetors
Selecting Power Valves

The power valve is the mainstay of the vacuum-operated power enrichment system in Holley carburetors. For best performance, the power valve must be matched to the engine's needs.

Power valves are available in single-stage and two-stage, and standard-flow and high-flow models, as well as a variety of calibrations. Single-stage models are recommended for performance applications over their two-stage brethren because they have one less restriction and only open once. Standard-flow valves are used in all applications except the Pro Series HP carburetors, and those using alcohol. Alcohol use requires the high-flow valve, due to the greater volume of fuel that's required in these applications.

You can check the calibration of a power valve by looking at its part number. The last two numbers after the hyphen indicate the vacuum reading at which the power valve will open. For example, if the part number reads 125-85, that power valve will open when engine vacuum drops to 8.5 inches of mercury. Power valves with just two digits after the hyphen are standard flow models. Those with a "1" immediately after the hyphen are high-flow units.

Power valve selection entails connecting an accurate vacuum gauge to a port below the throttle plates on the carburetor or to a tee in a vacuum fitting on the intake manifold. Determining which power valve is best-suited to an application depends on whether the engine has high (15+ inches) or low (less than 15 inches) vacuum at idle.

Edelbrock's Performer RPM Q-Jet carburetor offers the crisp throttle response of triple venturis and provides enough "juice" for 500+ horsepower.

Power valve selection impacts performance and fuel economy. The number stamped into the hex of the valve indicates its opening point in inches of engine vacuum. This particular valve is marked "65," so it opens at 6.5 inches of vacuum.

Here's a side-by-side comparison of two high-performance intake manifolds—rectangular on top and oval on the bottom. Oval-port manifolds are best for most street applications, while rectangular ports are for the racing set.

Engines with high manifold vacuum work best with the stock power valve. Engines with low manifold vacuum, like those with high overlap cams, require a selection technique based on whether the engine is backed up by a manual or automatic transmission.

If the vehicle uses a manual transmission, check the vacuum at idle when the engine is at normal operating temperature. If an automatic transmission is used, check the vacuum when the transmission is in Drive and the engine is thoroughly warmed. Then take the indicated vacuum reading, divide it in half, and select a power valve with that number rating. For example, if indicated vacuum is 14 inches, divide 14 by two, which equals seven. Then install a power valve with a rating of seven.

Intake Manifolds

Two types of intake manifolds are used on big blocks: wet and dry. As their names suggest, wet manifolds have the "wet" air/fuel mixture traveling through them. As expected, this group relies on a carburetor or throttle body to feed the engine. On the other hand, dry manifolds have no fuel flowing through them, only air. This type of manifold is used with port fuel injection systems. In this section, we'll focus on wet manifolds. However, the information presented here does apply to the intake manifolds used for throttle bodies, as well as carburetors (though not to dry-type port fuel-injected systems).

Most intake manifolds for the Chevy big block can be categorized into one of two types: dual-plane or single-plane. Although both types use a plenum and runners to direct fuel to the cylinder heads, they're designed for different purposes. Dual-plane manifolds willingly trade away some high rpm power to enhance engine performance at low- and mid-rpm. Single-plane manifolds are basically the opposite—they sacrifice some low-rpm power for better mid- and high-rpm punch. To achieve these goals, the plenums and runners of each type of manifold are significantly different.

Dual-Plane

Depending upon how plenum and runner volumes and lengths are juggled, dual-plane manifolds can be suitable for towing and RV use, as well as high-performance street and limited racing use. If your vehicle uses a low numerical axle ratio (for example, 3.08:1) and a transmission with one or two overdrive ratios, this type of gearing should put you in the fat part of a dual-plane manifold's power curve. The longer, smaller volume runners in dual-plane manifolds keep air velocity high at low- and mid-rpm, but restrict flow at high rpm.

We also have to consider that carburetor venturis work in response to engine vacuum. The higher the vacuum, the stronger the vacuum signal at the venturis. The stronger the vacuum signal, the greater the inertia of the air/fuel mixture. And the greater the inertia, the better throttle response.

To have as strong a vacuum signal as possible, the plenum of a dual-plane manifold is divided. Viewed from overhead, the two planes of a dual-plane manifold looks like two "Hs" nestled inside one another. With this configuration, four cylinders draw on just two carburetor barrels: one primary and one secondary. Furthermore, the runners are arranged two to each cylinder bank. This causes an intake pulse to act on alternating sides of the carburetor every 180 degrees of crankshaft rotation.

As engine rpm reaches a relatively high level, the constraints of a divided plenum become apparent. Since the four cylinders are only able to draw from two carburetor venturis, airflow through the venturis reaches its maximum fairly early on, strangling the engine. Also, since four of the eight runners are lower than the other for packaging reasons, they approach the cylinder head intake ports at a considerable angle, further reducing breathing capacity.

In spite of these drawbacks, a properly designed dual-plane manifold is best for most street applications because it produces the most power and torque in the rpm range that's typical for street and marine use—usually 1,500–6,500 rpm. It's also a good choice for a drag racing vehicle that weighs over 3,500 pounds with an automatic transmission.

Single-Plane

Single-plane manifolds have a plenum that's open to all four carburetor venturis and all eight runners.

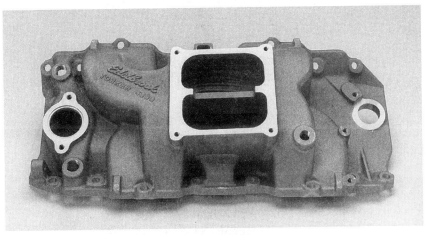

This Edelbrock Torker 2-R 4500 has been around since the early 1970s for good reason—it works well. Engineered for racing applications, this dual-plane design provides its best stuff from 3,500–8,500 rpm. *Edelbrock*

This Dart 4500 Series manifold is made for 525-cubic-inch and larger engines and is designed to be ported prior to installation. This is true of a number of aftermarket intake manifolds designed for racing engines. You can port your own manifold following the directions outlined in the text.

This promotes high-rpm power at the expense of low-rpm torque.

The runners in a modern, single-plane manifold are straighter than those in a dual-plane manifold. This reduces the turns that the air/fuel mixture has to make on its way to the cylinder head ports, increasing power. Also, since the runners don't have to pass over and under each other as they do in a dual-plane manifold, the entry angle to the cylinder head ports can be more optimal. Single-plane manifolds also have a greater volume compared to dual-plane manifolds because all the runners are tied to the open plenum as well as each other. This serves to increase flow at high rpm, but it also damps the vacuum signal that occurs as the intake valve closes, reducing low-rpm power and tractability.

Single-plane manifolds that work well on the street have an rpm range of about 2,500-7,500 rpm. Since big-block Chevys have so much bottom-end torque, a manifold like this could prove beneficial in a light vehicle that has trouble with traction from low speed, while having the bonus of significantly more top-end punch. Single-plane manifolds that are more suited to racing use have an operating range from 3,500 to 8,500 rpm. Although these manifolds could be used for a street vehicle, they're not the best choice for daily drivers, because they develop their power too far up the rpm scale. At low rpm, the air/fuel mixture tends to separate, causing hesitation, surging, and overall poor driveability.

Tunnel Ram

Tunnel ram manifolds are intended for serious street or racing use. When designed for two four-barrel carburetors, they provide the straightest path possible for the air/fuel mixture. Straight runners provide a direct path to the intake port, helping to "ram" the air/fuel mixture against the intake valves, increasing power. The volume of the plenum, along with the length and diameter of the runners, dictate the rpm range where these manifolds produce the most power. Long, small-volume runners produce power at a lower rpm range while short, high-volume runners push the power curve higher.

Street-style tunnel rams are usually outfitted with vacuum secondary 600-cfm carburetors because they provide the best compromise between performance and driveability. For Pro-Street fans, you might be able to get away with 750-cfm carbs with vacuum secondaries provided you're running a manual transmission with no overdrive ratios, use a 4.56:1 (or higher, numerically) rear axle ratio, and have the cam matched to the intake system.

Tunnel rams designed for racing most often use 4500 series Holley Dominators. This combination doesn't make much power below 4,500 rpm but will allow your engine to wind to 10,000 rpm, as long as it has the right parts and is properly assembled.

When selecting a street-style tunnel ram, be sure that it has provisions for power brakes if that's what your vehicle uses. Also be aware that tunnel rams don't have enough room to clear HEI distributors, so you'll have to use a small-bodied distributor, like the early GM point-type, ACCEL Super Stock, or MSD Pro-Billet. And because a tunnel ram is so tall, keep in mind that the hood on your car or truck will need to be cut out to clear it.

Carburetor Spacers and Adapters

Carburetor spacers are intended to give dual-plane intake manifolds a taste of what it would be like to be a single-plane intake manifold and vice versa.

If a single-hole spacer is used on a dual-plane manifold, its depth acts as a common plenum, just as with a single-plane manifold. And like a single-plane manifold, all cylinders get to draw from all the carburetor barrels.

When using a carburetor spacer, underhood clearance is usually at a premium, so a spacer with the optimum height may not fit without some hood modifications. And since a spacer adds to plenum volume, sometimes it's necessary to increase the jetting by a size or two to compensate for the somewhat weaker vacuum signal at the carburetor boosters. For this same reason, a greater accelerator pump shot may be required to ensure throttle response doesn't diminish.

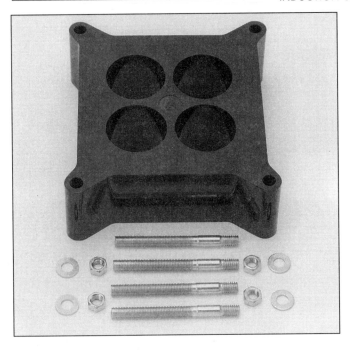 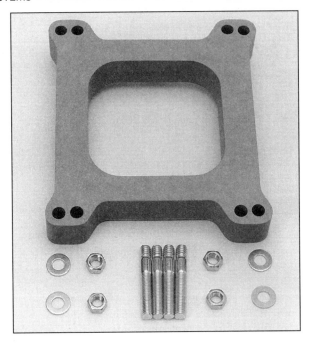

Carburetor spacers are a way of fine tuning a carburetor/intake manifold combination. Four hole spacers (left) strengthen throttle response of single plane manifolds, while single hole spacers (right) add top end punch to dual plane manifolds. *Edelbrock*

This can increase engine performance at higher rpm, but the effect depends on the height of the spacer, the characteristics of the particular manifold and carburetor (or throttle body injection unit) being used, and cylinder size. Also, you may lose a little low- rpm torque in the trade-off.

Four-hole spacers are also available and are intended for single-plane manifolds. Their mission is to strengthen the signal from each carburetor barrel so the manifold acts a little like a dual-plane manifold. This provides better low-end throttle response and torque, but it may take something away farther up the rpm scale.

Spacers also smooth the airflow from the carburetor to the intake runners by providing more room for the air/fuel mixture to turn as it exits the carburetor and enters the runners. This helps minimize the volume of air/fuel mixture that bounces off the plenum floor. It's especially important with dual-plane manifolds because of the decreased distance between the uppermost plenum floor and the bottom of the carburetor or throttle body.

Although carburetor spacers won't perform miracles, they are an effective tuning aid to get a few more horsepower out of your engine. Spacers vary in height from about 1/2 to 2 inches. Adjusting carburetor height by using different spacers or thick carburetor base gaskets and then testing will tell you what combination works best. Usually, the taller the spacer, the greater the shift in engine performance.

To ensure the best performance from a spacer, bolt it to the intake manifold and carefully grind or file it away until it matches the opening in the intake manifold perfectly. If the spacer tapers from the carburetor to the manifold, make the taper as gradual as possible to avoid any turbulence. And make sure that it clears the throttle blades at every throttle position, from idle to wide open.

Spacers are available from aftermarket suppliers such as Edelbrock and Moroso and are made from aluminum, phenolic plastic, or a wood fiber laminate. Since keeping the fuel temperature down to a manageable level always seems to be a problem with a high-performance engine, you may want to give preference to the wood fiber laminate or phenolic plastic spacers. Alternately, depend-ing upon the availability for your particular situation, you could use a plastic spacer coupled with an aluminum spacer, or a heat insulating gasket with an aluminum spacer.

Factory Intake Manifolds

If you had to divide the performance characteristics for factory intake manifolds into two categories, you could say that cast-iron intake manifolds were intended for low-performance applications, while most aluminum intake manifolds were fitted to high-performance engines.

Factory intake manifolds can be of either high- or low-rise design. High-rise designs provide more power thanks to their greater plenum volume. Low-rise designs were used where hood clearance was a problem, and although these manifolds may not produce as much top-end power as the high-rise manifolds, a number of them work well in street high-performance applications.

All factory big-block intakes were of the dual-plane design with the two planes separated by a divider. In most manifolds, this plenum divider is even with the carburetor mounting flange to provide good

HIGH PERFORMANCE FACTORY INTAKE MANIFOLDS

Port Type	Casting #	Carburetor Used	Original Engine Size	Material
Oval	3866948	Holley	396, 427	Cast Iron
Rectangular	3866963	Holley	396	Aluminum
Oval	3883948	Rochester	396, 427	Cast Iron
Rectangular	3885069	Holley	396, 427	Aluminum
Rectangular	3886093	Holley	427	Aluminum
Oval	3919849	Rochester	427	Aluminum
Oval	3931067	Rochester	396, 427	Cast Iron
Rectangular	3933163 [1]	Holley	396, 427	Aluminum
Rectangular	3933198	Holley	427	Aluminum
Oval	3937793	Rochester	427	Aluminum
Oval	3947801	Rochester	427	Aluminum
Oval	3955287	Rochester	454	Cast Iron
Rectangular	3963569	Holley	402, 454	Aluminum
Oval	3967474	Holley	454	Aluminum
Oval	3969802	Holley	454	Cast Iron
Rectangular	6269318	Holley	396, 427	Aluminum

[1] Available new from GM Dealers

This Weiand Team G manifold is slanted toward race rats. Designed to produce power from 2,500–8,200 rpm, this single-plane manifold requires high numerical gearing to perform at its best. *Weiand*

low-end power. However, in some of the high-performance manifolds, this divider was lower than the carburetor mounting flange, which helped increase top-end power, though it gave away some at lower rpm.

Some of the more desirable factory manifolds for high-performance applications—both low-rise and high-rise—are listed above.

Aftermarket Intake Manifolds

The aftermarket offers numerous types of intake manifolds—single quad, dual quad, single-plane, dual-plane, and tunnel ram. But no matter what type of intake manifold is used, it must be compatible with the carburetor(s) and camshaft being used, as well as the intended use of the engine.

Most rat motors run very well with a single four-barrel carburetor.

Here's the ticket for Pro Street and hot marine engines—Edelbrock's Street Tunnel Ram 2-O. It fits oval port heads and uses two 600 cfm carbs. Just remember, tunnel ram manifolds give up a considerable amount of low-rpm torque to provide high-rpm power. This manifold performs best from 3,500 to 7,500 rpm. *Edelbrock*

This Performer RPM manifold (#3261) is manufactured for marine use. All surfaces have a special finish that protect against corrosion from both salt and fresh water. *Edelbrock*

This Holley street performance manifold (#300-42) uses a dual-plane design engineered for low to mid-rpm performance. Its horsepower peak occurs at 5,200 rpm. *Holley*

This high-rise tunnel ram, which Weiand calls its "High Ram," is for a serious street/strip or racing engine. Designed for use with 600–850 cfm carbs, its power band runs from 2,500–7,800 rpm. *Weiand*

This is Holley's Street Dominator. Its low-rise single plane design strikes a balance between dual plane and more traditional single-plane manifolds—power comes in from idle-to-4,800 rpm. *Holley*

Weiand's Action Plus manifolds for rats use a dual-plane design for power from just above idle to about 6,500 rpm. For street use, a 600–750 cfm carb with vacuum secondaries works best. *Weiand*

AFTERMARKET INTAKE MANIFOLDS

Mfr.	Part #	Port Shape	Type	Operating Range (RPM)	Carburetor or EFI System	Notes
Brodix	HV 2000 HV 2006 (Tall Decks)	Rect.	Single-plane	3500-7500	Standard Holley flange	Racing. Fits Brodix and other standard aftermarket cast iron heads.
Brodix	HV 2001 HV 2005 (Tall Decks)	Rect.	Single-plane	3500-7500	Holley Dominator	Racing. Fits Brodix and other standard aftermarket cast iron heads.
Brodix	HV 2007	Oval	Single-plane	3500-7500	Standard Holley flange	Pro-street and racing
Brodix	HV 2008	Oval	Single-plane	3500-7500	Holley Dominator	Racing
Edelbrock	2161 (w/o EGR) 3761 (w/EGR)	Oval	Dual-plane	Idle-5500	Stock carb or 600-795cfm Performer Q-Jet	Street performance. Street legal. Matched camshaft kit available.
Edelbrock	7161	Oval	Dual-plane high-rise	1500-6500	750cfm Performer Q-Jet or 850cfm Holley double pumper	Street high performance. Not emissions certified. No provision for exhaust heated chokes. Matched camshaft kit available.
Edelbrock	7163	Rect.	Dual-plane high-rise	1500-6500	750cfm Performer Q-Jet or 850cfm Holley double pumper	Street high performance. Not emissions certified. No provision for exhaust heated chokes. Matched camshaft kit available.
Edelbrock	7164	Oval	Dual-plane high-rise	1500-6500	850cfm Performer Q-Jet	Street high performance. Not emissions certified. No provision for hot air style chokes.
Edelbrock	3764	Oval	Dual-plane	Idle-5500	Throttle Body Injection (TBI)	Street performance for 1987-90 454s with TBI. Street legal. Matched camshaft kit available.
Edelbrock	5061	Oval	Single-plane high-rise	2500-6500	750cfm Performer Q-Jet	Street high performance. Not emissions certified. Must use manual or electric choke carburetor. Matched camshaft kit available.
Edelbrock	5420	Oval or Rect.	Single-plane high-rise	1500-6000	Two 600cfm Performer Q-Jets	Street high performance. Not emissions certified. Matched camshaft kit available.

AFTERMARKET INTAKE MANIFOLDS (Cont'd)

Mfr.	Part #	Port Shape	Type	Operating Range (RPM)	Carburetor or EFI System	Notes
Edelbrock	2746	Rect.	Single-plane high-rise	3500-8500	Holley 4500 series carb	Racing use. Not emissions certified. Will not cover Bow Tie head intake ports.
Edelbrock	7115	Oval	Single-plane, street tunnel ram	3500-7500	Two 600cfm Performer Q-Jets	Pro Street or marine. Matched camshaft kit available.
Edelbrock	7075	Rect.	Single-plane tunnel ram	4500-10000	Two 4500 series Holley carbs	Track & marine racing and ski boats.
Edelbrock	2904 (Oval) 2902 (Rect.)	Oval or Rect.	Single-plane high-rise	3000-7500	850cfm Holley	Drag racing. Engines 502ci or less. #2902 will fit high-port Bow Tie heads #14044862.
Edelbrock	2909	Oval	Single-plane high-rise	3000-7500	One 4500 series Holley or standard flange Holley double-pumper	Drag racing and marine use. Fits stock, Bow Tie, Dart & Brodix heads.
Edelbrock	2907	Rect.	Single-plane high-rise	3500-8500	One 4500 series Holley or standard flange Holley double-pumper	Drag racing and marine use. Fits stock, Bow Tie, Dart & Brodix heads.
Edelbrock	2911	Rect.	Single-plane high-rise	3500-8500	One 4500 series Holley or standard flange Holley double-pumper	Drag racing and marine use with tall deck blocks. Fits stock, Bow Tie, Dart & Brodix heads.
Holley	300-42	Oval	Dual-plane	Idle-5200	4150 or 4160 series Holley carb.	Street performance. Non-emissions certified. No EGR provision.
Holley	300-3	Oval	Single-plane	Idle-4800	600-850cfm Holley w/vacuum secondaries	Street performance. 50-State street legal. EGR provision. Exhaust heat crossover provision.
Holley	300-4 (Oval) 300-5 (Rect.)	Oval or Rect.	Single-plane high rise	4500-8500	850-950cfm Holley w/ mechanical secondaries or 950cfm Holley with vacuum secondaries	Drag racing. No EGR or exhaust heat crossover provided.

AFTERMARKET INTAKE MANIFOLDS (Cont'd)

Mfr.	Part #	Port Shape	Type	Operating Range (RPM)	Carburetor or EFI System	Notes
Holley	300-45 w/ 300-206	Rect.	Single-plane tunnel ram	6500-10000	Two 4500 series Holleys	Drag racing. Runner length optimized for 8500+ rpm.
Weiand	8005	Oval	Dual-plane	Idle-6500	Stock Q-Jet or 600-750cfm carb w/ vac secondaries. Competition use: 700-850cfm double pumper.	Street/Strip performance. Matched camshaft kit available.
Weiand	8013	Oval	Dual-plane	Idle-6500	Street use: 600-750cfm carb w/ vac secondaries. Competition use: 700-850cfm double pumper.	Street/Strip performance. Matched camshaft kit available. Will fit tall deck blocks when used with spacer kit.
Weiand	8017	Oval (peanut)	Dual-plane	Idle-6000	Street use: stock Q-Jet Non-emission use: 600-750cfm carb w/ vac secondaries. Marine use: replaces stock MerCruiser manifold	Street & marine performance.
Weiand	7544 (Oval) 7513 (Rect.)	Oval or Rect.	Single-plane high-rise	1500-7000	Street use: 600-750cfm carb w/ vac secondaries. Competition use: 700-850cfm double pumper.	Street/Strip performance. Matched camshaft kit available. Will fit tall deck blocks when used with spacer kit.
Weiand	8018	Rect.	Dual-plane high-rise	Idle-7000	Street use: 650-750cfm carb w/ vac secondaries or double pumper Competition use: 700-850cfm double pumper.	Street/Strip & marine performance. Will fit tall deck blocks when used with spacer kit.

AFTERMARKET INTAKE MANIFOLDS (Cont'd)

Mfr.	Part #	Port Shape	Type	Operating Range (RPM)	Carburetor or EFI System	Notes
Weiand	8019	Oval	Dual-plane high-rise	Idle-7000	Street use: 650-750cfm carb w/ vac secondaries or double pumper Competition use: 700-850cfm double pumper.	Street/Strip & marine performance. Will fit tall deck blocks when used with spacer kit.
Weiand	7521	Rect.	Single-plane high-rise	2500-8000	750-850cfm double pumper carb w/square bore.	Drag & oval track racing. #7526 fits tall deck blocks.
Weiand	7522	Rect.	Single-plane high-rise	2800-8500	Use w/Holley 4500 series carb.	Drag & oval track racing. #7527 fits tall deck blocks.
Weiand	7523	Oval	Single-plane high-rise	2500-7900	750-850cfm double pumper carb w/square bore.	Drag & oval track racing. #7528 fits tall deck blocks.
Weiand	7524	Oval	Single-plane high-rise	2800-8300	Use w/Holley 4500 series carb.	Drag & oval track racing. #7529 fits tall deck blocks.
Weiand	3981 (Oval) 3985 (Rect.)	Oval or Rect.	Single-plane tunnel ram.	2500-7800	Use w/ 750-850cfm double pumper carb.	Street/Strip high performance. Tunnel ram design. Will fit tall deck block with proper spacers. HEI ignition will not clear.
Weiand	1981 (Oval) 1985 (Rect.)	Oval or Rect.	Single-plane Tunnel ram.	2500-7800	Street use: Two 600-700cfm performance or double pumper carbs. Track use: Two 650-850cfm double pumper carbs.	Street/Strip high performance. Tunnel ram design. Will fit tall deck block with proper spacers. HEI ignition will not clear.

AFTERMARKET INTAKE MANIFOLDS (Cont'd)

Mfr.	Part #	Port Shape	Type	Operating Range (RPM)	Carburetor or EFI System	Notes
Weiand	1980 (Oval) 1983 (Rect.)	Oval or Rect.	Single-plane Tunnel ram.	3600-9000	Street use: Two 650-750cfm performance or double pumper carbs. Track use: Two 750-850cfm double pumper carbs.	Street/Strip high performance. Tunnel ram design. Will fit tall deck block with proper spacers. HEI ignition will not clear.
Weiand	1952	Rect.	Single-plane Tunnel ram.	3000-10000	Use w/ Enderle, Hilborn, Kinsler or other fuel injection system.	Race only. Tunnel ram design. Will fit tall deck block with proper spacers. HEI ignition will not clear.
World Products	6301	Oval	Dual-Plane high-rise	1500-6500	Holley 4150 or 4160	Not emissions certified. Has provisions for direct port nitrous nozzles.
World Products	6302	Rect.	Dual-Plane high-rise	1500-6500	Holley 4150 or 4160	Not emissions certified. Has provisions for direct port nitrous nozzles.

Using a single carburetor also minimizes the time and effort required to dial-in an engine so that it runs properly. For those of you who desire something more exotic, a dual-quad manifold may be for you. With a dual-quad system, the total carburetor airflow from the two four-barrels can be greater than what you'd need from a single four-barrel. That's because the signal strength of eight smaller venturis is stronger than four larger ones in a single four-barrel carb. Dual vacuum-secondary 600-cfm carbs will provide both eye-popping performance and excellent throttle response when mated with a hot big block.

If you intend to use the engine in an emissions-controlled city or state, you also need to consider if the manifold has a provision for mounting an EGR valve. And keep in mind that if the cylinder heads on your engine have raised or symmetrical intake ports, an appropriate aftermarket intake manifold is required.

Listed nearby are some of the intake manifolds offered by the aftermarket. Compare the types that produce power in the rpm range you use your engine most, then look at the features each manifold offers. Those with matching camshaft kits are the easiest to tune once you get your engine together, but that might not be what you're looking for if you have a few successful engine "builds" under your belt. Keep in mind that most manifolds listed here are for normal "short-deck" blocks. To use these manifolds on a "tall-deck" block requires the use of intake manifold spacers to compensate for the increased distance between the cylinder heads on these blocks. Intake manifold spacers are available from Edelbrock and Weiand.

Intake Manifold Modifications

Before laying out your hard-earned money, consider what you're going to do or have done with the manifold. Consider a racing engine. Often, if you're going to take an intake manifold to a professional porter, they'll prefer using an intake manifold that's smaller than they want the end product to be because smaller manifolds have more material that porters can shape as they see fit. The object of this exercise is to get the same flow out of the smaller manifold so horsepower stays the same without sacrificing torque like a larger runner manifold would. To get the same results with a large-port intake manifold may require welding or the addition of epoxy in the right places before any porting work can begin. This situation varies by case, so talk to your porter before you buy.

Also be aware that some racing intake manifolds, like the Dart 4500, require porting before installation. On the other hand, CNC machined intake manifolds are designed to be installed as is. So find these things out before you buy.

No matter what the case, there are some things a careful amateur can do to an intake manifold to increase its performance dividends. By paying attention to areas that will disturb airflow, such as acute turns around a corner, increases in flow and performance can be realized.

To accomplish these modifications, you'll need a grinder such as a Dremel, along with some 60-grit sanding cones and a mandrel on which to mount them. Numerous companies offer the necessary sanding cones as

The walls that divide the port runners should be laid back about 15 to 20 degrees from vertical and have a gentle radius on their leading edge to keep the fuel suspended in the air. Also, the plenum floor should be free of any casting flash that could impede airflow through the manifold. When cleaning the manifold up, give it a fairly rough finish (about 150-grit) to prevent fuel from settling on the plenum floor.

part of a porting kit, which can be a worthwhile investment if you don't have an abrasive supply company nearby. Although carbide cutters sprayed with WD-40 can cut your modification time, they can also do a lot of damage quickly. So unless you have experience with these cutters (which aren't cheap), stick to the sanding cones. To protect yourself, safety glasses and a suitable dust mask are a must. Ear protection is a good idea, as well.

Although dual-plane manifolds are somewhat harder to modify than single-plane manifolds, because of their tighter port radii, worthwhile modifications can be accomplished by a patient and careful amateur. However, it's important to note that just hogging out the ports isn't the way to performance. Excessively large ports can be a detriment, even in a racing engine where engine response is key. Instead, you need to study the ports in your particular manifold and reduce the obstacles to airflow. By working in this manner, without increasing port volume substantially, the vacuum signal at the carburetor venturis remains nearly the same. And this minimizes any negative effects to throttle response.

Plenum and Runners

After the air and fuel pass through the throttle plates into the manifold, the air tends to swirl a bit

then hug the top of the intake runners, but a good portion of the fuel decides it's not along for the ride and drops to the bottom of the plenum. The sharp edges and turns where the carburetor mounting flange meets the intake runners contribute to this problem. Consequently, smoothing and careful blending of this area will result in measurable power gains.

As air flows into the manifold plenum, it has to make a hard turn to enter the manifold ports. And air prefers to be coaxed gradually to change its direction. By rounding the edges where the carburetor mounting flange meets with the ports, you'll ease the transition of the air from the plenum into the ports.

Turning your attention to the floor and sides of the plenum, make sure it blends smoothly into the bottom and sides of the ports. Hard edges, casting flash, and the like will cause the airflow within the plenum to be turbulent, which will impede airflow. Work to make any changes between the two as gradual as possible.

The divider between port pairs presents an opportunity for improve-

The carburetor mounting flange deserves some attention as well. Clean up any casting flash and put a gradual radius where the vertical portion of the mounting flange meets the top of the intake runners.

ment as well. If these dividers are vertical, angle them about 15 to 20 degrees to increase airflow. And put a gentle radius on their edges to minimize turbulence.

Port Matching

Considering the fact that it's difficult to perfectly match the intake manifold ports to the cylinder head intake ports, you're better off having the intake ports slightly smaller than the ports in the head. This will help

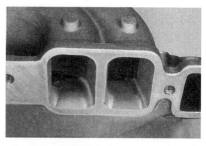

This Dart intake manifold's ports were professionally matched to the cylinder heads.

prevent a backwash of the air/fuel mixture into the manifold. However, if the ports in the head are smaller than those in the intake manifold, the airflow will have to "step" over the port edge to get into the head. This will change the path of the airflow, effectively reducing port size and significantly lowering flow. So be sure to avoid this situation as you're working to match the ports.

Depending upon what you want to do with the engine and how the parts have been manufactured, there are three ways to proceed with port matching, one slightly more involved than the other two. The first way uses a cardboard template to match the ports. Since this "template matching" method prevents removing excessive amounts of port material, thereby keeping flow velocity high, it's all that's really necessary for a street or marine high-performance application. The second way uses the intake manifold gasket as a template to match the ports. This "gasket matching" method may be the easiest and is used when the heads or intake manifold have been matched to a particular gasket by their manufacturer. The third process is more involved and requires marking the heads, installing them on the block (along with the intake manifold), and then transcribing those lines onto the manifold. This "race match" method is the most accurate way of matching the ports and should be used for racing applications.

To do the matching, you'll need a die grinder or Dremel Moto-Tool outfitted with a mandrel and some 60-grit sanding cones. As always, proper eye and ear protection is a must, as is a good dust respirator.

Template and Gasket Match Methods

To make the template, lay an intake manifold gasket over a length of paperboard from a cereal box. Use a sharp pencil to transfer the outline of the gasket, the intake ports, and the bolt holes onto the cardboard. Now remove the gasket and use an X-acto knife to cut the outline of the gasket and the bolt holes. Cut the bolt holes about 1/4 inch smaller than the outline indicates, so they'll fit snugly around the manifold bolts. But don't cut the ports out just yet.

Lay the template against the cylinder head and secure it with some 1/2-inch long x 3/8-inch diameter bolts run in finger tight. Using the port outlines you drew earlier strictly for guidance, slip the knife through the paperboard about 1/2 inch inboard of one of the lines then cut to the port wall. Follow the port wall around until you've cut the image of the port perfectly. Do the same for the remaining ports, then mark the template as to whether it fits the left or right cylinder head.

Clean the mating surfaces of the intake manifold with carb cleaner, then coat the area around each port with machinist's dye or a permanent marker. Now take six intake manifold bolts and wrap their upper half with about eight turns of masking tape. The masking tape will help center the bolts in the manifold. Next, place the template against the proper side of the manifold. Then slip the manifold bolts through the top side of the manifold and through the template. The template shouldn't move around. If it does, you may need more tape on the bolts to hold it in place. With the template secured, scribe the outline of the ports onto the manifold.

Now comes the fun part—grinding away the extra material. Just remember, stay inside the lines—don't grind them away or the port will be too large. To make a gradual transition from the newly enlarged area, blend it about 3/4 inch into the port. Don't go any farther than this or you may change the flow characteristics of the manifold.

The gasket match method is very similar to the template match method, it merely uses the intake

When performing either a gasket or a template match, you need to ensure the gasket (or template) is centered. Wrapping masking tape around some bolts helps to keep the gasket registered to the ports.

manifold gasket instead of the template. Just be sure the gasket is aligned with the bolt holes before you scribe the lines.

Race Match Method

Before you begin the actual "matching" process, your heads have to be mounted on your block. Also, the head gaskets you plan on using must be in place and the cylinder head bolts installed and torqued to specifications. All this work is necessary if you plan on matching the ports as closely as possible, which is what's necessary for a serious racing effort. Using your heads and block helps account for any differences in height that may have occurred as a result of decking the block or milling the heads.

After cleaning the port mating surfaces with carburetor cleaner, coat the area around each port with machinist's blue or a black permanent marker. Using a small straight edge, carry the lines of the port walls up to the top of the heads first using the marker, then a scribe. Likewise, use the straight edge to carry the lines of the port roof to the ends of the heads. These lines will provide the coordinates of where the cylinder head ports are when you install the intake manifold. And that's the next step.

With all four intake manifold gaskets in position (front, rear, and sides), carefully lower the manifold into place. Secure it by installing the manifold bolts and torquing them to specifications. Now run the marker across the tops of the ports where they meet the heads, then carry the port lines from the heads onto the manifold using a scribe. Do the same thing for lines that indicate the top edges of the ports, then remove the

To use the race-match method, extend the port lines to areas that are visible when the manifold is installed on the engine.

manifold. With the manifold off, transfer the lines from the top side of the ports to the cylinder head side of the manifold flange.

Now you'll need to determine how far away the bottom of the port is from the top of the port, using a set of calipers. Measure the height of each port on the heads and transfer these dimensions over to their respective ports on the manifold.

Once you have the port coordinates for the head transferred to the intake manifold, all that remains is to carefully grind the excess material away. Remember to stay inside the lines and limit your blending to about 3/4 inch into the ports.

Electronic Fuel Injection

Electronic fuel injection systems offer a number of advantages over carburetors, including better engine response, driveability, and fuel economy. When you couple these advantages with lower emissions, you'll understand why fuel injection has a lot going for it. One disadvantage of some street fuel injection systems, though, is that they don't produce as much peak power as a four-barrel carburetor coupled with a single-plane intake manifold. Another disadvantage is cost; there's a considerable price differential between electronic fuel injection and carburetion.

However, electronic fuel injection has a distinct advantage, because it can be tuned much more precisely than a carburetor, so you can have the best of both worlds—eye-popping performance on a race track, along with smooth, effortless driveability for street use. If you would attempt to do this with a carburetor, there are so many compromises that would need to be made because of the way carburetors meter fuel into the engine that you'd be extremely fortunate to meet these conflicting goals. And that's the beauty of electronic fuel injection.

Two types of fuel injection have been used or are available for the big block: electronic and mechanical. Electronic fuel injection systems for the big-block Chevy come in two varieties: throttle body injection (TBI) and port fuel injection (PFI).

Throttle Body Injection (TBI)

Throttle body injection (TBI) systems use what is essentially an empty carburetor (throttle) body atop of which two fuel injectors are mounted. Fuel is supplied constantly to the throttle body by an in-tank fuel pump, which pressurizes the fuel to 9–13 psi. Fuel that isn't used by the injectors is returned to the fuel tank. This ensures a supply of relatively cool fuel is available to the injectors at all times. The injectors spray fuel down through the venturis, as directed by the vehicle's electronic control module (ECM). The ECM calculates how much fuel should be injected, based on throttle opening, exhaust oxygen content, coolant temperature, engine load, engine speed,

vehicle speed, and altitude. TBI systems have a number of benefits over carburetors, such as improved cold weather starting, better fuel efficiency, and lower exhaust emissions.

Port Fuel Injection (PFI)

Port fuel injection (PFI) systems use the same basic inputs as a TBI system, just the method of fuel delivery is different. Instead of using two or four injectors mounted on a throttle body, a separate injector is used for each cylinder. These injectors are located in the intake manifold, just above each cylinder head intake port and are positioned so they spray fuel toward the backside of each intake valve. Another difference between TBI and PFI systems is fuel pressure. While TBI systems run low fuel pressure (9–13 psi), PFI systems require more fuel pressure, on the order of 43–45 psi.

PFI systems offer a number of advantages over TBI systems, including greater power and torque, better fuel efficiency, and improved throttle response.

System Components

Electronic fuel injection (EFI) systems require a number of components to do their job properly.

Fuel Injectors

A fuel injector is an electrical solenoid that controls fuel flow into the intake port. The finely atomized mist of fuel it delivers is one of the primary reasons a fuel-injection system can offer better driveability, mileage, and performance compared to carburetors.

Throttle Body

If you can picture a carburetor that doesn't allow fuel to flow, just air, you'll understand the job of the throttle body. Much like the throttle valves in a carburetor, the throttle body controls airflow into the intake manifold. The larger the throttle valves, the more air it can flow. Some throttle bodies resemble a carburetor, and like a carburetor, are mounted with their bores in a vertical position. Although systems that use this type of throttle body can be used in both low- and high-performance applications, they're rather tall, possibly entailing some hood modifications.

The other type of throttle body looks like a block of aluminum with an oval "mouth" to allow air to enter. This type of throttle body is mounted with its bores in a horizontal position and has internal passages so idle speed can be controlled via an idle air control (IAC) motor. This type of mounting lends itself to a shorter "packaging" height—an important consideration where underhood space is at a premium.

Plenum and Manifold

The plenum and manifold work together to hold and route air to the cylinders. Generally speaking, the larger the plenum, the greater the power output. The manifold keeps the velocity of the inlet air high as it guides it to the intake ports.

Electronic Control Module (ECM)

Electronic control module (ECM) used to be the factory's name for the computer that controlled all the operations of the emissions system, including the fuel-injection system. Nowadays, since this computer also controls transmission shift points and shift feel, the factory calls it the powertrain control module, or PCM, for short. To

Kinsler Fuel Injection offers a number of different fuel systems. This mechanical system uses a four-barrel throttle body mounted on a single plane high rise manifold. One fuel injector feeds each cylinder. *Kinsler Fuel Injection*

confuse matters further, aftermarket companies call this computer the electronic control unit (ECU).

Whatever the name, all these computers control the operation of the fuel-injection system. Inside the computer are calibration maps. These maps provide specific values on how much fuel and ignition timing to use under certain circumstances. Based on input from the oxygen sensor, throttle position sensor, coolant temperature sensor, MAP sensor, and engine rpm, the computer "looks up" the proper value from the calibration maps and adjusts the "on" time of the fuel injectors accordingly. These adjustments occur many times a second, to ensure optimum performance.

Throttle Position Sensor (TPS)

If you've ever played with slot cars, you have a good understanding of what a throttle position sensor (TPS) is and how it operates. The TPS is mounted on the end of the throttle valve shaft in the throttle body and is fed a voltage signal from the computer. As the throttle shaft opens (you squeeze the throttle), a wiper within the sensor moves, decreasing resistance (and increasing speed). The amount of voltage that's returned to the ECM indicates throttle position.

Manifold Absolute Pressure (MAP) Sensor

The manifold absolute pressure (MAP) sensor provides a way of measuring engine load.

Idle Air Control (IAC)

The idle air control (IAC) motor is what controls engine idle speed in an EFI system. Essentially an electric motor with a pointed tip, called a pintle, the IAC controls the amount of air that enters the engine via the throttle body based on commands from the ECM. The more the pintle moves away from its seat within the throttle body, the more air that's admitted to the engine and the more engine speed rises.

Coolant Temperature Sensor (CTS)

The coolant temperature sensor (CTS) provides information about engine coolant temperature to the ECM. This information is used by the ECM to determine if the fuel injection system should be in open or closed loop operation (whether it should use input from the oxygen sensor or not).

Oxygen Sensor

The oxygen (O2) sensor provides data to the ECM about how rich or lean the engine is running. It's usually positioned at a common point in the exhaust stream for all (or just one bank of) cylinders. As the exhaust gasses pass over the sensor, the elements within the sensor put out a voltage signal that varies based on the amount of oxygen flowing over it. The less oxygen in the exhaust, the richer the air/fuel mixture. Conversely, when there's more oxygen in the exhaust, the leaner the air/fuel mixture. Based primarily on the input from the O2 sensor, the ECM adjusts the "on" time of the fuel injectors. These adjustments occur a number of times a second to keep the air/fuel mixture at its optimum point, around 14.7:1.

There are a couple of things to remember when building an engine that's using an EFI system. Certain types of RTV sealers can give off fumes that will quickly put the oxygen sensor out to pasture. So when shopping for these sealants, make sure the package states that the sealant doesn't give off fumes that will harm an oxygen sensor.

Also, never install an oxygen sensor without first coating the threads with antiseize compound manufactured specifically for oxygen sensors. If you do, you'll probably never be able to remove the sensor without damaging both the sensor and the exhaust system.

Ignition System

The ignition system used with most fuel-injection systems is controlled by the computer. Using information on engine load and rpm, the ECM adjusts the ignition timing almost continuously to provide the best performance and fuel efficiency.

Open and Closed Loop Operation

The factory and some aftermarket fuel-injection systems have two operating modes: open loop and closed loop. During open loop, the engine is cold and requires a relatively rich air/fuel mixture to operate. During this phase, the ECM ignores the information from the oxygen sensor and turns the injectors "on" based on certain preprogrammed information within it. When engine temperature goes above a certain level, the system goes into the closed loop mode. At this point, the ECM uses the information from the oxygen sensor to operate the fuel injectors.

Fuel Injection System Requirements
Determining Injector Sizing

Peak engine power is what dictates fuel injector sizing. Typically peak power requires 1/2 pound of fuel per hour per horsepower. An easy way to determine this is to divide peak horsepower by two. For example, if an engine is putting out 480 horsepower, the total fuel flow from all the injectors should equal 240 pounds per hour (480 ÷ 2 = 240). If eight fuel injectors are used, each will need to deliver 30 pounds per hour (240 ÷ 8 = 30). But you also need to add 15 percent to the flow capacity to compensate for fuel that's returned to the fuel tank. So 30 x 1.15 = 34.5, which rounds up to 35 pounds per hour.

Determining Fuel Pump Size

The fuel pump needs to be considered, as well. Fuel pump capacity needs to be able to supply enough fuel to all the injectors. In this case, that works out to be 280 pounds per hour (35 x 8 = 280). However, fuel pumps aren't rated in pounds per hour, only gallons per hour. To convert pounds per hour to gallons per hour, divide pounds per hour by six. So our example engine would require a fuel pump that can delivers a minimum of about 47 gallons per hour (280 ÷ 6 = 46.67). Since fuel injection systems use a return line which reroutes unused fuel to the fuel tank, you have to add about 15 percent to the fuel pump capacity. Adding this to our 47-gallon requirement brings it to 54 gallons (47 x 1.15 = 54).

Performance Chips

One way to increase the performance of a stock, computer-controlled rat is to replace the stock

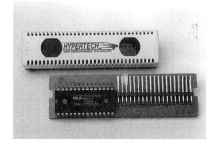

Performance "chips" are one way of gaining performance in computer-controlled vehicles. The performance increase varies between chip manufacturers and from vehicle to vehicle. *Hypertech*

PROM with a "performance chip." Generally speaking, these chips change the spark advance rate and fuel flow at wide-open-throttle to increase engine performance. They usually also allow the engine cooling fan to come on at a lower engine temperature, which helps increase performance by reducing the air temperature within the induction system.

Although these chips are designed to work with stock components, improvements like a low-restriction air filter and decreased exhaust system back-pressure will enhance its effects. Even a cam designed for use with a vehicle's stock computer (such as a Crane Comp-U-Cam) will complement this type of chip. Changes more radical than this will require the use of a custom chip. Typically, using a performance chip with a bone stock engine will net a performance increase of 0.2–0.4 second in the quarter mile. A general rule of thumb indicates that every 0.1 second decrease in quarter mile time equals one car length.

Aftermarket Fuel Injection Systems

Although some street-oriented fuel injection systems may not make any more power than a single four-barrel carb on a high-performance single-plane intake manifold, they offer a number of advantages over carburetors. Effortless starting, good driveability, greater midrange torque, increased throttle response, maximum fuel economy and minimal emissions are the hallmarks of a good street-style fuel-injection system. The mechanical fuel-injection systems offered by

Kinsler Fuel Injection also offers numerous styles of mechanical fuel injection systems for racing applications. When it comes to mechanical fuel injection, constant-flow systems work well for sprint car, drag racing, and road racing applications. It even offers better fuel economy than electronic fuel injection under some racing conditions. And in racing guise, it's substantially cheaper than electronic fuel injection. *Kinsler Fuel Injection*

Kinsler Fuel Injection are for serious racing applications where maximum performance is required.

ACCEL

ACCEL offers three different fuel injection systems for Chevy big-blocks: Stealth Oval Port, SuperRam, and Multi-Point.

Stealth Oval Port

ACCEL's Stealth Oval Port multipoint EFI system is made specifically for towing, RV, and marine applications where lots of low- and mid-rpm punch are required. Formerly known as the Injectork, this system features eight intake tubes of varying lengths contained in a common housing. These "tuned length" tubes are primarily responsible for the strong torque output. Designed for oval port-headed engines displacing 454–468 cubic inches, this system flows air at the rate of 1,000 cfm. According to ACCEL, this system provided an extra 90 pound-feet of torque over the stock GM intake manifold and carburetor at 3,500 rpm. It also

supplies significantly better driveability and fuel economy. But there are a couple of hitches.

This system's ECU is precalibrated to work with ACCEL's Super-Ram hydraulic, flat tappet cams, of which there are two to choose from. If one of these doesn't fit the bill for your particular application and you use a different camshaft, you'll need to recalibrate the system using ACCEL's CALMAP software and your PC or laptop computer. Also, the only distributor that's compatible with this system is the Camaro's computer-controlled HEI distributor if you want to retain the computer-controlled ignition timing.

SuperRam

ACCEL's SuperRam features a short-runner manifold base along with an intake plenum that's tuned to maximize power in the 3,500–6,500 rpm range. Available in both oval and rectangular port versions, this system works well for high-performance street applications.

ACCEL's testing of a 454-cubic-inch engine with a 8.8:1 compression ratio, 235/244-degree duration cam

ACCEL's Stealth Oval Port fuel injection system is designed for applications where torque is more important than top end power, like towing and marine applications.

with 0.561-inch intake lift and 0.571-inch exhaust lift running on 87 octane gas, produced 510 horsepower at 6,000 rpm, compared with 420 horsepower from the same engine fitted with a GM aluminum high-rise intake manifold and a 750-cfm Holley carburetor. Peak torque was 485 pound-feet at 4,000 rpm, versus 440 pound-feet for the carbu-

reted engine. Better yet, from 4,000 rpm on, the torque gap kept on widening, netting 440 pound-feet at 6,500 rpm against 315 pound-feet—great for street performance. Sallee Chevrolet's Dennis Baccus states that a 502 short block fitted with ported Gen V oval port heads and a Crower #1243 cam running on 92 octane pump gas kicked out 525

horsepower at 5,400 rpm and a whopping 624 pound-feet of torque at 4,000 rpm on their dyno. Just the ticket for high-performance street and marine applications.

Like the Stealth Oval Port system, the SuperRam system is precalibrated for certain ACCEL camshafts to maximize induction system tuning. If you opt not to use one of these cams, you'll need to recalibrate the system using the CALMAP software and your computer.

1,000- and 1,200-cfm Multipoint

Besides having one of the most cumbersome names in the business, the ACCEL 1,000- and 1,200-cfm Multipoint Spark Fuel Management Systems offer the performance of a single-plane, high-rise intake manifold with the advantages of electronic fuel injection. Engineered for either oval or rectangular port heads, this system will rev to 7,500 rpm using 8–36 pound-per-hour injectors. The 1,000-cfm version uses a horizontally mounted two-barrel throttle body. The 1,200- cfm version use a Lingenfelter-machined four-barrel throttle body mounted vertically. This system is completely programmable and is intended for off-road use only.

Edelbrock

Edelbrock offers a two-barrel throttle body injection system for Chevy big-blocks called the Performer Multi-Point System. Designed to upgrade the performance of the factory throttle body injection system, it retains the stock throttle body and ECM and combines them with individual fuel injectors for each cylinder. Engineered for mild street and towing applications, this complete system offers significant performance improvements over the stock TBI system. When combined with Edelbrock's TES headers, a gain of 66 horsepower and 70 pound-feet of torque were realized on a Mark IV engine. On a Gen V engine, a 38-horsepower and 45-pound-feet increase were found.

Holley

Holley offers a variety of TBI-type fuel systems for street and racing use. Their Pro-Jection (670 cfm) and Pro-Jection 4 (700 cfm) street

ACCEL's SuperRam system is slanted toward street high-performance engines. Tuned to produce maximum power in the 3,500–6,500 rpm range, this digital EFI system also provides great fuel economy and driveability. *ACCEL*

Here's a twist. This Edelbrock Multi-Point EFI system uses the stock GM throttle body to meter air and couples it with a manifold outfitted with separate fuel injectors for each cylinder. Together, this system increases power and torque substantially—up to 66 horsepower and 70 pound-feet of torque. *Edelbrock*

performance systems are designed for updating carbureted, noncomputerized V-8s to the advantages of a TBI fuel-injection system. These systems work well in RV and towing applications.

Holley offers a variety of TBI-type fuel-injection systems for street and racing use. Their Pro-Jection Digital "D" and "Di" fuel injection systems are designed for both street and high-

performance street applications. The 700-cfm "D" version will support up to 300 horsepower, while the 700-cfm "Di" version is good for up to 400 horsepower. Moving up to the 900-cfm rating, both the "D" and "Di" series will feed 500 horsepower. The "Di" (for Digitial-Interactive) series is a digitally controlled speed density system that allows the user to determine the fuel delivery rate of their

choice via an IBM PC-compatible computer. This system senses air inlet temperature, coolant temperature, manifold pressure, throttle position, engine rpm, exhaust oxygen content, and engine knock.

Holley's "big gun" is the Pro Series 2x2 Analog Pro-Jection 4 system. Featuring twin dual-injector throttle bodies with four 80-pound-per-hour fuel injectors, this system is for rats with rectangular heads, a tunnel ram, and at least 400 horsepower. This set-up combines the benefits of street driveability and drag strip performance. Fuel flow is handled by a

Holley's Pro Series 2x2 Analog Pro-Jection 4 system can make lots of power for rectangular port rats while retaining driveability. *Holley*

computer that controls the fuel flow from both throttle bodies.

All the above mentioned Holley TBI systems fit either stock or high-performance intake manifolds and are "stand-alone" systems. No other components are required for system operation.

Fuel Delivery Systems
Fuel Pumps

The fuel pump must be capable of flowing enough fuel to meet the needs of the engine. Since the need for fuel is greatest at wide-open throttle and engines typically require 0.5 pounds of fuel at wide-open throttle,

multiplying the engine's estimated horsepower by 0.5 will result in the number of pounds of gasoline required per hour. Alone, this figure won't do you much good, but if you divide it by six, which is the approximate weight of a gallon of gas, in pounds, the result will be the number of gallons per hour (gph) required. This number can be used to help you select the proper fuel pump.

For example, if engine output is 550 horsepower, the formula would look like this:

550 x 0.5=275 pounds per hour
275 ÷ 6=45.83 gallons per hour

So, a 550-horsepower engine will require a fuel pump capable of supplying about 46 gallons per hour. Typically, fuel pump volume ratings are rated in free-flow gallons per hour. But this is not the same environment that a carbureted (or fuel-injected) engine is working in. Consequently, you'll want to add about 10 to 15 percent to this figure so you have sufficient fuel volume under all operating conditions. If fuel volume is insufficient with one pump, two pumps plumbed in parallel with one another can be used.

Some fuel pumps have an internal regulator that controls output pressure. Other fuel pumps, usually those designed for high-horsepower applications, require an external fuel pressure regulator. Most carburetors require between 6 to 8 psi to operate properly. If fuel pressure is greater than required, fuel will work its way past the needle and seat in the float bowl and cause flooding. And for those of you using dual carbs, a separate pressure regulator is required for each.

Electric fuel pumps like these from Holley are less prone to vapor lock and don't take any horsepower to drive like mechanical pumps do. *Holley*

A high-performance mechanical fuel pump ensures enough fuel is available under most operating conditions.

High-performance fuel systems require high-performance fuel filters, like this billet aluminum unit from K&N. Capable of filtering down to 10 microns (0.0004 inch), it flows 15.3 gallons per minute. *K&N*

Fuel Lines

As you're considering fuel lines, remember that the inside diameter (ID) of the lines must be capable of flowing enough fuel for wide open throttle (WOT) operation. If there's not enough fuel available, the engine will bog at high rpm. Although the diameter of a 1/2-inch ID line is only one-third larger than a 3/8-inch ID line, its volume is nearly 78 percent greater! Consequently, 1/2-inch ID tubing has a much greater flow capacity than 3/8-inch ID tubing. That means that 3/8-inch ID (#6) fuel line is the smallest size that should be used to feed a rat. On applications with over 500 horsepower, fuel line ID must be 1/2-inch (#8) for best WOT performance.

When it comes to fuel line fittings, they should have the same ID as the fuel lines to prevent causing a fuel line restriction.

Fuel Filters

With the fuel line requirements in hand, you need to select a good, non-restrictive fuel filter. In-line filters are preferred to those in the carburetor because they offer more filtering area and, in turn, present less of a restriction. Holley, as well as other aftermarket manufacturers, offer fuel filters sized for both 3/8-inch and 1/2-inch ID fuel lines.

Fuel flow restrictions can be a big problem in large displacement engines, like a Chevy big-block. Years ago it was found that the sintered bronze fuel filter found just inside the fuel inlet nut on QuadraJet carburetors was the single largest impediment to fuel flow at high engine speeds. Accordingly, if your Q-jet has one of these fabulous filters, pitch it in the trash and replace it with a paper filter or use a good in-line filter.

This ACCEL 300+ Digital
Performance Ignition is a
multispark, capacitive discharge
system. It delivers high spark
current with low current draw.
ACCEL

CHAPTER TWELVE

IGNITION SYSTEMS

All the air and fuel in the world won't do any good if you can't ignite it—and that's the job of the ignition system. Although a good ignition system probably won't bring you any additional power, one that's not operating perfectly will take power away. And that's why you need to ensure your ignition system is working at its best.

Top engine performance depends on complete ignition of the air/fuel mixture at precisely the right moment. In turn, the air/fuel mixture must burn at as high a temperature and pressure as possible. This is easier said than done, especially in a high-compression engine.

One of the biggest problems is the inconsistency of the air/fuel mixture reaching the cylinders. As the air and fuel travel through the intake manifold, they have a tendency to separate from one another, and this tendency changes with rpm. Also, the intake port runners vary in length and volume because the distance between the intake plenum and the individual cylinder head ports varies. Combined, these factors cause a slight difference in the air/fuel ratio on practically every intake stroke for every cylinder.

Compression ratio plays its part as well. As compression rises, the increased cylinder pressure tries to blow the spark out like a candle on a birthday cake. In order for the spark to continue, ignition system voltage must increase. Increasing engine rpm also causes problems since there's less time for the coil to become saturated. In turn, this makes it more difficult for the spark to jump the gap at the plugs. So just when you need firepower the most, a conventional ignition system is starting to sign off. The usual sign is a misfire at high rpm.

To get around this problem, a capacitive discharge ignition (CDI) system should be used. The capacitors used in CDI ignition systems take far less time to reach their saturation point. This means, that at high rpm, significantly more voltage is available to fire the spark plugs.

Ignition System Requirements

Fuel atomization impacts ignition system requirements and varies based on the type of fuel system used, as well as its calibration. Fuel that's poorly atomized, such as with an overly large carburetor, takes more energy to ignite than fuel that's well atomized, like the fine spray that comes out of an electronic fuel injector. Intake manifolds that allow the fuel to puddle in the plenum or the runners, inadequate combustion chamber turbulence, and improper exhaust scavenging, all negatively affect the combustion process.

In addition to good fuel atomization, the air/fuel mixture needs to be exposed to the spark. Here, spark duration, length, and thickness are primary factors. Spark duration is measured in degrees of crankshaft rotation. Multiple spark ignitions have the advantage here because their sparks last for about 20 degrees of crankshaft rotation (at low rpm), whereas single-spark ignition systems produce a spark that lasts for about two degrees of crankshaft rotation. At higher rpm, multispark ignitions produce just one spark, but that spark lasts for around 10 to 15 degrees of crankshaft rotation.

Spark length is determined by the distance between the center and ground electrodes. The greater the spark plug gap, the greater the access the spark has to the air/fuel mixture. And this results in more complete combustion, provided the spark can jump the gap and is sufficiently thick. Spark thickness also determines how complete the combustion process is. A broad spark has more surface area to interact with the air/fuel mixture than a thinner one. This increases the efficiency of the combustion process.

Voltage and Amperage

Although the voltage in the system is important because it's what causes the spark to jump the electrode gap, it's not as important as amperage, or current as it's often called. The voltage rating represents the amount of pressure in an electrical system, amperage is the rate of flow, or volume, through the system.

To understand how voltage and amperage work together, think of a garden hose with an adjustable spray nozzle attached to it. The pressure that the water is under represents voltage. The volume of water that comes out of the hose represents amperage.

As the spray nozzle is opened, the water shoots for a considerable distance because the pressure is relatively high, but not much in front of the nozzle gets wet due to the low volume. As the spray nozzle is opened farther, the water will not flow as far, but the volume of water coming out of the nozzle increases considerably, drenching everything in front of it.

Remembering that voltage is pressure, we can see that a certain amount of voltage (pressure) is required to cover a certain distance. In the ignition system, this distance is represented by the gap between the center and ground electrodes. But voltage by itself results in a relatively thin spark. On the other hand, as the amperage (volume) increases, the spark can't shoot as far, but there's much more of it. Provided there's enough voltage to jump the gap, it's amperage that supplies the thicker spark. And a thicker spark provides more complete combustion. So, what you really need to look for in a high-performance ignition system is both amperage (current) and secondary voltage.

There can also be drawbacks to too much voltage or amperage. As you learned in school, electricity follows the path of least resistance. As system voltage increases, the pressure it exerts within the secondary ignition system (distributor cap, rotor, plug wires, and plugs) increases as well. If these components aren't capable of handling the higher voltage, or there's some problem with them, the voltage won't make the journey to bridge the spark plug gap. Instead, it will find and follow the path of least resistance to ground. And this leads to misfiring.

Ignition Advance System

Without some way to adjust the ignition timing for changing rpm or load, the engine wouldn't make much power, and it'd be pretty hard on a gallon of gas. These are the reasons for the ignition advance system. Three types of ignition advance are used in most street ignition systems; static, vacuum, and centrifugal. Together, they account for total ignition advance.

The static advance is the ignition timing that's set at the crankshaft. The vacuum and centrifugal advance systems help optimize ignition timing based on engine load and speed.

When the engine's idling, the spark plug must ignite the air/fuel mixture slightly before the piston reaches the top of its stroke. This ensures the majority of fuel is ignited and will begin to expand when the piston reaches the top of its stroke, pushing the piston down. This takes full advantage of the leverage effect of the connecting rod journal on the crankshaft and is known as static timing.

As engine rpm increases, piston speed goes up. But the burning and expansion rate of the fuel stays the same. To compensate for this, ignition of the air/fuel mixture needs to occur earlier so the fuel can begin expanding when the piston is at the top of its stroke.

If ignition begins too late, the piston is already moving down the cylinder and the pressure against the piston generated by the expanding fuel drops. This causes a drop in cylinder pressure with a resulting decrease in engine torque.

On the other hand, if the ignition timing becomes too far advanced, the fuel begins expanding before the piston reaches the top of its stroke. The pressure caused by the expanding fuel pushes down violently on the piston as it's still moving to the top of the cylinder, causing the hammering noise that is typical of detonation. It also slows the momentum of the crankshaft, resulting in a loss of power.

As you can see, the ignition must advance at a certain rate to take full advantage of the leverage effect of the crankshaft and to prevent engine damage.

The vacuum advance system is responsible for increasing ignition advance based on engine load. The lighter the engine load, the greater the advance. The greater the engine load, the less the advance.

The vacuum advance consists of a diaphragm within a metal housing.

Connected to one end of the housing is a source of manifold vacuum. On the other end, a plunger is connected to the diaphragm, which, in turn, is attached to the distributor breaker plate.

When the engine is lightly loaded, such as at idle and when cruising, manifold vacuum is high and ignition timing can be advanced without causing detonation. The high manifold vacuum pulls on the diaphragm. In turn, the diaphragm plunger pulls on the breaker plate, causing it to rotate. Since the ignition trigger (breaker points, magnetic switch, and so on) is mounted on the breaker plate, it begins to open earlier, relative to the distributor shaft. And this causes ignition timing to increase. This increase in ignition timing substantially improves fuel economy.

If the engine is accelerated, manifold vacuum drops. This allows the vacuum diaphragm, and in turn, the breaker plate, to ease back toward their neutral states, reducing ignition timing.

Where the vacuum advance system adjusts ignition timing based on engine load, the centrifugal advance system adjusts timing based on engine speed. The centrifugal advance system consists of two weights positioned at the top of the distributor shaft. The weights are held to the distributor drive shaft

with springs. As engine rpm increases, centrifugal force pulls the weights away from the distributor shaft causing the springs to expand. The weights are connected to the breaker plate assembly. As the weights move outward, they rotate the breaker plate within the distributor housing, causing the ignition timing to advance. The advance rate is controlled by the mass of the weights and the tension of the centrifugal weight springs.

The vacuum advance system works in concert with the centrifugal advance system in a type of see-saw routine. Whenever engine rpm increases, the vacuum advance system allows the ignition timing to ease back. But when engine rpm increases, the centrifugal advance system increases ignition timing. So they tend to help balance one another.

However, two things combine to make this an uneven trade-off. First, if the centrifugal advance weights and springs are selected for maximum performance, they won't add any more ignition advance above 2500 rpm or so. Second, the vacuum advance system is more sensitive than the centrifugal advance system; changes in throttle position that may change engine rpm only slightly and therefore cause no real change in centrifugal advance rate, can cause

Factory HEI ignitions systems work well on the street with their mechanical and vacuum advance systems. The vacuum advance system enhances part-throttle fuel economy substantially.

more significant changes in the vacuum advance system.

Overall, the more ignition timing you can run without causing detonation, the better the performance and fuel economy. And these are two good reasons for retaining the vacuum advance system for street operation.

HEI Ignition Systems

The factory high energy ignition (HEI) system is a transistorized ignition system that came on the scene in the 1974 model year to fulfill a need for decreased exhaust emissions.

Due to tightening emission standards mandated by the Clean Air Act of 1970, air/fuel mixtures had to become leaner. However, point-type ignition systems weren't capable of producing sparks hot enough to burn this leaner air/fuel mixture. And the changes in dwell due to point deterioration and rubbing

To give your stock HEI system a boost, try a high-performance ignition coil, like this Super Coil from ACCEL. It helps deliver hotter sparks for increased engine performance and is street legal in all 50 states. *ACCEL*

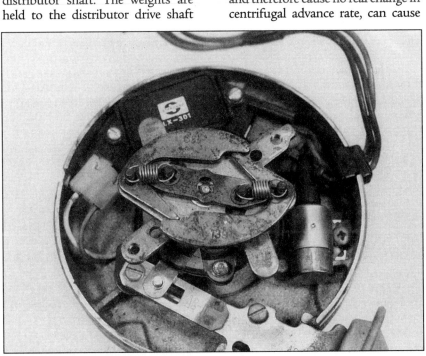

The mechanical advance system can be tailored for specific applications by using lighter or heavier weights and springs.

131

block wear also had a hand in increasing emissions.

By replacing the points with a magnetic triggering system, dwell changes caused by wear of the point rubbing block were a thing of the past. And where point type systems could put out only 25–40,000 volts, HEI systems could crank out over 60,000 volts. Combined, these features reduced exhaust emissions considerably, while increasing engine performance.

With the HEI's tremendous voltage increase, the terminals on the distributor cap needed to be moved farther away from each other to prevent arcing. In turn, this required an increase in distributor cap diameter, which makes it easy to identify an HEI distributor.

From a hot-rodding standpoint, HEI distributors produced before 1980 offer a considerable amount of "tunability" because they have both centrifugal and vacuum advance systems. Another good point is that millions are available at salvage yards across the country, because small-block and big-block V-8 distributors are the same, and this keeps the cost of purchasing one low.

Unfortunately, above 5,000 rpm or so, just when a high-performance engine really starts needing a good, strong spark, a stock HEI distributor begins signing off. The ignition

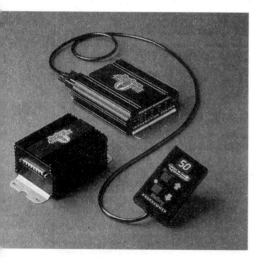

Holley's slant on multiple spark discharge ignition systems has resulted in its Annihilator Ignition Products line. This ProStrip Annihilator system is designed for professional drag racing and uses a microprocessor to control spark timing. *Holley*

module, which was designed for a relatively low-rpm production engine, starts losing spark energy. But don't fear. There are a number of aftermarket companies offering parts to upgrade the performance of the factory HEI system, including ignition modules, ignition coils, and high-performance caps and rotors.

MSD offers an ignition module (part number 8364) that's capable of 9,000 rpm when coupled with their High Energy HEI Coil (part number 8225). These modules replace four-pin HEI modules only.

If you're looking for a complete HEI distributor assembly, ACCEL offers blueprinted units made from stock distributor cores. They also include new magnetic pickups, a performance ignition module, a high-output coil, a harness, a high-performance cap and rotor, and OEM-style wiring.

If you're replacing a point-type ignition system with an HEI or other type of CDI system, remember that the HEI system requires 12 volts to operate properly. Since point-type ignition systems use a resistor mounted in the wiring harness to prevent burning the points, you'll have to either remove or bypass the resistor to ensure the HEI system receives sufficient voltage at all times.

An HEI system is a good choice for a street machine, as well as some kinds of racing, like circle track. They're reliable under a variety of environmental conditions, and hot-rodded versions are readily available through a number of aftermarket sources. However, for serious competition work, or where packaging constraints dictate the use of a smaller distributor, look to the aftermarket.

One last thing. Before you doctor up an HEI distributor for your boat, remember that they're not legal for marine use, because they lack spark protection. If you install one in a boat, it could ignite the fuel vapors in the bilge and cause a *deadly* explosion.

Capacitor Discharge Ignition (CDI) Systems

Transistor ignitions eliminated the problems inherent with ignition points, but one weak link remained—the time it took to induce a voltage in the coil. As engine rpm rises, there's less time available to induce a voltage

in the coil. Consequently, voltage from these systems drops off as engine rpm rises. A capacitor only takes about one-third the time to reach its saturation point as compared to a coil. By using a capacitor to do this part of the coil's job, voltage output doesn't start to drop off until 12,000–14,000 rpm—way beyond what most mortal engines will run to.

The downside to using capacitors in an ignition system is that spark duration is very short compared to a point or transistor ignition system. However, with the proper engineering, capacitor discharge ignition systems offer spark duration that can last for 20 degrees of crankshaft rotation—about 10 times greater than other ignition systems. Some of these ignition systems even use a computer chip that's programmable from inside the vehicle.

Single- and multiple-spark ignition systems are available from ACCEL, Crane, Holley, Jacobs, Mallory, and MSD.

Crankshaft-Triggered Ignition Systems

Crankshaft-triggered ignition systems use a wheel mounted on the crankshaft damper along with a pickup to trigger the coil. These systems offer increased timing accuracy over other types of ignition systems, because timing variations caused by timing chain stretch and distributor shaft vibration are eliminated. But they aren't for everyone.

Crank-triggered ignitions are required when an extra degree or two of ignition advance can make the difference between engine life and

This Flying Magnet Crank Trigger from MSD uses four magnets in the trigger wheel and a nonmagnetic pickup for accurate triggering of the ignition system. *Autotronic Controls Corporation/MSD*

death. And cylinder pressure is the primary determinant. If compression ratio or ignition timing or cam timing increase cylinder pressure to a point where the engine is on the verge of detonation, then you'll need to use a crank-triggered ignition.

With regular high-performance street and marine engines, a crank-triggered ignition system usually isn't necessary since you're not running cylinder pressure at its maximum. And if you are, you can often hear the detonation it causes if the vehicle has a good set of mufflers. However, for engines where you're trying to get that last bit of performance, like a serious street or race car, a crank-triggered ignition is just what the doctor ordered.

When installing a crank-triggered ignition, you need to lock out the centrifugal advance in the distributor. You also need to ensure the pickup is properly spaced from the trigger wheel. For engines with crankshaft strokes of 4.375 inches or less, set the "air gap" at 0.050 inch. For crankshaft strokes greater than this, enlarge the air gap to 0.060 inch to help prevent the trigger wheel from hitting the pickup due to the greater flexing that occurs with long-stroke crankshafts.

Ignition "Boxes"

In this section I'll use the term ignition "box" to differentiate between the ignition module that fits inside an HEI distributor, versus the externally mounted "box" that contains the controls for a CDI system.

Numerous types of ignition boxes are available from the aftermarket. All these boxes are designed for various applications and needs. Some are designed specifically to complement the factory HEI system. Others are designed for street-driven vehicles, while still others are engineered for marine or racing applications.

MSD offers four types of ignition boxes that can be used with point-type or HEI ignition systems and are legal in every state. For those of you looking for an all-round multiple spark discharge ignition for your land-operated vehicle, consider the MSD 6A ignition box. This ignition can be triggered using breaker points, a magnetic pickup, or the output side of an electronic amplifier. To ensure complete combustion, it provides a healthy 10 amps of power at 10,000 rpm.

Both ACCEL and Holley offer multiple spark discharge systems in their Digital and Annihilator lines, respectively. Although new to the multiple spark discharge scene, these systems are well-engineered and are a viable alternative for street, marine, and racing applications where healthy, long lasting sparks are required.

Most ignition system manufacturers offer ignition boxes with various types of rev limiters. A rev limiter simply prevents the engine from revving past a certain rpm. These can help prevent the engine from grenading if a shift is missed at high rpm, a driveshaft lets loose, or the prop comes out of the water.

There are two basic strategies for rev control—hard and soft. The hard type shuts off the spark to all the cylinders when a specific rpm is reached.

The problem with this type of system is that if mufflers or catalytic converters are used on the exhaust side, the fuel that continues to flow while the ignition is shut off collects in them. If a spark is introduced into the exhaust system courtesy of a backfire, the fuel is ignited and the mufflers and converters explode.

Soft rev limiters work by eliminating the spark on every other stroke. This keeps the engine from overrevving, while at the same time igniting the fuel in the combustion chambers. Not only does this save a street-type exhaust system, it's also easier on the camshaft drive system, because the engine isn't stopped suddenly. So if it's a rev limiter you want, this is the way to go.

To set a specific rpm limit, some ignition boxes use plug-in modules while others can be controlled via a rotary switch. The rotary switch type has a greater range of adjustability compared to plug-in modules since each module is calibrated for only one specific rpm. The Mallory HyFire IV with proportional rev limiter uses an approach that falls somewhere between these two types. This unit features a circuit board with a series of jacks. By inserting special plugs into the jacks, you set the rpm limit to whatever speed you decree is safe, anywhere from 3,000 to 10,000 rpm, in increments of 200 rpm.

When setting the rev limit of any engine, you're limited by your weakest component or system. For example, if the connecting rods are good to 8,000 rpm, but the valves begin floating at 6,500 rpm, you have to set the rev limiter based on 6,500 rpm. After determining the weakest link in your engine, set the rev limiter at least 200 rpm below its maximum rpm limit to ensure the engine will live.

Another consideration is ignition system draw. Remember that old adage: "It takes money to make money?" It can be paraphrased to apply to ignition systems as well—it takes power to make power. Most high-performance ignition boxes draw a significant amount of amperage from the battery, and this amperage requirement rises the faster you spin the engine. Accordingly, it's best to use an alternator to recharge the battery whenever possible. Conversely,

This ignition "box" from MSD features multiple spark discharge technology combined with a "soft touch" rev limiter. This type of rev limiter helps prevent damaging engine components when the rpm limit is reached. *Autotronic Controls Corporation/MSD*

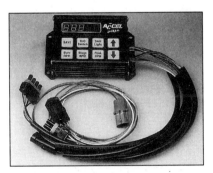

This ACCEL three-stage rev limiter is designed for drag racers. It can control engine rpm for burnouts, staging, and peak rpm. It also can set the rpm level for nitrous activation. *ACCEL*

if an ignition box is used without having an alternator to recharge the battery, its output, along with the battery's, will drop rather quickly. And this will lead to misfiring.

Tips and Adjustments
Centrifugal Advance
By discarding the factory weights or springs and replacing them with aftermarket pieces, you can tailor the ignition advance for your particular application. Heavier weights or lighter springs allow ignition advance to begin sooner. Conversely, lighter weights or heavier springs cause ignition advance to begin later. What's right for your application depends on a number of things including compression ratio, camshaft timing, fuel octane, and altitude.

For most street/strip applications, you want all the advance in by 2,500–3,200 rpm, depending upon the other components used in the engine and the octane rating of available gas. For racing applications, total ignition timing is typically 20 degrees until 1,800 rpm or so, climbing to a maximum of 36–38 degrees at 3,000 rpm.

Distributors
Tall deck blocks, decking of the block, milling of the cylinder heads, and thicker or thinner intake manifold distributor base pads can result in misalignment of the distributor driven gear with the camshaft drive gear. To accommodate these situations, use a distributor that has an adjustable slip collar.

Distributor caps and rotors are another consideration. With today's high-voltage CDI systems, there's considerable potential for the spark to jump from the rotor to the plug terminal in the cap, either before or after it's perfectly aligned with it. Depending on when this happens, it will either advance or retard the ignition timing for that particular cylinder. Neither situation is good for power output nor engine longevity and requires that you check rotor phasing.

Rotor Phasing
To check rotor phasing, the ignition timing must be set. You'll also need to cut a hole in the top side of the distributor cap directly above the

Distributor rotors must be properly phased to the terminals in the distributor cap. MSD offers a two-piece rotor that allows you to correct rotor phasing problems. *Autotronic Controls Corp/MSD*

To reduce the potential for cross-firing between cylinders, MSD offers its Cap-A-Dapt system. This system installs on your stock HEI distributor, spacing the cap terminals farther apart to reduce the chances of cross-firing. *Autotronic Controls Corporation/MSD*

terminal for cylinder #1 or use a clear distributor cap. Then scribe a line in the center of the rotor terminal and the cap terminal. To help see them, fill the lines with a china marker or crayon. Next, connect a timing light to the plug wire for cylinder number one and run the engine at idle. If the marks on the rotor and cap terminals are aligned with each other, rotor phasing is correct.

If the distributor uses a vacuum advance, run the engine at 1,000 rpm, then at 4,000 rpm. Mark the rotor position on the cap at each rpm level, then determine the midpoint between these marks. If the midpoint coincides with the center of the terminal, rotor phasing is where it should be.

If rotor phasing is incorrect, it means that the triggering device (points, etc.) is opening too soon or too late. You can fix this problem by moving the triggering device forward

or backward from where it currently is relative to the distributor shaft. Alternately, MSD offers a two-piece rotor that allows you to move the rotor terminal independently of the rotor base.

Other Considerations
The type of intake manifold used sometimes determines what type of distributor can be used. All low- and high-rise manifolds that use a single four-barrel carburetor can use practically any type of distributor, because there's lots of space rearward of the carb. However, an HEI distributor won't work with many tunnel ram manifolds because there's just not enough room for it. So don't go out and buy a distributor until you're sure what your intake manifold will accept.

Spark Plug Wires
Years ago, when you wanted some high-performance spark plug wires for your engine, you'd slap on a set of solid core wires and motor on off into the sunset. However, if you wanted to listen to the radio, you couldn't, because the music would be masked by a hissing sound known as radio frequency interference (RFI). Thankfully, things have changed.

Radio Frequency Interference (RFI)
Today's modern ignition systems are a blessing from both an emissions and performance standpoint. They provide enough current flow to keep emissions in check

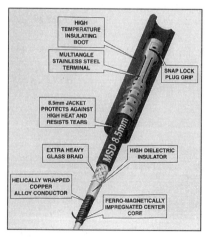

HIGH TEMPERATURE INSULATING BOOT

MULTIANGLE STAINLESS STEEL TERMINAL

SNAP LOCK PLUG GRIP

8.5mm JACKET PROTECTS AGAINST HIGH HEAT AND RESISTS TEARS

EXTRA HEAVY GLASS BRAID

HIGH DIELECTRIC INSULATOR

HELICALLY WRAPPED COPPER ALLOY CONDUCTOR

FERRO-MAGNETICALLY IMPREGNATED CENTER CORE

This MSD Heli-Core Ignition Wire features a helically wrapped copper conductor to fight RFI. *Autotronic Controls Corporation/MSD*

while at the same time boosting engine performance, courtesy of more complete combustion. But they're more prone to giving off RFI.

When current flows through a wire, it causes a magnetic field around the wire. The strength of this magnetic field is directly tied to the amperage or voltage running through the wire—the higher the amperage or voltage, the stronger the magnetic field.

The factory computer system relies on sensors that operate on thousandths of an amp, which are referred to as milli-amps. These milli-amp signals provide the computer with information so it can make the appropriate changes to the fuel and ignition systems.

Problems begin when high-amperage wires, like the feed wire from the alternator, or high-voltage wires, like spark plug wires, are routed too close to the wires running to and from these sensors. The RFI radiating from the high amperage or voltage wires causes a change in the electrical signals from the sensors. Since the computer is reading electrical signals that don't reflect what's actually going on with the sensors, it makes the wrong adjustments to the fuel or the ignition system. And this makes for one strangely acting rat that can misfire or backfire.

To prevent this from happening, route all high-amperage and high-voltage wires, like alternator and spark plug wires, away from any wires that lead to the computer sensors. A distance of 1 1/2 inches will be sufficient to prevent RFI from causing any driveability problems.

For vehicles equipped with rev limiters, timing controls, and other electronic components, the drill is the same. Keep all high-amperage wires away from these components and their wiring.

Spark plug wire design can also impact RFI. Some spark plug wires, like the carbon core resistor type, do a fair job of shielding RFI, but they can have lots of internal resistance, up to 10,000 ohms per foot. This high resistance reduces the voltage that gets to the spark plugs, which obviously is not a good situation. And as the carbon core ages, it breaks, which causes its resistance to

increase. Those of you on a tight budget may be lured by carbon core wires since they're relatively cheap. But their cheaper initial cost is outweighed by their shorter service life and poor performance.

For best performance and value, choose spark plug wires that use a spiral-wound metal core with a high-temperature silicone jacket. These wires are effective at shielding RFI but have internal resistance as low as 40 ohms per foot. Spark plug wires that use this design include:

- ACCEL Super Stock Spiral Core
- Jacobs Energy Core
- Mallory Pro Sidewinder
- Moroso Blue Max Spiral Core
- MSD 8-mm Heli-Core and Super Conductor

Keep in mind that in order to carry as much voltage to the spark plugs as possible, you want to use spark plug wires that have the least amount of resistance. Since resistance varies between brands, shop around.

Spacing and Routing

The spacing and routing of spark plug wires is important to optimal and lasting ignition performance.

If spark plug wires are closer than 1/2 inch to each other and are parallel to one another, each can cause the other cylinder to fire, just like an ignition coil. This out-of-time firing, called crossfire, can be troublesome, but it's particularly bad for cylinder seven. Remember, in a big-block Chevy, the firing order of cylinders five and seven are one right after the other. Also keep in mind that cylinder seven is just starting its compression stroke when the spark plug for cylinder five is fired.

Now, if the spark plug wire for cylinder five is positioned so that it causes cylinder seven to fire, ignition timing for cylinder seven will be severely advanced. With this much advance, it won't take long for the piston, rings, and rod bearings for cylinder seven to die a quick but painful death.

To avoid this situation, use non-conductive wiring spacers to keep the spark plug wires at least 1/2 inch apart from one another. If they must be routed closer together than this,

position them so that they cross each other at a right angle. This will significantly reduce the chance for crossfiring. Also, be sure to use spiral-wound spark plug wires, as mentioned earlier.

Besides crossfiring, routing also impacts spark plug wire longevity. For longest life, route the wires away from headers and other sources of extreme heat. In this respect, it's beneficial to route the wires underneath the headers. Also, keep the wires away from sharp edges that could chafe or cut the insulation. If the wires must pass near sharp edges or hot areas, use insulated sleeving to protect them.

To help prevent pulling the plug ends off the wires, apply a dime-size amount of dielectric grease to the inside of each spark plug boot. This grease also helps seal out moisture and protects against voltage leaks.

Spark Plugs
Heat Ranges

The heat range of a spark plug refers to the ability of a spark plug to transfer heat from the end that's exposed to the combustion process to the cooling jacket in the cylinder head. A "hot" spark plug sheds it heat rather slowly to prevent fouling and misfire when combustion chamber or cylinder head temperatures are relatively low. A "cold" spark plug does the opposite; instead of retaining heat, it transfers it more quickly to prevent overheating the plug core and causing preignition. As you would imagine, this type of plug is used where combustion or cylinder head temperatures are high.

Lots of things influence the selection of a spark plug with the proper heat range. Whenever compression rises, the temperature inside the combustion chamber rises. This means the spark plugs need to be colder to keep the heat load balanced. Things that raise compression include boring the cylinders, decking the block, using heads with smaller combustion chambers (by milling or by design), using higher compression ratio pistons, a thinner head gasket, or a supercharger, turbocharger, or nitrous oxide.

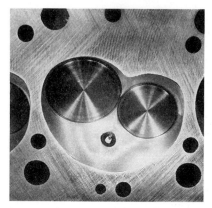

Indexing spark plugs can further add to engine performance. As the piston moves up to the top of its stroke, it compresses the air/fuel mixture. Most of the air/fuel mixture that's located between the quench area of the piston and the head gets squeezed out toward the spark plug. By "indexing" the ground electrode so it points toward the top of the combustion chamber, the spark is fully exposed to the air/fuel mixture being squeezed toward it. This results in more complete combustion and adds a few more ponies as well. This plug is 180 degrees from where it should be.

Plug Gap

Adjusting spark plug gap is another way of increasing engine performance, especially after installing a high-performance ignition system. After gapping the plugs at the manufacturer's recommended gap and checking engine performance, increase the gap by 0.005 inch, then test again. When performance drops, the gap is too large, so go back to the previous setting. Although normally aspirated, carbureted and fuel-injected engines respond well to plug gap increases, the extra pressure of nitrous oxide, supercharging, or turbocharging tends to blow out the spark when large plug gaps are used. In these cases, you're usually best off with the standard plug gap.

Reading Plugs

Reading plugs is one way of determining if a spark plug is too hot or too cold for particular application. To "read" a spark plug, you need to carefully examine the color and texture of the base of the ceramic insulator where it surrounds the center elec-

trode. On a fresh set of plugs, these indications can be quite subtle. Consequently, you're best off by using an illuminated magnifying glass to see all the detail in this area. You also need to examine the condition of the center and ground electrodes, as well as the ends of the threads. Although spark plug reading has been elevated to an art form, an amateur can gain enough expertise to avoid major engine problems through careful study of the plugs and the accompanying chart.

Select a baseline plug with which to begin your testing by looking at the spark plug manufacturer's recommendation chart, or by asking the company you purchased your cylinder heads from. If you have any doubts about what heat range plug to use for your trial runs, always use a colder plug to prevent preignition and detonation. Detonation will eat your engine alive and leave you with a fat dinner check to pay.

With the engine properly tuned, ignition timing set, and a fresh set of plugs installed, the engine needs to be run at full throttle in high gear for a mile or so. All runs must be made where this is legal and will not endanger anyone or anything. For all the people driving the 1320, you'll need about four runs to color the plugs sufficiently. At the end of the run, disengage the clutch or put the transmission in neutral to prevent changing the plug coloring.

As you remove the plugs, note which cylinder they came from so you can troubleshoot as necessary. Also remember that fuel distribution may be uneven cylinder-to-cylinder. The degree to which this occurs depends upon whether a single- or dual-plane intake manifold is used, or if the engine is fitted with fuel injection. Whatever the case, what you want to strive for is equally colored plugs. This indicates all the cylinders are performing equally, which contributes to developing maximum power.

Another way to check if the air/fuel ratio is right is to remove the headers and take a look at the exhaust ports. If the air/fuel ratio is where it should be, the ports will be medium gray in color. If they're darker, the engine is running too rich. Conversely, if they're lighter, the air/fuel ratio is too lean.

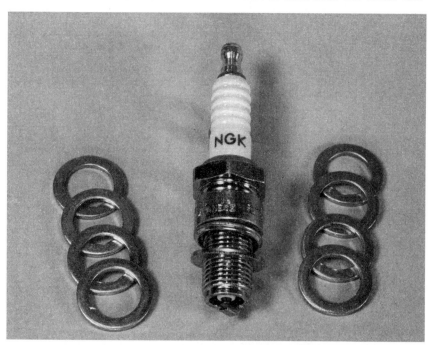

To index spark plugs, you'll need a set of indexing washers. These washers are made from varying thicknesses of copper and are available from speed shops. Draw a line on the spark plug hex that is directly opposite where the ground electrode is welded to the spark plug. Then screw the spark plug into the cylinder head and torque it to specifications. The ground electrode should point toward the top of the combustion chamber, within a 10 to 2 o'clock window as you sight down the plug toward the head. If it doesn't, use a thicker or thinner washer as necessary to gain the proper ground electrode orientation.

SPARK PLUG DIAGNOSIS CHART

PLUG CONDITION	APPEARANCE	CAUSES
Normal	• Insulator greyish tan or brown • Insulator around center electrode not blistered • Ground electrode not discolored or eroded	• Heat range correct • Air/fuel ratio good • Ignition system good • Oil control sufficient
Pre-ignition	• Insulator blistered, satin white with brown spots • Ground electrode blue	• Heat range incorrect • Air/fuel mixture lean • Engine cooling poor • Combustion chamber deposits
Detonation	• Small aluminum beads on insulator next to center electrode • Insulator cracked (in extreme cases)	• Ignition timing overly advanced • Air/fuel mixture lean • Fuel octane too low
Overheated	• Insulator clean and white • Ground electrode overly eroded	• Ignition timing overly advanced • Air/fuel mixture too lean • Engine cooling poor
Carbon Fouled	• Insulator black with dry, sooty deposits	• Heat range too cold • Air/fuel mixture too rich • Ignition output low
Oil Fouled	• Insulator black and possibly wet with oil	• Valve guide clearance excessive • Valve stem seals leaking • Piston rings not sealing • PCV valve faulty

CONTENTS

CHAPTER THIRTEEN

EXHAUST SYSTEMS

The exhaust system is the final link in the airflow path through the engine. Properly selected components will complement the induction system, camshaft, and cylinder heads, resulting in big dividends. The main objectives of a high-performance exhaust system is to help scavenge the exhaust gasses out of the cylinders and reduce back pressure.

By pulling the exhaust gasses out of the cylinders, you make more room available for the fresh air/fuel charge. And the more fresh air/fuel charge that's available, the more power the engine will make, provided it can be burned completely.

Back pressure is another concern. Think of it as someone holding a pillow over your face as you try to exhale. You may be able to do it, but it takes more effort than when there's no pillow on your face. So, the less back pressure, the better.

Computer simulation reveals that for Chevy rats outfitted with stock cylinder heads, an efficient exhaust system—specifically one incorporating headers—provides about the best bang for the buck. And this is borne out by real world experience.

Headers

There's nothing like a set of headers to wake up a sleeping giant like the big-block Chevy. As the nearby computer simulation charts show, slapping some small tube headers on an otherwise stock rat, shakes out another 43 horsepower and 56 pound-feet of torque. It also fattens up the torque curve all the way from

If you're driving a car or truck that must meet emission standards, but you still desire the additional performance that headers provide, look into systems like this Edelbrock Tubular Exhaust System. This system is 50-state legal. *Edelbrock*

2,000 rpm to 6,500 rpm, while extending the curve another 500 rpm—results so good they're almost like free money. Gains like this are even greater when the engine has been modified with things like a more aggressive cam or single plane intake manifold, due to the more efficient exhaust flow provided by headers. And it's not uncommon to see a fuel economy improvement of 10 to 15 percent. With results like these, it shouldn't be a question of *if* you'll buy headers, it should be a question of: "Can I get those headers today?"

Headers Versus Exhaust Manifolds

Purely on the basis of weight, headers are better than cast-iron exhaust manifolds. Typically, headers will save 20 pounds over cast-iron exhaust manifolds. This increases the power-to-weight ratio of the vehicle, and just as important, improves handling, since this weight comes off the front of the vehicle.

Before you can fully appreciate the functional aspects of headers, you need to think about how stock exhaust manifolds are designed and work. Compared to headers, exhaust manifolds use very short primary "tubes" to route the exhaust gasses from each cylinder to the "log" or "collector." These short primary tubes don't allow each cylinder to be isolated from the others during engine operation, and this hurts power production.

Consider this: Each cylinder in a cylinder bank is connected to one common manifold. As the engine runs, each cylinder in the cylinder bank is at a different point in its operating cycle; when one cylinder is on the power stroke, another is on the compression stroke, and so on.

When one cylinder is on its exhaust stroke, the burned air/fuel mixture is pushed out of the cylinder into the exhaust manifold. Because the primary tubes on an exhaust manifold are so short, the pressurized exhaust gasses coming out of this cylinder find their way into the other cylinders that have lower pressure before the exhaust can be routed away. In turn, these exhaust gasses take space in the combustion chambers that would have been used for the

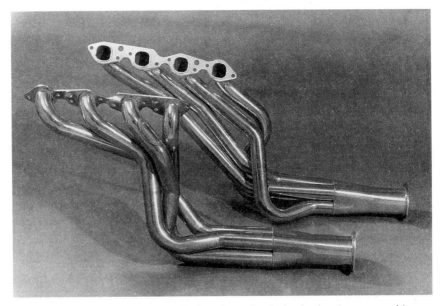

Dollar-for-dollar, headers provide the best bang for the buck when it comes to big-block Chevys. However, they must be of the correct dimensions for best performance. The thermal barrier coating on these Hooker headers helps increase exhaust efficiency even further. *Hooker*

fresh charge of air and fuel. With less room in the combustion chambers for the fresh air and fuel, power drops off.

Compared to exhaust manifolds, headers have much longer primary tubes before they join together into a common collector. Since it takes more time for the exhaust gasses from one cylinder to reach the collector than it takes for the other cylinders to produce their own exhaust stroke, the exhaust gasses aren't forced into the other cylinders. The allows more room for the fresh air/fuel charge, which, in turn, produces more power.

Headers also increase power by "scavenging." As the exhaust gasses from one cylinder pass by the ends of the other primary tubes in the collector, they create a vacuum. When the next exhaust valve on the cylinder bank opens, the gasses move out of the combustion chamber faster, due to the vacuum in the collector helping to suck them out of the cylinder. This scavenging effect also helps draw the fresh air/fuel charge past the open intake valve and into the cylinder.

Sizing

When it comes to sizing, header dimensions should complement the characteristics of the camshaft being used. Changing the length or diameter of the primary tubes changes the

timing at which the scavenging occurs. In turn, this affects the point in the rpm band where the extra power is realized. Generally, smaller diameter or longer primary tubes boost power at low- and mid-rpm and are typically used with short duration, low-overlap cams. On the other hand, larger diameter or shorter primary tubes prove most beneficial at mid- to high-rpm. These headers work best with high overlap cams.

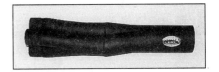

Those in the hunt for more low- and mid-rpm power can slip on a pair of these split flow collectors from Hooker. Using the same principle as Tri-Y headers, they pair the cylinders that are farthest apart from one another in the firing sequence to enhance performance. *Hooker*

Header dimensions can be calculated. "Rough" tuning of headers entails selection of a specific primary tube diameter. Once primary tube diameter is chosen, engine output can be "fine" tuned by adjusting the length of the primary tube, as well as the length of the collector.

To determine primary tube diameter, use the following formula:

$$\frac{\text{Engine size (in cubic inches)} \times 1,900}{\text{Tube length} \times \text{torque peak rpm}}$$

After this equation is complete, you'll need to find the square root of the result to determine the primary tube outside diameter.

Plugging some figures into this formula, let's say engine size is 468 cubic inches, that you want to use a tubing length of 34 inches, and that the engine is built to produce peak torque at 5,600 rpm.

Our formula would then look like this:

$$\text{Primary tube diam.} = \frac{468 \times 1,900}{34 \times 5,600}$$
$$\text{Primary tube diam.} = \frac{889,200}{190,400}$$
$$\text{Primary tube diam.} = 4.670168$$

Since the square root of 4.670168 is 2.1610571, you'll need a primary tube outside diameter of approximately 2.16 inches to match your engine. Realistically, you won't be able to find primary tubes with an OD of 2.16 inches, so you'll need to choose between ODs of 2 1/8 (2.125) or 2 1/4 (2.250) inches. The smaller tube will move the torque peak down the rpm scale and the larger one will move it up the scale.

The formula for primary tube length is:

$$\frac{\text{Engine size (in cubic inches)} \times 1,900}{\text{Tube diameter}^2 \times \text{torque peak rpm}}$$

For example, let's say engine size is 502 cubic inches, primary tube diameter is 2.25 inches, and peak torque comes in at 6,200 rpm. The formula would then look like this:

$$\text{Primary tube length} = \frac{502 \times 1,900}{(2.25 \times 2.25) \times 6,200}$$
$$\text{Primary tube length} = \frac{953,800}{31,388}$$
$$\text{Primary tube length} = 30.387409 \text{ inches}$$

If the engine is equipped with nitrous or a supercharger and used for racing, you'll want to increase primary tube diameter by 1/8 to 1/4 inch to allow for the increase in exhaust flow generated by these sys-

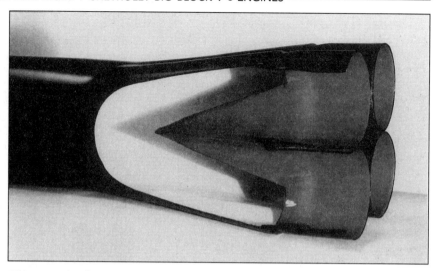

This merged collector from Hooker helps the exhaust flow transition into the header for decreased turbulence and more high-rpm power. *Hooker*

tems. Just don't do this for vehicles that aren't normally raced, or you'll hurt torque, and fuel consumption will suffer.

Like the primary tubes, collector volume helps determine torque output, though to a lesser degree. Greater volume (through increases in length or diameter) raise torque output. Conversely, a smaller volume decreases torque.

Stepped Headers

Stepped headers are a recent development in exhaust system technology. The idea behind them is pretty simple. By using two different primary tube diameters, the first tube smaller than the second, less force is required to accelerate the gasses in the pipe. This reduces exhaust back pressure, but it also allows the extension of camshaft exhaust lobe timing. In turn, this allows more power to be produced without losing low-rpm torque.

Header Coating and Wraps

One of the great things about headers is that they reduce underhood heat compared to cast-iron exhaust manifolds. Instead of acting like a big heat sink the way cast-iron manifolds do, they shed their heat much more readily. This lowers underhood temperatures, which increases power.

Taking a good thing one step further are the various coatings and wraps available from header manufacturers,

as well as other aftermarket sources. By insulating the headers from the rest of the engine compartment, underhood temperatures are further reduced. With cooler, denser air under the hood, horsepower goes up.

However, there's another benefit to using header coatings or wraps that isn't visible, and that's an increase in exhaust scavenging. As exhaust gasses pass through the header primary tubes, they pass their heat fairly rapidly. And the cooler the gasses are, the slower they move. By wrapping or coating the tubes with one of these heat-insulating materials, more heat is retained within the headers, so the speed of the gasses remains high, which leads to better scavenging.

However, unlike header coatings, which most of the header manufacturers offer themselves, use of header wraps may void the header warranty because they make the tubes brittle and prone to cracking. So check the warranty before you buy.

Regulations

If you plan on running headers on your street-driven vehicle, check your local regulations first. In many areas of the country where exhaust emission testing takes place, it's illegal to modify the exhaust system upstream of the catalytic converter. However, as long as the headers have received an exemption from the California Air Resources Board, you'll be on solid, legal ground. As part of the exemption process, the headers must be able to accept all the emissions hardware that the stock exhaust manifolds accepted, including AIR fittings, and the oxygen sensor(s).

Adjustments

After you install your headers, you'll need to make fuel delivery and ignition timing changes for the engine to run at its best. Remember, with headers and a high-flow exhaust system, airflow through the engine will increase. This will necessitate enrichment of the air/fuel mixture to compensate. You'll also need to advance ignition timing one-to-two degrees to take advantage of the greater fuel flow and airflow.

Balance Tubes

A balance tube connects the exhaust on one side of a V-8 to the other side. By adding more volume to the exhaust system, a balance tube helps lessen the pulsing within the exhaust. This increases low-rpm torque and decreases sound. It also allows each cylinder bank to share the opposite muffler of a dual exhaust system, further reducing exhaust system back pressure.

A larger balance tube reduces noise more effectively than a smaller one because of its greater volume. It also increases low-rpm torque courtesy of its larger reduction in back pressure. A "small" balance tube is considered to be one size smaller than the exhaust system tubing (e.g., using a 2.25-inch diameter balance tube with a 2.50-inch diameter exhaust system) and is sometimes necessary to retain sufficient ground clearance. A "larger" tube is equal in size to the exhaust system tubing.

Position of the balance tube is important to its effectiveness. For best results, it needs to be placed in the exhaust pipes just behind the collectors. The farther downstream it is from this point, the less effective it is. If you're not using headers, the best place for a balance tube is as close to the engine as possible.

Exhaust Tubing

Like header primary tube selection, exhaust tubing can be thought of as a tuning aid. Exhaust tubing diameter is dictated by peak engine power. Pipes that are too small create

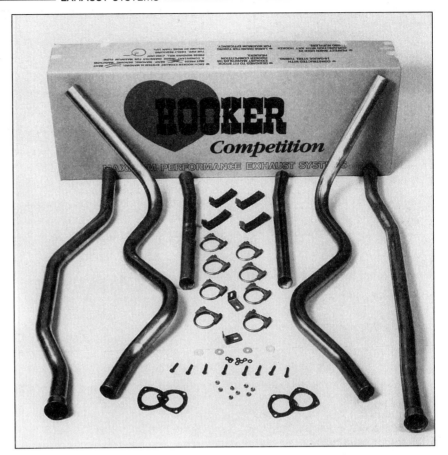

Mandrel-bent exhaust tubing is one sure way toward more power. This Header Dual Exhaust System from Hooker does just that. Designed to be mated with their Competition Series headers, this system is available for a variety of car, trucks, and vans. *Hooker*

enough back pressure to cause a decrease in power. On the other hand, oversized exhaust tubing, like oversized intake ports, cause a drop in low- to mid-rpm response and torque.

The method used to bend exhaust tubing also has an effect on flow. Three types of bends are used: wrinkle, compression, and mandrel.

Wrinkle bends are typical of factory exhaust systems. In order to get the tubing to bend, it's simply pushed on its ends until the required bend radius is achieved. The effects

RECOMMENDED EXHAUST TUBING INSIDE DIAMETER (O.D.)	
Horsepower (Net)	Tubing O.D. in Inches (Dual Exhaust)
200-300	2.25
300-400	2.50
400-550	3.0
550-800	3.5
800-950	4.0
950-1100	4.5
over 1,100	5.0

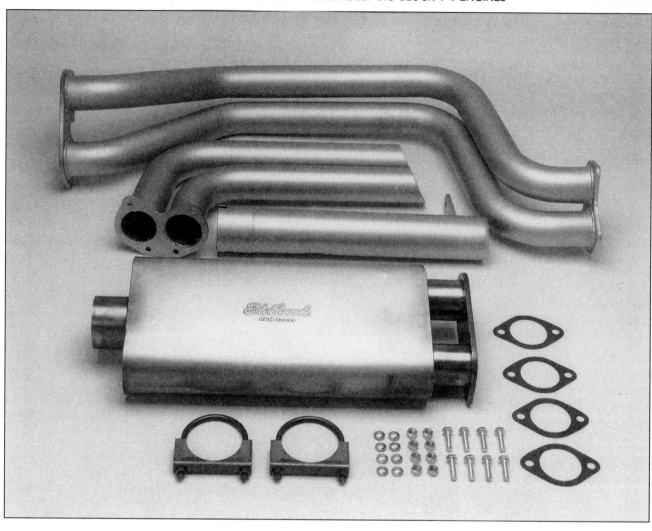

"Cat-back" systems like this one from Edelbrock increase exhaust system efficiency rearward of the catalytic converter. To do this, they use mandrel bent tubing and a high-flow muffler. *Edelbrock*

of this process is a series of wrinkles on the inside diameter of the bend and lots of areas where the exhaust flow can be trapped or disrupted. Cheap and fast are the hallmarks of this production process.

Compression bends are made with equipment that works just the exterior of the tubing. Without any support inside the tubing, the inside radius of the bend is pushed in farther than the tubing immediately surrounding it. This increases airflow restriction within the tubing because the tubing diameter is decreased at the bend. Most muffler shops use compression bending equipment to make their exhaust systems.

Mandrel bends are made with dies positioned inside the tubing in the area of the bend while bending

shoes work the outside of the tubing. The result is a smooth bend that maintains the original tubing diameter—with no increase in restriction.

So what's best? It depends on what you want the vehicle to do. Wrinkle-bent exhaust tubing is just fine for the grocery-getter, but from a performance standpoint, compression bending is a better choice. It flows considerably more air than wrinkle-bent tubing, and although it flows less than mandrel-bent tubing, you really won't notice much difference on the street. It's also considerably cheaper than mandrel-bent tubing. However, if maximum performance is what you're after and you've got the bucks to belly up to the bar, ask for a double shot of mandrel-bent tubing. Many aftermarket

exhaust system manufacturers, such as Walker/Dynomax, offer complete systems with mandrel-bent tubing for a variety of applications.

Mufflers

It used to be that mufflers were to be avoided at all costs on a high-performance street machine—straight pipes were king. However, today's high-performance mufflers impose little, if any, horsepower penalty. In fact, in some cases, a properly designed muffler can actually increase torque, because it provides some scavenging of the exhaust system.

It used to be that when people thought of a performance muffler, they thought of glasspacks. Glasspacks are okay if you're into the retro thing, but they'll also retro your engine's power output. Although simple in construction, using louvers and fiberglass packing, the louvers add a considerable

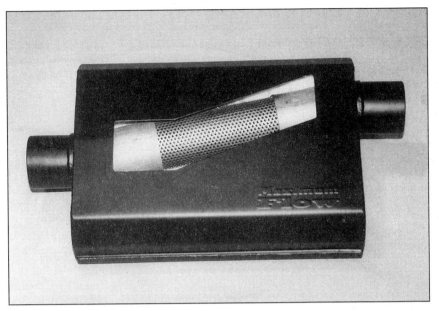

Hooker offers this "straight-through" muffler which is most effective when used with compression ratios of 8.5:1 and lower and in combination with a catalytic converter. *Hooker*

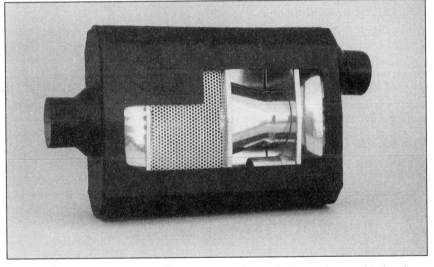

This Hooker Aero Chamber muffler uses a step design similar to that used in headers to minimize turbulence and provide a high flow rate. *Hooker*

amount of turbulence to the exhaust. And just like intake manifolds, turbulence isn't a good thing when it comes to exhaust systems because it makes it harder to flush out the spent exhaust gasses.

Modern high-performance mufflers can use tuned chambers, perforated tubing, and reflectors, separately or in combination, to control sound while minimizing exhaust back pressure.

Perforated tubing, whether the perforations are holes, slits, or any other type of void, work by breaking the sound down into smaller "chunks." These smaller chunks of sound are easier to control than the one large chunk of sound that's delivered from the engine.

Reflectors help reduce exhaust back pressure by creating a low-pressure area to help draw the exhaust gasses out. This action makes them more efficient than using straight pipes without mufflers.

Mufflers must be sized to the exhaust system to minimize back pressure. High-horsepower engines produce a tremendous volume of exhaust gasses. Because of this, they demand a high-flow exhaust and muffler system. Some companies, like Flowmaster, offer mufflers with inlets and outlets as large as 5 inches in diameter. A pair of these mufflers can handle the exhaust from a 1,100-horsepower engine, which covers 99.99 percent of all street and racing vehicles.

CHAPTER FOURTEEN

COOLING SYSTEMS

Proper engine cooling is a necessity for optimal engine operation. If the engine is undercooled or overcooled, problems will arise.

If engine cooling is insufficient, ignition timing has to be retarded to prevent the engine from detonating. The amount of ignition retard is directly proportional to the drop in power output. In extreme cases, camshaft timing or compression ratio has to be compromised to avoid detonation. On the other hand, if the engine runs too cool, power will be down, because the heat that's necessary to produce the most power isn't available. So either way, you lose.

What are the usual causes of a cooling system deficiency?
- Low coolant level
- Externally blocked or internally plugged radiator
- Bad thermostat
- Leaking or collapsed radiator hoses
- Faulty fan clutch
- Faulty radiator cap
- Missing radiator shroud

For maximum cooling efficiency, all components in the cooling system must be in good working order. A high-performance radiator or water pump may cure an overheating problem if the system is marginal, but sometimes it can't make up for the deficiencies listed above. So you need to take stock of the total system. Adequate flow rate, system pressure, and heat transfer area are key to keeping your rat cool. And temperature balance between both sides of the block is strategic to maximizing engine power.

Radiators

The number of tubes in the radiator core, as well as the density of the cooling fins determines a radiator's capacity to shed heat to the atmosphere. Typically, radiators for big-block Chevys use three or four rows of tubes. The more tubes, the greater the volume of coolant that passes through it. In turn, the coolant

High-performance engines are harder to cool than normal street engines because they produce more heat. Proper cooling system operation is key to allowing maximum ignition timing for peak power production.

passes through the radiator slower, allowing it to shed more heat. As the hot coolant passes through the tubes, the heat it contains is transferred to the radiator fins and then to the air flowing around the fins. The greater the number of fins per inch, the greater the cooling capacity. Big-block Chevys driven on paved roads require a minimum of 12 fins per inch to ensure proper cooling.

Radiator position in the vehicle is important, as well. Since the water pump relies on gravity to feed it coolant from the radiator, the top of the radiator and the level of the coolant inside of it must be higher than the water pump under all operating conditions. If not, cavitation and overheating are just a short time away.

And don't forget that a radiator depends on airflow to do its job. To ensure adequate airflow through the radiator, make sure no bugs, leaves, or anything else covers the radiator core.

Radiator Caps

The radiator cap regulates the pressure within the cooling system and has a significant effect on its efficiency.

If you'll think back to your school science classes, you'll recall that pressure affects the boiling point of liquids. The greater the pressure, the higher the boiling point. When a liquid starts to boil, it's composed of mostly air. Since air is 25 times less effective at transferring heat than a liquid, the potential for engine detonation and durability problems increases significantly if the coolant boils. By increasing the pressure within the cooling system, you can raise the point at which the coolant begins to boil.

Radiator construction and materials are the most significant limiter in terms of how much pressure the cooling system can stand, with radiator hoses coming in a close second. Street-driven vehicles can get by with an 18-psi radiator cap in most instances. Race vehicles squeak by with a 22-psi cap and frequent visual inspection of the radiator and hoses. Raising pressure beyond this may prove beneficial, but you'll need to re-engineer the radiator and use steel-braided radiator hoses to prevent blowing them apart. Remember, you'll be checking out new fron-

Cooling fin density has a direct bearing on how much heat the radiator can shed. The closer the fins are to one another, the better the cooling. However, when you increase the thickness of the radiator, greater fin density can cause a problem because it restricts airflow to the fins on the back side of the radiator. In light of this, it's better to use a wider or taller radiator than one that's thicker but smaller.

tiers if you decide to do this, but it may prove to be quite an advantage.

Overflow Reservoirs

An overflow reservoir doesn't sound like a big thing, but it can help prevent an overheating problem.

As the coolant heats up, it expands far enough to unseat the

pressure relief valve in the radiator cap. To prevent losing the coolant onto the ground and causing an overheating problem, it should be routed to an overflow reservoir. As the engine cools the vacuum created in the cooling system will draw the coolant in the reservoir back into the radiator. To ensure the coolant is siphoned out of the reservoir as the engine cools, make sure the tube between the reservoir and the radiator is well-sealed.

Shrouds

The radiator shroud is an important part of the cooling system. It increases the efficiency of the radiator fan because it allows the fan to draw from the entire surface of the radiator, not just the area directly in front of it. For best cooling performance, the shroud should end in the middle of the fan blades (viewed from the side). If this isn't the case, use spacers between the nose of the pump and the fan to gain the proper fan positioning. Just don't use spacers longer than 4 inches in length or you'll put the water pump bearings and shaft out to pasture in a hurry. If a spacer longer than 4 inches is required, extend the shroud instead. Also, foam stuffers made from roll bar padding should

Cooling systems are designed to allow easy flow of coolant, but casting processes can muck up the works. These coolant passages are obstructed by casting flash that impedes coolant flow and can lead to premature detonation. Just below this casting flash is even more flash. All this flash should be removed with a die grinder and grinding burrs or sanding cones.

seal any gaps between the shroud and the radiator so the fan draws entirely from the radiator core.

Fans

Although it's not obvious, an engine fan is only required at speeds below 30 miles per hour or so. Above this speed, airflow through the radiator is sufficient to draw the heat from the radiator.

Two types of fans are available for Chevy rats: engine driven and electrically driven. No matter how they're driven, all fans rely on the number of blades, angle of the blades (blade pitch), and drive speed to do their jobs. The greater the number of blades, pitch, or speed, the greater the airflow.

Engine-Driven Fans

Engine-driven fans take horsepower to drive compared to electrically driven fans, but are a lower-cost alternative.

Factory steel fans that are directly mounted to the water pump take the greatest amount of horsepower to drive. If this describes your situation, you may want use a fan with a fan clutch, a flex fan, or an electrically driven fan.

When the vehicle is equipped with air conditioning or a heavy-duty cooling package, a fan clutch is usually included. These packages are pretty efficient when it comes to cooling and don't take lots of horsepower to run. The downside to a fan clutch is that it's more expensive than a high-quality flex fan, if you didn't inherit it when you purchased the vehicle.

Flex fans are a relatively inexpensive way of keeping your rat cool while saving some parasitic power loss. At low engine speeds, the blades of a flex fan keep their shape and draw air through the radiator. At higher engine speeds, when vehicle speed is high enough to cool the radiator, the blades flatten out, reducing the horsepower required to drive it.

Electrically Driven Fans

To save the horsepower that's taken by an engine-driven fan, you can use one or two electrically driven fans. Some of these fans can be configured to either push the air through the radiator, or to pull it through, depending upon your needs and the space available between the front of the engine and the radiator. When searching for this type of fan, look for those that move the most air with the lowest amperage draw. Also, look for fans that have an adjustable thermostat to give you some flexibility in adjusting engine coolant temperature for all the driving conditions you encounter. Flex-a-Lite, Mr. Gasket, and Perma-Cool all offer electrically driven fans.

Water Pumps

Water pumps are sometimes considered as an afterthought. If that's how you think, the heathens of heat will be eating your engine for lunch. A good water pump helps minimize hot spots in the engine, hot spots that rob your engine of power, increase the potential for detonation, and can shorten engine component life.

Aftermarket companies improve on factory water pumps by increasing water pump efficiency. One key determinant of water pump efficiency is the clearance between the impeller and housing. Factory water pumps have a liberal tolerance here, which prevents moving a considerable portion of the coolant that enters the pump. Aftermarket high-

For street-driven vehicles, Weiand offers this Action-Plus pump. It uses a stamped steel impeller designed to limit cavitation at high rpm, and it's available in both short and long leg versions. *Weiand*

performance pumps have tighter and more-consistent tolerances between the impeller and housing, consequently they can move considerably more coolant than a factory pump.

This increase in flow also provides greater pressure within the engine. Greater pressure helps overcome hot spots in the block and heads by forcing its way into these areas, which, in turn, increases cooling.

When comparing aftermarket pumps, use their flow rating in gallons-per-minute (GPM) to compare their performance. And just as important is their ability to flow equal amounts of cooling through both

This Team G water pump from Weiand is designed for racing applications. It features a 3/4-inch-diameter shaft, extra heavy-duty bearings, and a high-efficiency impeller. *Weiand*

sides of the block. The more equal the flow, the higher the ignition advance can be before detonation sets in. And this leads to more power.

As they come from the factory, big-block Chevys are limited in the amount of ignition timing they can utilize because of the temperature differential between the left and right cylinder banks. When engine temperature increases beyond a certain point, the potential for detonation increases. By having one cylinder bank run hotter than the other, the amount of ignition advance that can be used is limited by the hotter running bank. With ignition timing reduced from the optimum, cylinder pressure decreases and torque goes along with it. However, if we can achieve a better balance between the temperatures of the left and right cylinder banks, ignition timing can be advanced a little more, providing more torque. One of the best and easiest ways to do this is through the use of a high-performance water pump with a high-efficiency impeller.

Impeller Design

With most water pumps, it doesn't matter which way the impeller is driven, clockwise or counterclockwise, the pump flows about equally well in both direc-tions. This is great from a production standpoint because you don't have to worry about putting the wrong pump on a particular engine. However, it leaves considerable room for improvement if the impeller is optimized to provide flow in a specific direction. Some high-performance water pumps use a "preferred direction" impeller to take advantage of the additional flow provided by this type of system. Temperature balance through the block improves, as well, paving the way for more ignition advance and power.

Edelbrock, Milodon, Moroso, and Weiand all offer high-performance water pumps for big-block Chevys.

Electrically Driven Pumps

Electrically driven water pumps have an advantage over crank-driven water pumps in that they don't take any horsepower to drive. Although these pumps are mainly used for drag racing applications, some are available for street use. Before buying this type of pump, make sure that it will provide adequate flow and pressure for your specific application.

Water Pump Pulleys

The flow rate of a water pump is linear; the faster you spin it, the more coolant it puts out. The ratio between the diameter of the water pump pulley and the crankshaft pulley dictates how fast the water pump is driven. Because it takes between 15 and 20 horsepower to drive a water pump at speeds above 6,000 rpm, rarely do you see a water pump driven faster than 100 percent of crankshaft rpm. Although the 15–20 horsepower draw is something to consider for a street application, it's critical in racing, where it can mean the difference between winning and losing. If you're using a high-performance water pump, there are a couple of ways you play this.

Since high-performance water pumps increase cooling efficiency and therefore allow more ignition timing, you can run the pump at a 1:1 ratio, and even though it's eating some horsepower at higher rpm, you'll also have more power to offset the water pump losses. On the other hand, you can run the pump slower, at about 65–70 percent of engine speed, thereby reducing pumping losses, but you may have to dial back the ignition timing to prevent detonation. And with reduced timing, horsepower drops.

Although either of these approaches work, the first scenario is preferred for most street applications because it provides a cooling reserve for when you're stuck in traffic. Alternately, underdriving the water pump is usually better for a race car because engine rpm is often kept significantly higher than a street car, preventing overheating problems. In fact, the trick is to drive the water pump as slowly as possible (to avoid parasitic losses), while ensuring the engine is cooled sufficiently under all operating conditions.

Whichever approach you try, be sure to keep an eye on the coolant temperature gauge, and keep an ear out for detonation. If coolant temperature is excessive, or the engine begins detonating, you'll need to change your approach.

Thermostats

To get the most power out of an engine, you want to regulate its heat load with the proper thermostat. If the engine runs at too low of a temperature, the heat that's essential to

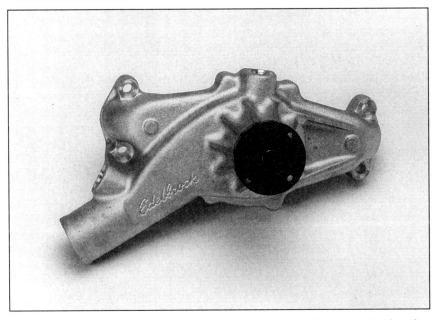

This Edelbrock Victor water pump is noted for its nearly equal flow to both sides of the block. When both sides of the block are the same temperature, more power can be made. *Edelbrock*

Thermostats play an important role in the cooling system. From a power production standpoint, it increases pressure within the engine, which helps eliminate air pockets. And with coolant laying against all the interior surfaces of the block and heads, more ignition timing can be used before detonation sets in.

producing power is transferred to the cooling system and power drops. On the other hand, if the engine runs too hot, detonation or piston and ring scuffing will follow, which will also cause power to drop. With big-block Chevys, the optimal operating range is 180 to 200 degrees Fahrenheit. This leaves about a 20- to 40-degree cooling reserve for situations like being caught in traffic, either on the road or on the track.

Besides regulating the temperature of the coolant as it flows out of the engine into the radiator, the thermostat increases pressure within the engine. By doing this, it helps force air out of the system the same way a high-performance water pump does. This helps prevent localized boiling within the cooling system which allows greater ignition advance and

more power. So don't run your engine without a thermostat.

Anti-Freeze/Coolant

The ratio of anti-freeze to water is critical to the operation of the cooling system. Anti-freeze provides protection from coolant freezing, as well as boiling. Why not use just straight anti-freeze and forget the water? Because straight anti-freeze can't transfer heat as well as a solution of water and anti-freeze. If you use straight anti-freeze, it'll cause localized boiling within the cooling system, usually in the cylinder heads or at the tops of the cylinders—places that can least tolerate more heat. The best balance between anti-freeze and antiboil protection is achieved with a 2:1 ratio of anti-freeze to water. This will provide protection between -45 and about 240 degrees Fahrenheit.

CONTENTS

CHAPTER FIFTEEN

BREAK-IN

Now that you've spent numerous hours painstakingly cleaning, measuring, and assembling your engine, your excitement begins to build and you can't wait to start it. This is definitely the time for the pay-off pitch, but don't rush now. If you do, you stand a good chance of shortening your engine's life or worse. Instead, discipline yourself to work slowly and methodically. This will help prevent mistakes.

Priming the Lubrication System

Of all the work you've done thus far, maybe the most important job is to prime the lubrication system. It's best to do this while the engine is on the stand because if anything's wrong with the lubrication system, you can repair it with relative ease there compared to when the engine is in the vehicle. If everything's all right, prime it just before you're ready to start it as well.

Begin by filling a new oil filter with fresh SH-rated 10W30 or 10W40 conventional engine oil. Don't use synthetic engine oil or the engine will not break-in properly. Then apply a light coating of oil to the filter seal and screw the filter onto the engine or adapter.

Before you add the oil to the crankcase, pour in a quart of General Motors' Engine Oil Supplement (EOS). The antiwear additives in this supplement will ease component break-in. Then fill the crankcase to the "Full" mark on the dipstick with SH-rated engine oil.

To monitor oil pressure, connect a mechanical oil pressure gauge to the boss near the oil filter on the block. Then position the gauge where you can easily read it as you drive the oil pump.

To prime a wet-sump system, use the bottom half of an old (but clean) distributor, or use one of the commercially available priming tools. Using a drill (1/2 horsepower or better works best) to drive the priming tool, start at a low RPM and watch the gauge carefully. Oil pressure may be nonexistent for the first few revolutions as the oil begins to flow through the engine and oil filter. In a short time, it should rise to about 30–40 psi when you've got the trigger on the drill pegged, depending upon the speed of the drill and the ambient temperature. If oil pressure is building, the drill motor will begin to labor.

If you don't get any oil pressure, make sure your drive "tool" is engaged with the oil pump drive shaft. If everything's okay here, take a close look at the line to the oil pressure gauge. When you're driving the pump, you should see the oil in the line move. If it moves but the needle on the gauge doesn't move, the gauge is probably dead. However, if the oil in the line doesn't move, something's wrong with the oil pump, the bearing clearances are too large or you've forgotten to install one or more of the threaded plugs in the camshaft gallery feed holes.

When the pump is running, have someone slowly rotate the crankshaft a couple of turns as this helps ensure complete lubrication of the engine.

If oil pressure doesn't build, assume the oil filter is plugged and replace it. I know, you've used a new oil filter so there shouldn't be any problem with it. Unfortunately, this problem can happen, because I've experienced it. So replace the filter and check for oil pressure once again while cranking the engine.

When the oil pressure is all right, check fuel flow. The cranking of the engine should have allowed the fuel pump to prime the fuel lines and carburetor or fuel injection system. To check fuel flow with a carburetor, quickly open the throttle. You should see a stream of gas squirt into the carburetor venturis, from the accelerator pump(s).

If the engine is equipped with any type of fuel-injection system, prime the system by turning the ignition key to the "Run" position. You should hear the electric fuel pump in the tank run for a few seconds then shut off. If you don't hear it run, check its fuse.

One last thing. Get a friend to start your car so you can watch what's happening in the engine compartment. Also watch for any "surprises" that may occur when the engine starts running, such as a fuel line leak, or a radiator cooling fan that isn't working. And keep a fire extinguisher handy. It's not that you're necessarily going to use the extinguisher, but you'll wish you had one if the need arises.

Starting the Engine

Before you start the engine, check all the belts and hoses to make sure they're securely connected. Also, take a look at all the electrical connections to be sure they're where they belong and aren't hanging where they can be caught by a spinning belt or be burned. In addition, check the coolant and oil levels to make sure they're up to the proper level. And be sure there's enough fuel in the fuel tank to start the engine and run it for at least 45 minutes. This is very important, because once you start the engine, it needs to be run between 2,000 and 2,500 rpm for half-an-hour. This helps break-in the camshaft and lifters properly, preventing them from dying a quick but unmerciful death.

It's also best to have the exhaust system connected and fully operational before you start the engine, as this will allow you to listen for any unusual noises as the engine starts and runs.

It's also imperative that you check the operation of the throttle. It must return to the fully closed position otherwise you may have a V-8-powered hand grenade in the engine compartment rather than an engine. If the throttle doesn't fully close, the cable may be kinked or the return springs may be missing from the lever or not attached to the engine.

As your friend tries to start the engine, be ready at the distributor. If the engine doesn't start in about three seconds or so, and doesn't sound like it will, stop cranking the engine. This will save wear and tear on the cam and lifters if they're new. Then put your hand around the middle of the distributor cap, halfway between the spark plug wires and metal housing, rotate the distributor a few degrees, and have your friend try again. If the engine coughs and sputters, try rotating the distributor in that direction until it starts. If it doesn't sound like it's going to start, try turning the distributor in the opposite direction.

If it still doesn't start, stop the cranking. It's possible you've installed the distributor 180-degrees out of position. With cylinder number one at TDC on the compression stroke, check the position of the distributor cap rotor. It should line up with the #1 spark plug wire terminal in the distributor cap. If it's within a quarter inch or so, you just have to rotate the distributor until it does. If it's farther away than this, you'll have to remove the distributor and rotate its shaft until you get a satisfactory alignment.

As soon as the engine starts, run it at 2,000–2,500 rpm. Engine oil pressure should be at least 30 psi with 10W30 in the crankcase. If it isn't, stop the engine immediately!

Unfortunately, if the oil pressure is this low and all the galley plugs are in, usually the oil pump is bad or excessive bearing clearance exists.

After the engine is started, smoke may rise from it. A moderate amount of smoke can be expected if the engine has been freshly painted (the engine's heat cures the enamel paint, creating smoke). It will also smoke if you happen to spill oil on the exhaust system or the headers or exhaust system are new. This is normal and is nothing to be alarmed about. However, if the smoke lasts more than five minutes or so, or it's in tremendous volume, chances are something is wrong. Stop the engine immediately and find the cause of the problem.

Strange noises are another concern. Clicking noises in the area of the valve covers can signal a valvetrain problem—most likely loose rocker arms. However, the fuel injectors in a multi-port fuel-injected engine make a clicking noise as they open and close, so don't mistake this noise for a valvetrain problem.

As the engine runs, have your friend keep an eye on the coolant temperature and oil pressure gauges, as well as the tachometer. Engine temperature shouldn't rise above 220 degrees Fahrenheit. If it does, place an electric fan in front of the radiator to provide additional cooling. If the engine temperature still rises, shut the engine off. When the engine has cooled, carefully check the coolant level, as well as for any leaks that may have caused the elevated temperature.

The First Oil Change

After the engine has been run 25 minutes or so, you'll need to change the engine oil filter. That's because the molybdenum disulfide lubricant you used on the camshaft, lifters, and other internal parts will completely plug an oil filter in about 30 minutes of engine operation.

ENGINE BUILD SHEETS

ENGINE BUILD SHEET

Engine:		Date:		

Bore:	Stroke:	Displacement: (0.7853981 x bore² x stroke x .8)	Compression Ratio: (Comb. chamber volume + cylinder volume ÷ comb. chamber volume)	Octane Reqm't:

Cylinder Block Manufacturer and casting #	**Material** Aluminum Cast Iron	**Main Bearing Cap Fasteners (# & dia.)**	**Main Bearing Weight (grams)**	**Deck Height** 9.8in 10.2in Other:	**Camshaft Location** Std. +0.400in Other:

Crankshaft Manufacturer and casting or forging #	**Material**	**Balancing** Internal External	**Stroke** 3.76in 4.00in Other:	**Cross-drilled?** Yes No	**End Play** (0.005-0.007in)

Main Bearing Inside Diameter	**Main Bearing Journal Diameter**	**Main Bearing Clearance** (Main Bearing I.D. minus Main Journal Diameter) Strokes to 4.500in - 0.0026-0.0030in Strokes over 4.500in - 0.0029-0.0032in
Mcap #1	Jnl. #1	Jnl. #1
Mcap #2	Jnl. #2	Jnl. #2
Mcap #3	Jnl. #3	Jnl. #3
Mcap #4	Jnl. #4	Jnl. #4
Mcap #5	Jnl. #5	Jnl. #5

Connecting Rods Manufacturer and part #	**Ctr-to-Ctr Length** 6.135in 6.485in 6.535in Other	**Rod Bolts** Manufacturer Type Diameter	**Rod Bolt Torque (or Stretch)**	**Rod Bearing Weight (grams)**

Connecting Rod Inside Diameter	**Small End**	**Large End**	**Small End Weight (grams)**	**Large End Weight (grams)**
Cyl. #1				
Cyl. #2				
Cyl. #3				
Cyl. #4				
Cyl. #5				
Cyl. #6				
Cyl. #7				
Cyl. #8				

Rod Bearing Inside Diameter	Rod Bearing Journal Diameter	Rod Bearing Clearance (Rod Bearing I.D. minus Rod Journal Diameter) (0.002-0.003in)	
Cyl. #1 Cyl. #2	Jnl. #1	Cyl. #1 Cyl. #2	
Cyl. #3 Cyl. #4	Jnl. #2	Cyl. #3 Cyl. #4	
Cyl. #5 Cyl. #6	Jnl. #3	Cyl. #5 Cyl. #6	
Cyl. #7 Cyl. #8	Jnl. #4	Cyl. #7 Cyl. #8	

Rod Bearing Journal Width	Connecting Rod Paired Width	Rod Side Clearance (Rod Bearing Journal Width minus Rod Paired Width) Steel rods - 0.015-0.018in Aluminum rods - 0.020-0.025in
Jnl. #1	Rods 1&2	
Jnl. #2	Rods 3&4	
Jnl. #3	Rods 5&6	
Jnl. #4	Rods 7&8	

Pistons Manufacturer and part #	Type Cast Hypereutectic Forged	Dome Type Open Closed	Dome Vol. (cc)	Compression Height	Pin Type & Dia.	Deck Height Typical Values Steel rods - 0.005in Alum. rods - 0.020in
Pin-to-Piston Clearance	Pin-to-Rod Clearance (0.0005-0.0008in)	Pin End Clearance (0.000-0.005in)	Pin Weight	Lock Type Pressed Spirolox Tru Arc	Lock Weight	

Cylinder Bore Diameter	Piston Diameter (Measure 90° Away From Piston Pin)	Piston-to-Bore Clearance (Bore Diameter - Piston Diameter) Refer to Manufacturer's Recommendations
Cyl. #1	Cyl. #1	Cyl. #1
Cyl. #2	Cyl. #2	Cyl. #2
Cyl. #3	Cyl. #3	Cyl. #3
Cyl. #4	Cyl. #4	Cyl. #4
Cyl. #5	Cyl. #5	Cyl. #5
Cyl. #6	Cyl. #6	Cyl. #6
Cyl. #7	Cyl. #7	Cyl. #7
Cyl. #8	Cyl. #8	Cyl. #8

Piston Rings Manufacturer and part #	**Type** Moly Plasma Moly Gapless	**Width** Top Compression Middle Compression Oil Control	
Piston Ring End Gap	**Top Compression** (0.018in Minimum)	**Middle Compression** (0.016in Minimum)	**Oil Control** (0.016in Minimum)
Cyl. #1			
Cyl. #2			
Cyl. #3			
Cyl. #4			
Cyl. #5			
Cyl. #6			
Cyl. #7			
Cyl. #8			

Camshaft Manufacturer and part #:	**Lift** Intake: Exhaust:	**Duration @ 0.050in lift** Intake: Exhaust:	**Lobe Separation Angle**
Valve Lash Intake: Exhaust:	**Valve-to-Piston Clearance @ TDC** (0.100in recommended) Intake: Exhaust:	**Camshaft Gear** (° Advanced or Retarded)	**Crankshaft Gear** (° Advanced or Retarded)

Cylinder Head Manufacturer and part #	**Valve Sizes** Intake: Exhaust:	**Port Volume** Intake: Exhaust:	**Rocker Arm Ratio** Intake: Exhaust:	**Head Gasket Volume (cc)**
Valve Springs Manufacturer and part #	**Spring Type & Dia.**	**Installed Height** Intake: Exhaust:	**Closed Pressure** Intake: Exhaust:	**Open Pressure** Intake: Exhaust:

SUPPLIER DIRECTORY

Air Filters
K&N Engineering
561 Iowa Ave.
PO Box 1329
Riverside, CA 92507
PH: (800) 858-3333

Bearings
Childs & Albert
24849 Anza Dr.
Valencia, CA 91355-1259
PH: (805) 295-1900

Camshaft Drive Systems
Cloyes Gear and
Products, Inc.
4520 Beidler
Willoughby, OH 44094
PH: (216) 205-7500

Jesel Inc.
PO Box 1407
Wall, NJ 07719
PH: (908) 681-5344

Camshafts and
Valvetrain Components
Competition Cams
3406 Democrat Rd.
Memphis, TN 38118
PH: 800-999-0853 (info)
(901) 795-2400

Crane Cams, Inc.
530 Fentress Blvd.
Daytona Beach, FL 32114
PH: (904) 258-6174
Crower Cams &
 Equipment
3333 Main St.
Chula Vista, CA
91911-5899
PH: (800) 222-2267
(619) 422-1191 (info)

Edelbrock Equipment Co.
2700 California St.
Torrance, CA 90503
PH: (310) 781-2222

Erson Cams
550 Mallory Way
Carson City, NV 89701
PH: (702) 882-1622

Iskenderian Racing Cams
16020 S. Broadway
PO Box 30
Gardena, CA 90247-9990
PH: (213) 770-0930

Lunati Cranks &
Cams, Inc.
4770 Lamar Ave.
Memphis, TN 3
8181-0021
PH: (901) 365-0950
FAX: (901) 795-9411

Manley Performance
1960 Swarthmore Ave.
Lakewood, NJ 08701
PH: (908) 905-3366

Wolverine/Blue Racer
4790 Hudson Rd.
Osseo, MI 49266
PH: (800) 248-0134

Carburetors and
Fuel Injection Systems
Barry Grant Fuel Systems
& Nitrous Works
Route 1
PO Box 1900
Dahlonega, GA 30533
PH: (404) 864-8544

Carburetor Shop
1457 E. Philadelphia #24
Ontario, CA 91761
PH: (909) 947-7744

Edelbrock Equipment Co.
2700 California St.
Torrance, CA 90503
PH: (310) 781-2222

Hilborn Fuel Injection
25891 Crown Valley
Parkway
Laguna Nigel, CA 92677
PH: (714) 582-1170
FAX: (714) 582 3795

Holley Performance
Products
1801 Russellville Rd.
PO Box 10360
Bowling Green,
KY 42102-7360
PH: (502) 843-8630

Kinsler Fuel Injection
1834 Thunderbird
Troy, MI 48084
PH: (810) 362-1145

Computer PROMS
Hypertech, Inc.
1910 Thomas Rd.
Memphis, TN
38134-6315
PH: (901) 382-8888

Performance Resource
12 Barbara Dr.
Fairfield, NJ 07004
PH: (201) 343-0680

Computer
Simulation Programs
DeskTop Dyno
Mr. Gasket
Performance Group
8700 Brookpark Rd.
Cleveland, OH 44129
PH: (216) 398-8300 (info)

Performance Trends, Inc.
PO Box 0573
Dearborn Hts, MI 48127
PH: (810) 473-9230

Connecting Rods
Carrillo Industries
33041 Calle Perfecto
San Juan Capistrano,
CA 92675
PH: (714) 498-1800 (info)
FX: (714) 498-2355

Childs & Albert
24849 Anza Dr.
Valencia, CA 91355-1259
PH: (805) 295-1900

Crower Cams &
Equipment
3333 Main St.
Chula Vista, CA
91911-5899
PH: (800) 222-2267
(619) 422-1191 (info)

Eagle Specialty
Products Inc.
3075 Norbrook Dr.
Memphis, TN 38116
PH: (901) 345-5886

Crankshafts
Callies Performance
Products
110 W. Jones Rd.
Fostoria, OH 44830
PH: (419) 435-2711
FX: (419) 435-2625

Cola Performance
Products
19122 S. Santa Fe Ave.
Rancho Dominguez,
CA 90221
PH: (800)366-COL

Crower Cams &
Equipment
3333 Main St.
Chula Vista, CA 91911-
5899
PH: (800) 222-2267
(619) 422-1191 (info)

Lunati Cranks &
Cams, Inc.
4770 Lamar Ave.
Memphis, TN
38181-0021
PH: (901) 365-0950
FAX: (901) 795-9411

Cylinder Blocks
GM Performance Parts
Local General
Motors Dealers

Donovan Engineering
2305 Border Ave.
Torrance, CA 90501
PH: (310) 320-3772
FAX: (310) 320-1090

Rodeck, Inc.
2134 Tractor St.
Paso Robles
PH: (805) 237-6040

Cylinder Heads

Brodix, Inc.
301 Maple
PO Box 1347
Mena, AR 71953
PH: (501) 394-1075
FAX: (501) 394-1996

Dart Machinery, Ltd.
353 Oliver St.
Troy, MI 48084
PH: (810) 244-9822

Edelbrock Equipment Co.
2700 California St.
Torrance, CA 90503
PH: (310) 781-2222

World Products
29 Trade Zone Drive
Ronkonkoma, NY 11779
PH: (810) 244-9822

Dampers

BHJ Dynamics Inc.
37530 Enterprise Court
Newark, CA 94560
PH: (510) 797-6780
Fluid Damper
Vibratech Inc.
537 E. Delavan Ave.
Buffalo, NY 14211
PH: (714) 895-5404
FAX: (714) 895-7258

Pro/Street Performance
2060 Dawson Ave.
Signal Hill, CA
90806-5929
PH: (310) 597-1190

Engine Builders

Scott Shafiroff
Racing Enterprises
76A Dell Street
West Babylon, NY 11704
PH: (516) 293-2220

Gaerte Engines
615 Monroe St.
Rochester, IN 46975
PH: (219) 223-3016

Gianino/Lukovich
Racing Engines
4812 Leafdale Blvd.
Royal Oak, MI 48073
PH: (248) 280-0240
FX: (248) 280-9755

Fasteners

ARP Automotive
Racing Products
250 Quail Court
Santa Paula, CA 93060
PH: (800)
826-3045 (orders)
(805) 525-5152 (info)

GM Performance Parts

Sallee Chevrolet
Performance
Parts
1003 S. Main St.
Milton-Freewater,
OR 97862
PH: (800)
545-0048 (orders)
(503) 938-6982 (info)

Scoggin-Dickey
Parts Center
5901 Spur 327
Lubbock, TX 79424
PH: (800)
456-0211 (orders)
(806) 798-4108 (info)

Headers & Exhaust Systems

Borla Performance
Industries
5901 Edison Dr.
Oxnard, CA 93033
PH: (805) 986-8600
FAX: (805) 986-8999

Edelbrock Equipment Co.
2700 California St.
Torrance, CA 90503
PH: (310) 781-2222

Flowmaster, Inc.
2975 Dutton Ave., #3
Santa Rosa, CA 95407
PH: (800) 544-4761

High Performance
Coatings
550 W. 361 N. Glade
Oklahoma City,
OK 73127
PH: (800) 456-4721
(801) 262-6807

Hooker Headers
1024 West Brooks St.
Ontario, CA 91762
PH: (909) 983-5871

Jet Hot Coatings
Bridgeport, PA
Tempe, AZ
PH: (800)
432-3379 (orders)
 (610) 277-5646 (info)

Stahl Headers
1515 Mt. Rose Ave.
York, PA 17403
PH: (717) 846-1632

SuperFlow
3512 E. North Tejon
Colorado Springs,
CO 80907
PH: (719) 471-7900

Walker Manufacturing
1202 Michigan Blvd.
Racine, WI 53402
PH: (800) 767-DYNO

Ignition Systems
ACCEL
8700 Brookpark Rd.
Cleveland, OH 44129
PH: (216) 398-8300

Champion Spark Plug
Motorsports Racing
Hotline
PH: (419) 535-2443

Jacobs Electronics
500 N. Baird St.
Midland, TX 79701
PH: (800) 627-8800

Mallory, Inc.
550 Mallory Way
Carson City, NV 89701
PH: (702) 882-6600

MSD Ignition
Autotronic
Controls Corp.
1490 Henry
Brennan Drive
El Paso, TX 79936
PH: (915) 857-5200
Performance Distributors
2699 Barris Dr.
Memphis, TN 38132
PH: (901) 396-5782

Intake Manifolds
Weiand Automotive
2316 San Fernando Rd.
PO Box 65301
Los Angeles, CA 90065
PH: (213) 225-1346

Also see "Cylinder
Heads" on page 156

Oil Pans and Pumps
Canton Racing Products
14 Commerce Dr.
North Branford,
CT 06471
PH: (203) 484-4900

Hamburger's High
Performance
1501 Industrial Way N.
Toms River, NJ 08755
PH: (908) 240-3888

Milodon Inc.
20716 Plummer St.
Chatsworth, CA 91311
PH: (818) 407-1211

Moroso
Performance Products
80 Carter Drive
Guilford, CT 06437
PH: (203) 453-6571

Weaver Brothers, Ltd.
1980 Boeing Way
Carson City, NV 89701
PH: (702) 883-7677

Pistons and Rings
Arias Pistons
13420 S. Normandie Ave.
Gardena, CA 90249
PH: (213) 532-9737

JE Pistons
15681 Computer Lane
Huntington Beach,
CA 92649
PH: (714) 898-9763
FX: (714) 898-7873

Keith Black Systems
5630 Imperial Hwy.
South Gate, CA 90280
PH: (213) 861-4765

Ross Racing Pistons
11927 S. Prairie Ave.
Hawthorne, CA 90250
PH: (800)
392-7677 (orders)
PH: (310) 644-9779 (info)

Total Seal Inc.
2225 W. Mountain
View #6
Phoenix, AZ 85021
PH: (602) 678-4977

TRW Speed-Pro
26555
Northwestern Hwy.
Southfield, MI 48034
PH: (810) 354-7700

Wiseco Pistons, Inc.
7201 Industrial
Park Blvd.
Mentor, OH 44060-5396
PH: (216) 951-6600

Water Pumps
Edelbrock Equipment Co.
2700 California St.
Torrance, CA 90503
PH: (310) 781-2222

Stewart Components
P.O. Box 5523
High Point, NC 27262
PH: (910) 889-8789

Weiand Automotive
2316 San Fernando Rd.
PO Box 65301
Los Angeles, CA 90065
PH: (213) 225-1346

INDEX